The politics of participation in sustainable development g

The United Nations University Institute of Advanced Studies (UNU-IAS) is a global think tank whose mission is "advancing knowledge and promoting learning for policymaking to meet the challenges of sustainable development". UNU-IAS undertakes research and postgraduate education to identify and address strategic issues of concern for all humankind, for governments and decision makers and, particularly, for developing countries. The Institute convenes expertise from disciplines such as economics, law, and social and natural sciences to better understand and contribute creative solutions to pressing global concerns, with research focused on Biodiplomacy, Sustainable Development Governance, Science Policy and Education for Sustainable Development, and Ecosystems and People.

Website: http://www.ias.unu.edu

The politics of participation in sustainable development governance

Edited by Jessica F. Green and W. Bradnee Chambers

United Nations University Press
TOKYO · NEW YORK · PARIS

© United Nations University, 2006

The views expressed in this publication are those of the authors and do not necessarily reflect the views of the United Nations University.

United Nations University Press
United Nations University, 53-70, Jingumae 5-chome,
Shibuya-ku, Tokyo 150-8925, Japan
Tel: +81-3-3499-2811   Fax: +81-3-3406-7345
E-mail: sales@hq.unu.edu
General enquiries: press@hq.unu.edu
www.unu.edu

United Nations University Office at the United Nations, New York
2 United Nations Plaza, Room DC2-2062, New York, NY 10017, USA
Tel: +1-212-963-6387   Fax: +1-212-371-9454
E-mail: unuona@ony.unu.edu

United Nations University Press is the publishing division of the United Nations University.

Cover design by Mea Rhee

Printed in India

Library of Congress Cataloging-in-Publication Data

The politics of participation in sustainable development governance / edited by Jessica F. Green and W. Bradnee Chambers.
   p. cm.
 Includes index.
 ISBN 9280811339 (pbk.)
 1. Sustainable development—Management—International cooperation.
2. Developing countries—Foreign economic relations—Developed countries.
3. Developed countries—Foreign economic relations—Developing countries.
4. Equality. I. Green, Jessica F. II. Chambers, W. Bradnee.
HD75.6.P65   2006
338.9′27091724—dc22   2006029372

Table of contents

List of figures and tables vii

About the contributors viii

Preface xi

Acknowledgements xiii

List of acronyms xiv

Introduction
Understanding the challenges to enfranchisement 1
   Jessica F. Green and W. Bradnee Chambers

Part I: Actors 19

  1 Increasing disenfranchisement of developing country
     negotiators in a multi-speed world 21
     Joyeeta Gupta

  2 In tension: Enfranchising initiatives in the face of aggressive
     marginalisation 40
     John W. Foster

3 Business-society interaction towards sustainable development
– Corporate social responsibility: The road ahead 62
Mikoto Usui

4 Developing country scientists and decision-making:
An institutional perspective of issues and barriers 90
W. Bradnee Chambers

5 The legacy of Deskaheh: Decolonising indigenous
participation in sustainable development governance 108
Leanne Simpson

Part II: Models 131

6 Civil society and the World Trade Organization 133
Kevin R. Gray

7 The politics of inclusion in the Monterrey Process 153
Barry Herman

8 The Åarhus Convention: Engaging the disenfranchised
through the institutionalisation of procedural rights? 179
Marc Pallemaerts

9 Promoting enfranchisement: New approaches for the climate
talks 204
Gunnar Sjöstedt

10 Toward inclusion and influence: Strategies for
enfranchisement 227
Jessica F. Green

Index 247

List of tables and figures

Figures
Figure 9.1   Basic elements of a multilateral negotiation 206

Tables
Table 3.1   International codes related to corporate social responsibility 68
Table 4.1   Researchers in developing countries 100
Table 9.1   Association between *process stage* and *pattern of interaction* in the climate talks 217
Table 9.2   Association between negotiation on particular *regime element (outcomes)* and *pattern of interaction (games)* 219

About the contributors

W. Bradnee Chambers is Senior Programme Officer at the United Nations University-Institute of Advanced Studies. Chambers' current research is on finding ways of improving cooperation between major multilateral environmental agreements based on an interlinkages approach. He works and publishes on issues related to climate change, biodiversity, biotechnology policy and trade and environment. In addition to his responsibilities at UNU-IAS, Chambers is a convening lead author in the Millennium Ecosystem Assessment and the Global Environmental Outlook 4 and a Senior Legal Research Fellow at the Centre for International Sustainable Development Law in Canada.

John W. Foster is Principal Researcher at the North-South Institute (Ottawa, Canada), with a focus on civil society and global governance. He is chair of the Coordinating Committee of the Social Watch, and an active participant in UBUNTU, the International Facilitating Group in Financing for Development, and the Commonwealth Civil Society Advisory Committee. He is a member of the Global Treatment Action Group (GTAG), and Common Frontiers in Canada, as well as a former director of Greenpeace Canada and the Canadian Council for International Cooperation. Foster worked for many years in social justice in the United Church of Canada and the ecumenical justice coalitions in Canada. He has more recently been CEO of Oxfam-Canada (1989–1997) and Ariel F. Sallows Professor of International Human Rights at the Law College of the University of Saskatchewan (1997–1999).

Kevin R. Gray holds an LLM and is currently Counsel at the Trade Law Bureau at the Canadian Department of Foreign Affairs and International Trade after one-and-a-half years as Senior Policy Analyst at the Trade and Environment Branch at Environment Canada. He is an international lawyer and academic, having taught at the London School of Economics and the School of Oriental and African Studies. He has also been a research fellow at the Royal Institute of International Affairs and the British Institute of International and Comparative Law. He is the current co-chair of the American Society of International Law International Environmental Law Interest Group and sits on the ILA Committee on Sustainable Development.

Jessica F. Green is a doctoral candidate at the Woodrow Wilson School at Princeton University and a visiting researcher at UNU-IAS. Her research focuses on the role of non-state actors in global governance, particularly in the area of sustainable development. She is co-editor of *Reforming International Environmental Governance: From Institutional Limits to Innovative Reforms*, and was a lead author in the recently concluded Millennium Ecosystem Assessment. She holds a master's degree in public policy from Columbia University's School of International and Public Affairs.

Joyeeta Gupta has been working at the Institute for Environmental Studies at the Faculty of Earth and Life Sciences in de Vrije Universiteit in Amsterdam since 1993, and is currently Professor of Climate Change Law and Policy. She also holds a part-time position as Professor in Policy and Law of Water Resources and the Environment at the UNESCO-IHE Institute for Water Education in Delft. She has published extensively in the area of environmental governance, climate change and North-South relations. Gupta is editor-in-chief of the journal *International Environmental Agreements: Politics, Law and Economics*, a member of the scientific steering committees of a number of international organisations and initiatives and serves as vice-chair of the Global Change Commission of the Netherlands and of the Netherlands Research Programme on Climate Change. She is a lead author with the Inter-governmental Panel on Climate Change, and is presently a lead author for the Millennium Ecosystem Assessment. She holds a PhD in law from de Vrije Universiteit.

Barry Herman is a Senior Adviser in the Financing for Development Office in the United Nations Department of Economic and Social Affairs. He was part of the UN Secretariat team that prepared the Monterrey Summit on Financing for Development in 2002. Earlier he led the team that produced the UN's annual *World Economic and Social Survey*. He began his UN career in 1976, when he worked on promoting personal savings mobilisation in developing countries. Before joining the Secretariat he taught development and international economics. He holds a PhD from the University of Michigan and an MBA from the University of Chicago. He has edited three books and published articles and chapters in books on North-South financial issues.

Marc Pallemaerts holds graduate degrees in law and political science from the Vrije Universiteit Brussels and Harvard University. He teaches European and international environmental law at the Université Libre de Bruxelles and the Vrije Universiteit Brussels. He has also acted as legal and policy adviser to several environment ministers and was Deputy Chief of Staff of the Belgian State Secretary for Energy and Sustainable Development from 1999 to 2003. He is currently a Senior Fellow and Head of the Governance Team at the Institute for European Environmental Policy, an independent, non-profit research institute with offices in London and Brussels.

Leanne Simpson is of Anishinaabeg ancestry and holds a PhD from the University of Manitoba. She has served as director of Indigenous Environmental Studies at Trent University in Peterborough, Ontario, and on delegations to the United Nations' Ad Hoc Open-Ended Working Group on the Biosafety Protocol, the Ad Hoc Open-Ended Inter-Sessional Working Group on Article 8(j) and Related Provisions of the Convention on Biological Diversity and the Permanent Forum on Indigenous Issues. She is currently working with several indigenous communities on land issues and is a Steering Committee member of Call of the Earth/ Llamado de la Tierra.

Gunnar Sjöstedt is Senior Research Fellow at the Swedish Institute of International Affairs, and Associate Professor at the University of Stockholm. He is a member of the Steering Committee of the Program on the Processes of International Negotiation at the International Institute for Applied Systems Analysis (IIASA), and a member of the Editorial Advisory Board of *Negotiation Journal*. Recent publications edited or co-edited by Sjöstedt include *International Economic Negotiations, Models versus Reality* (Edward Elgar, 2000), *Transboundary Risk Management* (Earthscan Publications, 2001); *Containing the Atom. International Negotiations on Nuclear Security and Safety* (Lexington Books, 2002); *Professional Cultures in International Negotiation. Bridge or Rift?* (Lexington Books, 2003); *Systems Approaches and their Application. Examples from Sweden* (Kluwer Academic, 2004); and *Global Challenges. Furthering the Multilateral Process for Sustainable Development* (Greenleaf Publishing, 2005).

Mikoto Usui is Professor Emeritus at the University of Tsukuba, Japan. Currently he teaches international negotiation and development at Seisa University. He has taught at Shukutoku University and Keio University SFC. He has been a Visiting Professor at the UNU-Institute of Advanced Studies since 1997. From 1986 to 1989 he served as Director of Research at UNIDO in Vienna, Austria.

Preface

The United Nations University Institute of Advanced Studies (UNU-IAS) began its research on the politics of participation by releasing a research agenda entitled *Engaging the Disenfranchised: Developing Countries and Civil Society in International Governance for Sustainable Development*. The report set forth a framework for investigating the problems and questions surrounding the participation of state and non-state actors from developing nations in regimes for sustainable development. Following the release of the report, UNU-IAS convened a group of scholars and practitioners to present work related to issues of disenfranchisement and to discuss potential remedies. In collaboration with the International Institute for Applied Systems Analysis (IIASA) and with support from the Austrian Ministry of Foreign Affairs, this group identified the major challenges and developed recommendations for improving the engagement of a variety of state and non-state actors. This volume represents the final product of that research.

Sustainable development will require expanding both the breadth of actors involved in creating and implementing policy and the depth of their involvement. This volume will be a useful contribution to our collective thinking about how to achieve these goals. It offers a careful analysis of the obstacles facing both state and non-state actors from developing nations in their efforts to participate in the policy-making process. Of particular use to policy-makers, civil society and others involved with sustainable development governance, the book also proposes concrete measures to help remedy this problem.

It is particularly appropriate that UNU-IAS, an advanced studies institute mandated to focus on the challenges facing developing countries, should undertake research on engaging disenfranchised actors in international governance for sustainable development. UNU-IAS is one of the 13 research and training centres that comprise the United Nations University. It contributes creative solutions to key emerging issues of global concern by providing neutral policy analysis and intensive capacity development. This book is just one example of these efforts.

A. H. Zakri
Director, UNU-IAS

Acknowledgements

The editors gratefully acknowledge the support of the Austrian Ministry of Foreign Affairs, which supported the research presented in this volume, and in particular Walther Lichem and Aloisia Woergetter for their support and participation. Collaboration with the International Institute for Applied Systems Analysis in Laxenburg, Austria, greatly improved the quality of the project. Special thanks to Mahendra Shah and Tanja Huber for their work on the meeting held in June 2004. The contributions of other participants at that meeting are reflected throughout the book; they include Meryem Amar-Samnotra, Dana R. Fisher, Ana Flavia Barros Platiau, Eva-Maria Hanfstaegel, Veit Koester, Adil Najam, Jeremy Wates and Farhana Yamin. Valuable comments on various elements of the project and this volume were given by Barry Herman, Sam Johnston, Jibecke Jonsson, Mikoto Usui and A. H. Zakri.

List of acronyms

ABS	CBD Ad-Hoc Open Ended Working Group on Access and Benefit Sharing of Genetic Resources
ACP	African, Caribbean and Pacific
AEETC	Asia-Europe Environmental Technology Centre
AFN	Assembly of First Nations (Canada)
ANPED	Northern Alliance for Sustainability
AOSIS	Association of Small Island States
ART	Alliance for Responsible Trade (USA)
ASEAN	Association of South-East Asian Nations
ASEM	Asia-Europe Meeting
BASD	Business Action for Sustainable Development
BIAC	Business and Industry Advisory Council
BWI	Bretton Woods institution
CAIPAP	Canadian Arctic Indigenous Peoples Against POPs
CASDP	Center for Advancement of Sustainable Development Partnerships
CBD	UN Convention on Biological Diversity
CCBI	Coordinated Committee of Business Interlocutors
CCC	Clean Clothes Campaign
CCD	UN Convention to Combat Desertification
CERES	Coalition for Environmentally Responsible Economies
CI	Consumers International
CIDSE	Cooperation Internationale pour le Developpement et la Solidarité
CITES	Convention on International Trade in Endangered Species
CLRTAP	Convention on Long Range Transboundary Air Pollutions

COE	The Call of the Earth
COP	Conference of the Parties
COPOLCO	ISO Consumer Policy Council
CSD	UN Commission on Sustainable Development
CSO	civil society organisation
CSR	corporate social responsibility
DC	developing country
DESA	UN Department of Economic and Social Affairs
DEVCO	ISO Committee on Developing Country Matters
ECE	UN Economic Commission for Europe
ECO	environmental citizens' organisation
ECOSOC	UN Economic and Social Council
ENGO	environmental non-governmental organisation
ESCAP	UN Economic and Social Commission for Asia and the Pacific
FCCC	UN Framework Convention on Climate Change
FfD	Financing for Development
FIELD	Foundation for International Environmental Law and Development
FLA	Fair Labor Association
FoEI	Friends of the Earth International
FSC	Forestry Stewardship Council
FTAA	Free Trade Area of the Americas
GATT	General Agreement on Tariffs and Trade
GATS	General Agreement on Trade in Services
GC	UN Global Compact
GEO	Global Environment Outlook
GRI	Global Reporting Initiative
HSA	Hemispheric Social Alliance
ICC	International Chamber of Commerce
ICFTU	International Confederation of Free Trade Unions
IFBWW	International Federation of Building and Wood Workers
IFG	International Facilitating Committee on Financing for Development
IGO	inter-governmental organisation
IIASA	International Institute for Applied Systems Analysis
ILO	International Labour Organization
IMF	International Monetary Fund
IMFC	IMF International Monetary and Financial Committee
ING	Intergovernmental Negotiation Committee
IP	intellectual property
IPCC	Intergovernmental Panel on Climate Change
IPR	intellectual property right
ISC	International Support Committee
ISO	International Standardization Organization
JPOI	Johannesburg Plan of Implementation
KPCS	Kimberley Process Certification Scheme
LDC	least developed country

MA	Millennium Ecosystem Assessment
MAI	Multilateral Agreement on Investment
MEA	multilateral environmental agreement
MERCOSUR	Southern Cone Common Market
MNC	multinational corporation
MNE	multinational enterprise
MSC	Marine Stewardship Council
NAFTA	North American Free Trade Agreement
NCP	national contact point
NEPAD	New Partnership for Africa's Development
NGO	non-governmental organisation
OAS	Organization of American States
ODA	official development assistance
OECD	Organization for Economic Cooperation and Development
OHCHR	Office of the UN High Commissioner on Human Rights
OPEC	Organization of Petroleum Exporting Countries
ORIT	Organización Regional Interamericana de Trabajadores
PFII	Permanent Forum on Indigenous Issues
POP	persistent organic pollutant
RMALC	Red mexicana al frente de libre comercio (Mexican Network on the Free Trade Agreement)
RQIC	Reseau Quebecois sur la integration continentale (Canada)
SMEs	small and medium-sized enterprises
SRI	socially responsible investment
TRIMs	Agreement on Trade-Related Investment Measures
TRIPs	Agreement on Trade-Related Aspects of Intellectual Property Rights
TUAC	Trade Union Advisory Council
UNCED	UN Conference on Environment and Development
UNCTAD	UN Conference on Trade and Development
UNDP	UN Development Programme
UNEP	UN Environment Programme
UNHCR	UN High Commissioner for Refugees
UNIDO	United Nations Industrial Development Organization
UNITAR	UN Institute for Training and Research
UNPO	Unrepresented Nations and Peoples Organization
UNRISD	UN Research Institute of Social Development
WBCSD	World Business Council for Sustainable Development
WIPO	World Intellectual Property Organization
WMO	World Meteorological Organization
WRAP	Worldwide Responsible Apparel Production
WRC	Workers Rights Consortium
WSIS	World Summit on the Information Society
WSSD	World Summit for Sustainable Development
WTO	World Trade Organization

Introduction: Understanding the challenges to enfranchisement

Jessica F. Green and W. Bradnee Chambers

Introduction

The word "participation" is widely used, if not over-used, in current discussions of global governance. Indeed, the word appears frequently in the outcome document of the 2005 Millennium+5 Summit. It is used in conjunction with developing countries, civil society, the private sector, local authorities, women and the general citizenry, always stressing the importance of promoting the participation of these groups. The call for participation is echoed in landmark documents such as the Rio Declaration, Agenda 21, the Johannesburg Plan of Implementation and a host of other international agreements. Attempts to implement the UN's commitment to collaborative efforts are further seen in initiatives such as the Global Compact, Type II partnerships and agencies such as the UN Fund for International Partnerships.

While these efforts advance, critics argue that they are insufficient. As the *Report of the Panel of Eminent Persons on United Nations-Civil Society Relations* suggests, "[j]ust when more issues demand global responses than ever before, the haphazard processes of global governance seem to generate as many contradictions as complementarities".[1] Globalisation has greatly enhanced the need for global governance as well as the need for greater decentralisation of that governance.[2] The democratic deficit of global governance persists, and it threatens to undermine the legitimacy of multilateralism.[3] The protests against the WTO in Seattle, Genoa and Cancun, for example, are in effect a call for broader participation.

1

Though some critics have dismissed these events as the responses of a small minority of anarchists or other equally untrustworthy ideologues, these criticisms cannot be brushed aside forever. Similarly, the breakdown of the WTO negotiations in Doha in 2001 and the subsequent "July package" suggest not only that meaningful engagement with the developing world is needed, but also that it will lead to consensus and progress that will ultimately aid sustainable development.[4] In sum, effective participation of developing countries, particularly delegates, is urgently needed in the current globalised system. Global rules cannot be actively made by some and passively accepted by others.

The question of participation is inextricably linked to sustainable development, for without a plurality of actors and approaches, sustainable development cannot be realised. The importance of broad-based participation, particularly the inclusion of the developing world, has emerged as a consistent theme in many major international agreements – the Rio Declaration, Agenda 21, the Millennium Development Goals, the Monterrey Consensus and the Johannesburg Plan of Implementation. Although participation of diverse groups of actors has been widely accepted and codified as a fundamental tenet of sustainable development, the international policy-making system is still struggling with ways to realise this principle. That is, despite the growing participation of a variety of non-state actors – scientists, business organisations, civil society of all stripes and indigenous peoples – in many cases, there has not been a correspondent growth in their input. Participation is uneven and unequal across and among these groups. Thus, the central challenge of this volume is to understand how these different actors can overcome obstacles to participation and improve the quality of their engagement in sustainable development governance.

This volume contributes to the collective efforts to improve both the levels and the quality of the engagement of various actors in the policy process – with a particular focus on the developing world. Specifically, the goals of the volume are twofold.

- To identify and understand barriers towards enfranchisement that developing countries and non-state actors encounter in international policy-making processes for sustainable development.
- To propose strategies to enhance the engagement of these actors, particularly those from the developing world.

Understanding enfranchisement

What does it mean to be enfranchised? Alternatively, can we say that representatives of developing countries and civil society actors are currently disenfranchised from international policy-making? Certainly, different groups vying to have their voices heard could be construed as a simple case of democracy at work. The authors maintain, however, that attempts by both negotiators and civil society actors from developing nations to become more involved and influential in international policy-making is a symptom of a more systemic problem. The current practices, institutional arrangements and political realities have hindered their engagement in international policy-making processes.

In this volume, enfranchisement is defined as the ability to both participate in and influence agenda-setting and decision-making in international regimes for sustainable development.[5] It is important to be clear that both developing country actors and civil society may be considered disenfranchised from multilateral policy-making, but that this phenomenon occurs very differently for each set of actors. Some delegates from developing nations would bristle at the thought of being labelled disenfranchised from international policy-making. These countries are accorded the same rights under international law as their developed counterparts, are recognised as sovereign nations and are free to negotiate agreements with other nations. In some cases, however, they lack the authority to influence agenda-setting or to affect outcomes.[6] As Gunnar Sjöstedt explains in chapter 9, a weak (and often developing) country, may "perform only as a silent observer for long periods of time". Thus, actors must be able not only to voice their opinions (and have them heard) but also have some influence on the outcomes of the decision-making process. Therefore, a crucial distinction exists between participation and influence; the former is a necessary but not sufficient condition for the latter. This definition of enfranchisement recognises both of these aspects. In considering the concept of enfranchisement, it is also important to note that this is not a dichotomous choice, but rather occurs on a spectrum. Not all developing countries should automatically be considered disenfranchised; the ability to participate and influence can be a matter of degrees, varying by institution, forum and policy.

Thus, according to this construction of the concept, legal rights do not ensure effective participation. Civil society does not, and should not, enjoy the same rights or privileges as states. But rules and practices about their participation are varied and inconsistent, and the ability to influence discussions is often limited to a few groups. Despite these differences, the obstacles to engagement of both state and non-state actors should be considered jointly, because failure to resolve each will have similar consequences for global governance: a heightened legitimacy crisis that will threaten the future functioning and effectiveness of these organisations.

When discussing enfranchisement, it is also important to clarify what is meant by sustainable development governance. Keohane and Nye define governance as "the processes and institutions, both formal and informal that guide and restrain the collective activities of a group".[7] According to this definition, governance includes both formal intergovernmental processes as well as "governance from below".[8] This broad depiction is important because it includes both state *and* non-state actors as well as what Karkkainen has referred to as "post sovereign" forms of governance – those that are not solely organised around and executed by the state.[9] Governance for sustainable development includes those activities related to each of the three pillars of sustainable development – economic, environmental and social. This book examines a range of actors and regimes for sustainable development, including the World Trade Organization, the Framework Convention on Climate Change, Financing for Development and the Convention on Access to Information, Public Participation in Decision-making and Access to Justice in Environmental Matters (hereafter referred to as the Åarhus Convention). Throughout this volume, international policy-making and the multilateral arena will be used to refer to the sites and processes where sustainable development governance takes place.

Although the majority of the research presented in this book focuses on the formal processes through which international policies for sustainable development are negotiated and implemented, it is important to underscore that enfranchisement need not be restricted to formal institutional processes. The research in this volume distinguishes between institutional and non-institutional pathways for influence. Institutional pathways are defined as the modes of participation sanctioned by international processes and organisations. These pathways can include roles and activities such as proposing policies, responding to policy proposals, voting and membership practices and reporting. Because not all influence is derived from organisational norms and rules of engagement – particularly for non-state actors – the research also examines non-institutional pathways, which are defined as those tactics outside the policy-making arena that actors use to influence policy decisions. Though it appears that non-state actors would be more likely to employ non-institutional pathways because of their observer status, state actors may also use them to increase their leverage, lessen the demand on their resources or simply as another way to be heard.

The framework for examining institutional and non-institutional pathways for participation is a means of operationalising (in a qualitative way) the characteristics of enfranchisement described above.[10] Being able to put forth proposals is one way actors may be able to participate in the multilateral process; this type of engagement might include conducting policy research and development, submitting position papers or comments during negotiations and intergovernmental meetings or contributing to expert panels that may shape future proposals. Similarly, actors may use established procedures to respond to proposals, such as through a public comment period; this practice is especially applicable to civil society. Voting and membership are also critical in exercising influence. The weight and number of votes are an important consideration, as is membership on committees, expert groups and boards. Finally, monitoring state compliance – either through intergovernmental bodies, independent commissions or civil society actors – may be another way to influence the policy process. Exposing non-compliance can serve as an important incentive for countries not wishing to be perceived as laggards. By contrast, countries that lead in implementation or innovation can spur a race to the top.

Since many non-state actors have limited official recognition in international policy-making, it is also necessary to examine the informal ways that they exercise influence through non-institutional pathways. One such example might include creating different organisational forms – such as coalitions or transnational groups – to increase leverage. In chapter 2, John Foster describes the transnational advocacy network that brought together diverse civil society organisations to lobby diplomats in the Financing for Development process. For developing countries, alliances with other nations in negotiating blocs may make for more complex policy positions but at the same time offer the possibility for greater leverage, a tactic often used by the Group of 77 and China, a negotiating bloc representing the majority of the developing world.[11]

Alternatively, actors might try to garner media attention in an attempt to sway public opinion in favour of a certain policy. The media is also an effective way to "sound alarms" about the gravity of a certain problem, the lack of compliance or upcoming decisions about a policy.[12] Agenda-setting is another non-institutional tactic which can put a certain issue in the public eye or into policy discussions. Again, this tactic is often used by civil society organisations. Finally, lobbying and mobilising constituencies are an important pathway for exerting pressure on the domestic level, either to influence local or national policies or to try to influence a state's position on international policies. Though these are some examples of non-institutional pathways, they are not always discrete tactics; they can, at times, blend together.

A second important point in understanding how actors are enfranchised in the multilateral arena concerns the issue of scale. According to the definition of *Webster's Revised Unabridged Dictionary*, to enfranchise is "to incorporate into a body politic and thus to invest with civil and political privileges".[13] Extrapolating from this definition, enfranchisement takes place on two levels – within the body politic, and within each group that interacts with the body politic. In the context of sustainable development governance, an actor can belong to a group that is enfranchised, and/or that actor can himself be enfranchised by exercising voice and power within his group. Enfranchisement on the "micro level", of actors within a group, is an important component of the research presented in this volume, since it is directly related to issues of accountability and legitimacy. As will be explored in the following section, the issue of scale is also important *vis-à-vis* actors' perceived legitimacy; if it is known that there are disenfranchised actors within a group, then the validity and legitimacy of its views may be called into question within a larger discussion of the body politic.

Can all actors be enfranchised?

When discussing the issue of engagement, particularly through institutional pathways, a frequent critique of the argument to promote greater inclusion is the fear of being overrun by both people and opinions. Too much deliberation causes paralysis. Consensus is impossible. Such criticisms cannot be ignored. But consider the opposite perspective: how can sustainable development governance be sustainable itself if it is not sufficiently inclusive? Integrating social, economic and environmental concerns will require the involvement of many different types of actors, all of whom approach these three pillars with different attitudes and priorities. Without this input, decision-makers may not be capable of devising solutions to the myriad challenges presented by sustainable development. More importantly, however, policy processes that exclude certain actors – either in name or in practice – risk jeopardising their legitimacy. Legitimacy is enhanced through deliberation and discussion, which bolster the "normative belief by an actor that a rule or institution ought to be obeyed".[14] Thus, by allowing the input and opinions of civil society and other actors, the policy-making process is perceived to be legitimate. Civil society and other non-state actors also have a growing role in sustainable development governance – including through agenda-setting, developing usable knowledge, monitoring, rule-making (through principled standards), policy verification, enforcement and capacity-building.[15] In addition, these non-state actors are more frequently responsible for policy implementation and service provision on the ground.[16] Their input on how policies may fare on the ground is a vital part of evaluating successes and failures and adjusting policies accordingly.

This volume will argue that delegates from developing countries and a variety of non-state actors must be able to engage meaningfully in sustainable development governance for it to be both legitimate and effective. At the same time, it is acknowledged that one of the inherent difficulties in elaborating on this problem is defining the appropriate roles and level of engagement for these actors. One cannot simply open the doors to all who wish to voice their opinion. There is no definitive answer to this problem; rather it must be discussed so that some consensus can emerge, or at least a middle ground can be reached. Indeed, some might argue that such an outcome is already emerging: the current rules and practices within the United Nations (and to a lesser extent other international institutions) reflect a norm of public and non-state participation. The current systems do allow and promote participation in specific ways, but they are imperfect in their implementation. Barriers to enfranchisement persist. This book contributes to the larger discussion about the appropriate level of engagement for different actors by first attempting to understand these obstacles and then offering potential solutions.

Given the breadth of sustainable development governance, no work, including this book, could possibly investigate all of the relevant institutions and their practices. This volume casts its net widely, examining the roles of a variety of different actors: delegates from developing countries, civil society actors, scientists, the business community and indigenous peoples. The span is intentionally broad, to try to survey the extent of disparity in engagement across actors and the types of obstacles encountered. It is particularly useful because it pulls together a variety of key actors in sustainable development governance to get a picture of the participatory "landscape". The disadvantage of this approach is that it makes proposing solutions across such diversity more challenging. However, the final section of this chapter, which gives an overview of the organisation of the book, will provide some insight into how lessons gleaned from this cross-section of actors and regimes can be understood within a larger context of enfranchisement.

Obstacles to enfranchisement

The discussion thus far has suggested that delegates from developing nations and civil society actors face different types of obstacles to effective engagement with the multilateral arena. Yet increasing engagement is not simply a matter of more training, but also of larger structural considerations. Similarly, engaging civil society actors, particularly those from the developing world, is not just about changing accreditation procedures or other institutional rules, but also remedying the disparity in capacity and representation between North and South. In short, both the structure of international policy-making (including constraints on participation at the domestic level) and the capacity of the actors have direct bearing on the level of participation and influence that both developing country delegates and civil society actors enjoy.

To gain a fuller understanding of both structure and capacity issues facing these actors, the book is divided into two parts. The first part examines the challenges for specific types of actors, including developing country delegates, non-governmental organisations (NGOs), scientists, indigenous peoples and business. Each chapter makes recommendations specific to each set of actors. The second half examines specific regimes and institutions to see what lessons can be gleaned from them. That is, these chapters focus on different structures to see if they can serve as models for enhancing engagement at the international level.

Developing country delegates

Developing countries face a distinct set of barriers to enfranchisement. All delegates have equal rights of participation. Thus, delegates representing developing nations have the right to address the floor, introduce proposals and negotiate text. However, due to their individual capacities, these same delegates may be unable to exercise power or influence the discussions of multilateral policy-making. This may be because it is not their area of expertise; because they have an extremely large and varied portfolio; or because they have been recently assigned a new one. The result is a significant disparity in power. Often this disparity falls along North-South lines; countries with economies in transition commonly encounter similar obstacles as countries from the developing world. On the macro level, the obstacles that developing country delegates encounter more frequently than their developed country counterparts include the following.

- Small or one-person delegations – precludes attendance at multiple, simultaneous sessions in one meeting, or sending delegations to different meetings that occur at the same time.[17]
- Lack of knowledge of English – although plenary sessions are translated into the six official languages, small contact groups and late-night sessions are often not.
- Lack of funds to travel to meetings – makes it costly to attend the numerous meetings held each year, particularly when no financial support is available. It should be noted here that the uniform designation of developing countries could obscure which ones are in most need of financial aid.
- Lack of experience in multilateral negotiations.
- Lack of technical knowledge about the issues being discussed – can be further exacerbated by scarce access to information technology. In-

creasingly, both raw data and analysis of specific issues are available on the internet, so lack of internet access (or poor-quality connections) can create serious obstacles to participation. Access to information technology such as the internet improves access not only to information, but also to other people who can serve as information resources and provide contact with social networks.
- Lack of expert knowledge – means that developing countries send diplomats to international negotiations while developed countries have a team of experts negotiating. Developing country delegates may thus be outnumbered, as mentioned above, or may experience difficulties in communicating about technical or scientific issues.

Another obstacle identified includes the lack of instruction from state capitals. Without a clear understanding of desired outcomes, developing country negotiators are left to decide what policies would be most beneficial and how to negotiate this position effectively. An absence of instruction can also lead to what Gupta, in chapter 1, terms "a hollow mandate", where developing countries have a bare skeleton of ideas that lean heavily on other national positions. These ideas may not necessarily be well suited to the regime at hand. In addition, a lack of instruction from capitals may arise because there is insufficient discussion at the national level, which may simply reflect domestic policy priorities. If the international agenda is being driven by other nations with different priorities, the issue being discussed may not overlap with domestic policy objectives. Alternatively, because domestic discussions evolve at differing paces and timeframes, some developing nations may not have arrived at the conclusion that a particular issue merits national-level debate. In either case, states may remain marginalised *because* they are marginalised; with other nations driving the international agenda, they may be ill-equipped to influence the multilateral discussion, thus perpetuating the problem.

On the micro level, that is, among actors within a given group, one of the main obstacles to enfranchisement identified by contributors was the potential "hijacking" of a coalition agenda. For example, to increase their influence, developing countries have joined together in a number of different negotiating blocs, the largest of which is the G-77 and China. However, some have criticised this on the grounds that, despite consultations among all the members, the agenda is often skewed toward the most powerful countries within the G-77.[18] Some of the smaller countries may sign on to G-77 positions because it is their best opportunity for some degree of influence, even if they have been relatively uninvolved in the formulation of the negotiating positions. In some cases there may be deal-making within the G-77, so that while certain nations may not endorse the overall package, the side payments are sufficiently attractive to secure their support.[19] The G-77 also illustrates obstacles to enfranchisement on the macro level. The G-77 often reverts to a defensive position, spending more time opposing than proposing. At best, this defensive strategy will allow them to block policies to which they object but not implement those from which they would benefit.

In chapter 1, Joyeeta Gupta delves into the problems that developing negotiators are facing through a case study of the climate change regime. She reaffirms many of the problems outlined above, but also points to a more serious trend. She argues that the playing field is likely to continue to be skewed and uneven, particularly as the current trend for law-making speeds up. This expansion and acceleration of international law-making for sustainable development will place further pressure on developing countries to understand their relevance for their national positions. If the trend is sustained in the long run, and the disadvantages viewed by developing country negotiators are not addressed, then there may be implications for the legitimacy of international law itself.

Non-state actors

Civil society

There is a similar disparity of power between developed and developing countries among civil society actors. Often, civil society organisations (CSOs) from the developed world have more staff, funding and experience with international policy-making than those from the developing world. Although this is a general characterisation of the problem, the numbers confirm there is more than a little truth to the statement. Despite the dramatic increase in civil society actors active in international governance for sustainable development, a disproportionate number of civil society groups are from the developed world. Indeed, statistics bear this out: in 2004 almost 70 per cent of NGOs in consultative status with the UN Economic and Social Council (ECOSOC) were from North America and Europe, and only 17 per cent were from Africa, Latin America and the Caribbean.[20] Thus, the level of development of civil society on the national level may not be reflected in the international arena.

The disparity of participation and influence between the developed and developing worlds is further exacerbated by civil society's still-evolving role in the multilateral process. Indeed, some scholars have argued that civil society participation in sustainable development governance remains, in many ways, *ad hoc*.[21] Moreover, the fragmentation of formalised accreditation processes makes it difficult for civil society actors to participate in different realms of policy-making. There are other logistical difficulties, including:

- number of intergovernmental meetings;
- cost of attending these meetings;
- difficulty in procuring visas, and the frequency of meetings held in the developed world;
- limited ability to participate in some forums due to forum-specific rules and practices.

Lack of capacity is particularly applicable to CSOs of the developing world. For many, effecting influence is beyond the scope of reasonable expectations; simply participating – finding the financial and human resources to attend meetings and follow policy processes – is the first order of business. Limited access to the proceedings of a particular process can be doubly problematic. CSOs may be unable to participate on the international level; without access to drafts and documents it is difficult both to lobby and to offer proposals.

Access to UN discussions can also be difficult. NGOs can be accredited to participate in intergovernmental meetings through ECOSOC; moreover, they can gain access to information and to UN headquarters through accreditation with the Department of Public Information. However, as noted by the High Level Panel on UN-Civil Society Relations, this process is fragmented, complex and often overwhelming.[22] At times accreditation can also be a political procedure, since states have the final say in who is approved. It can be a difficult process to navigate, particularly for small, understaffed and underfinanced NGOs. Consequently, the accreditation of NGOs is skewed to those who have the resources; often groups based in North America and Europe. Access to meetings of other international institutions is even more restricted, as Kevin Gray points out in his discussion of the World Trade Organization in chapter 6.

Even for those NGOs that are accredited, some argue that this institutional pathway affords them participation, but little to no influence. As Barry Herman points out in chapter 7, follow-up roundtables in the Financing for Development process offered ample opportunity for interaction between civil society and policy-makers – except that during this part of the process, fewer policy-makers showed up.

In addition, there are a number of more substantive political obstacles that limit the participation and influence of a variety of civil society actors. For instance, many states are wary of allowing an expanded role for civil society, and they often use the obstacles listed above to reaffirm that civil society is not necessarily representative of their purported constituents. This self-selected group is not accountable, and thus many have argued that there are serious and credible concerns about their legitimacy.[23]

In chapter 2, John W. Foster looks generally at the political terrain that has led to increased tension between civil society groups and the multilateral system. He uses what he calls the atypical case of the negotiations of the Free Trade Area of the Americas (FTAA) to examine the institutional and non-institutional pathways of civil society and compares these in a number of categories, such as the ways in which CSOs are able to respond to proposals made by governments, to make policies and proposals themselves in the negotiations, the reporting processes and the voting they use and membership and procedural rights of CSOs. Foster then turns to more systemic issues of macro-economic policy, Financing for Development and the development framework for the Millenium Development Goals to make a similar comparison. He argues that though there are several good examples of how multilateral processes could be improved, and civil society is offering useful proposals, he is concerned that these will not be effective until the United Nations creates a "strategic process" or an "occasion" for these changes to be adopted.

Business

Given the enormous power the business sector can exercise in lobbying and influencing sustainable development governance, the challenge for this group is to envision ways they can credibly and effectively collaborate with other actors. For example, UN Secretary-General Annan's initiative for broadening UN-business partnerships through the Global Compact elicited criticism from civil society and calls for a legally binding framework to govern corporations – viewing this as the only way to rein in what civil society perceives to be undue influence on international policy-making. Civil society did not achieve its desired outcome, but these objections contributed to the creation of the High Level Panel on UN-Civil Society Relations. Since corporate social responsibility is quite firmly on the agenda of the Global Compact and many other advocacy networks for sustainable business, the question is no longer whether business will be involved, but how its involvement can promote sustainable development and the enfranchisement of other actors. These networks now endeavour to include or enfranchise more of the weaker segments of their stakeholders – particularly small and medium-sized enterprises in the developing world. A key challenge is to create a policy environment which ensures that business leaders and civil society activists can collaborate credibly to consolidate and implement internationally acceptable standards for corporate social responsibility, and thus to maintain an appropriate balance of influence between business, government and civil society actors.

In chapter 3, Mikoto Usui discusses the nuances between state regulation and self-regulation, and some of the main hurdles that must be overcome in order to forge a more legitimate relationship between what he defines as the business sector and civil society in sustainable development governance processes. He finds that most pathways for bringing business into the realm of global governance are non-institutional (or what he terms quasi-institutional pathways), which is quickly becoming the more common route for participation under current models of governance. But unlike civil society, the business sector places much less emphasis on formalising these pathways. In the wake of mounting pressure to create legally binding rules of corporate conduct, business has preferred to adopt what it views as concrete actions by agreeing to greater corporate responsibility through voluntary action. This area, which Usui describes as a "subtle combination of 'confronting' and 'conflating' the engagement between business and CSO leaders", still requires further research and understanding; nevertheless, there is an interesting policy space between a *laissez-faire* approach and that of binding regulation. This scope exists in areas of corporate social responsibility that could be further operationalised through a standardised code of conduct and by mainstreaming corporate responsibility into international and national policy- and decision-making.

Scientists

Scientists are not often regarded as directly involved in the multilateral process, and their neutrality has necessitated that they play a role from afar as independent observers. Yet this distanced and impartial role is no longer possible. Because the scientific issues surrounding sustainable development are complex and require high levels of expertise, and because uncertainty over the facts has led to major debates over scientific evidence, scientists must be involved in the policy-making process. Increasingly, they are conducting assessments and voicing their opinions as experts in international policy forums. This raises questions of legitimacy, balance and the role that scientists should play. For example, the Millennium Ecosystem Assessment launched by the United Nations in 2001 was formed in large part by concerned scientists who believed there was a real need for an integrated assessment that offered a global picture of the state of the earth's ecosystems. To undertake such a study as a strictly intergovernmental process would have been a much more difficult endeavour. But where are the boundaries between agenda-setting and advocacy? If science is important to policy-making, how can it be made more salient? Is science really neutral or does perspective (i.e. gender, culture, developing or developed) matter and affect research priorities? And how can decisions be taken when the science remains uncertain? In chapter 4, W. Bradnee Chambers explores these and other questions by looking at formal assessment processes and scientific mechanisms directly linked to policy-making and through informal or non-institutionalised pathways, in the form of social networks and epistemic communities.

Indigenous people

As holders of traditional forms of knowledge, and important actors in the preservation of this knowledge, indigenous peoples must be included in international policy-making for sustainable development. The creation of the Permanent Forum on Indigenous Issues (PFII) in 2000 has underscored the growing recognition of the role they must have. The forum is charged with, among other things, "providing expert advice and recommendations on indigenous issues to the Council, as well as to programmes, funds and agencies of the United Nations through the Council".[24] Despite this new institutionalised pathway for input, there is a long path to enfranchisement, and indigenous people continue to encounter a number of obstacles to achieving this goal.

First, as is evidenced by the PFII, indigenous peoples are not recognised as having international standing. In chapter 5, Leanne Simpson argues that such recognition must be the end result of indigenous enfranchisement in sustainable development governance. In the interim there are institutional pathways available, but they sometimes offer participation without any real opportunity for influence. For example, although a number of nations invite indigenous representatives to sit on their delegations, in some cases they may not have any real input into the state position. This reduces indigenous participation to tokenism, which is used to enhance the image or credibility of the delegation. A similar phenomenon of "participation in name only" can be seen in the Commission on Sustainable Development, where indigenous people are one of the nine major groups. However, their participation is often reduced to brief interventions in a body that has been criticised for its lack of impact on sustainable development policy and governance. Thus, this is not a problem that is singularly applicable to indigenous peoples, but, as interventions are one of the main institutional pathways available to them, it is an important one.

A corollary to the problem of participation without influence is the lack of inter-institutional (and even intra-institutional) exchange. The importance of traditional knowledge to the achievement of sustainable development is signalled by international agreements such as the Convention on Biological Diversity and the Desertification Convention, and processes and forums within these conventions such as the Working Group on Article 8(j) of the Convention on Biological Diversity on traditional knowledge, innovation and practices. These have considerable participation and buy-in from indigenous peoples, yet Simpson argues that their recommendations often miss the target of where effective change can be made. Traditional peoples are willing to use their knowledge to protect the environment and work towards sustainable futures, but they also want to protect this knowledge from commercial exploitation and receive due recognition of the origin of the knowledge. These concerns cannot be achieved effectively through multilateral environmental agreements (MEAs), but require protection through *sui generis* systems created in intellectual property agreements under the World Intellectual Property Organization and enforceable in the Trade-related Intellectual Property Agreement of the WTO. Representation and access to these processes by indigenous groups, however, is much less, and in some cases, such as the WTO, virtually non-existent. Even after many years of lobbying by indigenous groups to get the traditional issues on the WTO Ministerial agendas, the Doha Round is likely to finish without any significant progress made on recognising that traditional knowledge does not fit into the existing intellectual property rights system and may require tailored measures for its adequate protection.

The second half of the book begins with Kevin Gray's examination of the current engagement of civil society within the WTO. He notes that both institutional and non-institutional pathways for influence are minimal within the WTO. Thus, the NGO community involved in trade-related issues has tried to forge its own pathway by submitting *amicus* briefs to the dispute settlement body, yet even this practice has proven to be contentious. He notes, however, that the increased pressure brought to bear on the WTO regime by civil society has, to some extent, prompted the institution to begin to allow limited interaction through public symposia, its website and, at times, observer status at committee and council meetings. Gray's chapter thus demonstrates some tactics that have been useful in starting the process of enfranchisement through the creation of basic mechanisms for participation. In chapter 7, Barry Herman explores how developing countries were effective at influencing the debate surrounding the Financing for Development process. He demonstrates the ways that developing countries involved in the discussion were able to reshape the debate and create more favourable conditions for exercising influence through non-institutional pathways.

The final two chapters examine ways that both civil society actors and developing countries can enhance their influence through already established institutional pathways for participation. Marc Pallemaerts describes the precedents in public participation mechanisms established by the Aarhus Convention, the "first multilateral treaty on the environment whose main aim is to impose obligations on states in respect of their own citizens". These citizens' rights are of a procedural nature and thus have the effect of codifying institutional pathways for both participation and influence of civil society. Gunnar Sjöstedt examines ways to improve the capacity of developing countries in the climate change regime to enhance their ability to influence the formal negotiating process. The concluding chapter by Jessica F. Green offers some conclusions and recommendations for promoting enfranchisement.

Notes

1. United Nations (2004) *We the Peoples: Civil Society, the United Nations and Global Governance*, A/RES/58/817, para. 178.
2. Slaughter, A. M. (2004) *A New World Order*, Princeton, NJ: Princeton University Press.
3. See, for example, O'Brien, Robert, Goetz, Anne Marie, Scholte, Jan Aart and Williams, Marc (2000) "Contesting Governance: Multilateralism and Global Social Movements", in Robert O'Brien, Anne Marie Goetz, Jan Aart Scholte and Marc Williams, eds, *Contesting Global Governance: Multilateral Economic Institutions and Global Social Movements*, Cambridge: Cambridge University Press, pp. 1–23.
4. See *July Package*, available from www.wto.org/english/tratop_e/dda_e/draft_text _gc_dg_31july04_e.htm.
5. This definition was first used in the framework document for this project: Green, J. (2004) *Engaging the Disenfranchised: Developing Countries and Civil Society in International Governance for Sustainable Development*, UNU-IAS report.
6. Najam, A. and Robins, N. (2001) "Seizing the Future: The South, Sustainable Development and International Trade", *International Affairs* 77(1): 49–68.
7. Keohane, R. and Nye, J. (2002) "Governance in a Globalizing World", in R. Keohane, ed., *Power and Governance in a Partially Globalized World*, London: Routledge.
8. Appadurai, A. (2001) *Globalization*, Durham, NC: Duke University Press.
9. Karkkainen, Bradley (2004) "Post-Sovereign Environmental Governance", *Global Environmental Politics* 4(1): 72–96.
10. The authors acknowledge different uses of the word institution, which tends to be defined broadly as a "persistent and connected sets of rules and practices that prescribe behavioural roles, constrain activities and shape expectations" (Keohane, Robert O., Haas, Peter M. and Levy, Marc A. (1993) "The Effectiveness of International Environmental Institutions", in P. Haas, R. Keohane and M. Levy, eds, *Institutions for the Earth: Sources of Effective International Environmental Protection*, Cambridge, MA: MIT Press, p. 5). In this volume, the term is used more narrowly to distinguish between those processes and practices sanctioned by international organisations and intergovernmental rule-making, and similar activities which occur *beyond* this context. Although this is not the traditional use of the word, as invoked by institutionalists, it is felt that it is important to distinguish between insider and outsider approaches to engagement.
11. Najam, Adil (1995) "An Environmental Negotiation Strategy for the South", *International Environmental Affairs* 7(3): 249–287.
12. Mazur, Allan and Lee, Jinling (1997) "Sounding the Global Alarm: Environmental Issues in the US National News", *Social Studies of Science* 23(4): 681–720; Raustiala, Kal (1997) "States, NGOs and International Environmental Institutions", *International Studies Quarterly* 41(4): 719–740.
13. *Webster's Revised Unabridged Dictionary*, Webster-Merriam, 1998 edition.
14. Hurd, Ian (1999) "Legitimacy and Authority in International Politics", *International Organization* 53(2): 379–408.
15. Haas, Peter, Kanie, Norichika and Murphy, Craig (2004) "Institutional Design and In-

stitutional Reform for Sustainable Development", in Norichika Kanie and Peter Haas, eds, *Emerging Forces in Environmental Governance*, Tokyo: United Nations University Press, p. 267.
16. Tussie, Diana and Riggirozzi, Maria Pia (2001) "Pressing Ahead with New Procedures for Old Machinery: Global Governance and Civil Society", in Volker Rittberger, ed., *Global Governance and the United Nations System*, New York: United Nations University Press, pp. 158–180.
17. These obstacles have been discussed elsewhere, not only in the research agenda for this project, "Engaging the Disenfranchised: Developing Countries and Civil Society in International Regimes for Sustainable Development", UNU-IAS, February 2004, but also in Chandhoke, Neera (2002) "The Limits of Global Civil Society", in M. Glasius, M. Kaldor and H. Anheier, eds, *Global Civil Society*, Oxford: Oxford University Press, pp. 35–53; Clark, A. M., Friedman, E. and Hochstetler, K. (1998) "The Sovereign Limits of Global Civil Society: A Comparison of NGO Participation in UN World Conferences on the Environment, Human Rights and Women", *World Politics* 51(1): 1–35.
18. Discussion at "Engaging the Disenfranchised" meeting, Laxenburg, Austria, 22 June 2004.
19. Najam, Adil (2004) "Dynamics of the Southern Collective: Developing Countries in Desertification Negotiations", *Global Environmental Politics* 4(3): 128–154.
20. UN DESA, NGO Section. "NGOs in Consultative Status with ECOSOC, 2004", available from www.un.org/esa/coordination/ngo.
21. Gemmill, Barbara and Bamidele-Izu, Amibola (2002) "The Role of NGOs and Civil Society in Global Environmental Governance", in Daniel Esty and Maria Ivanova, eds, *Global Environmental Governance: Options and Opportunities*, New Haven: Yale School of Forestry and Environmental Studies, pp. 77–101. See also Oberthur, Sebastian, Buck, Matthias, Muller, Sebastian, Pfahl, Stefanie and Tarasofsky, Richard (2002) *Participation of Non-Governmental Organisations in International Environmental Governance: Legal Basis and Practical Experience*, Berlin: Ecologic.
22. United Nations (2004) "We the Peoples: Civil Society, the United Nations and Global Governance. Report by the Panel of Eminent Persons on UN-Civil Society Relations", A/58/817.
23. Fox, J. A. and Brown, L. D. (1998) *The Struggle for Accountability: The World Bank, NGOs and Grassroots Movements*, Cambridge, MA: MIT Press; Edwards, Michael and Gaventa, John (2001) *Global Citizen Action*, Boulder, CO: Lynne Rienner Publishers.
24. "Permanent Forum: Origin and Development", available from www.un.org/esa/socdev/unpfii/aboutPFII/mandate_home_2.htm.

Part I
Actors

1
Increasing disenfranchisement of developing country negotiators in a multi-speed world

Joyeeta Gupta

Introduction

Globalisation has shrunk our world, lessening the geographic, cultural and linguistic distances and differences between us. Yet at the same time, we live in a divided world which works at two speeds: in one, developed countries, enjoying the benefits of development and from a position of relative comfort, are motivated to address global problems largely because of the potential negative impacts they may endure; in the other, the developing world is struggling to keep abreast of the rapid pace of developments in the international arena, and to participate in rule-making processes that may eventually affect them.[1]

Globalisation enthusiasts argue that trade liberalisation will spread wealth around the world and will be a panacea to help developing countries develop. For example, Bhagwati notes that critics of globalisation miss the tremendous opportunity within it to accelerate socially relevant solutions.[2] Das argues that trade liberalisation will release developing countries from their self-imposed shackles of protectionism.[3]

Sceptics, on the other hand, believe that globalisation may spread wealth to the top layer of society but is unlikely to stimulate economic growth in the bulk of developing countries or reduce income inequalities.[4] De Rivero argues that the development model being exported today is a myth and a non-viable option for the developing world.[5] He claims that the wealth of nations agenda is based on a mistaken perception of the global reality.

Banuri argues that the world is in fact a third world country, in that almost all the social, political and economic features seen in a classic third world country are reflected in the global context.⁶ Continuing with Banuri's logic suggests that power politics at the global level is no different from the processes of politics in countries with poor governance. The rule of law is an unfinished project and good governance is still a dream at global level, leaving some nations more vulnerable and less influential than others. It is in this imperfect governance system that the forces of globalisation have been unleashed. In this globalised world, multiple actors are engaged in competitive governance patterns in different international forums, and there is increasing scope for self-regulation, for public-private partnerships and for autonomous processes that implicitly lead to new rules at international level. Hence there is well-founded concern that in this competition, accountability, legitimacy and even legality certainty and predictability will be sacrificed.⁷ This reality calls for an overhaul of the global governance system, for without it the disenfranchisement of the weak and less powerful will continue.

Against this background, this chapter examines the disenfranchisement of developing country negotiators within the specific context of the climate change negotiations. The author has argued for several years that developing countries are becoming increasingly disenfranchised in the negotiating process, and that there are major questions of legitimacy and compliance-pull.⁸ By compliance-pull is meant that countries should feel inclined to comply with an agreement because this is what they have agreed to and not only because there are controls to check that they are complying. This chapter builds on the theoretical framework put forth in the introduction discussing the role of developing country negotiators in using institutional and non-institutional pathways for influencing policies. It uses the results of more than 600 interviews conducted with negotiators in the course of several projects⁹ as well as the literature that is increasingly being devoted to this subject.

This chapter takes an ideal-typical approach: it focuses on the generic developing country, the generic developing country negotiator and the generic problems of the developing country negotiator in the international negotiating process. This does not imply ignorance of the vast differences between developing countries or the vast differences between negotiators or negotiating situations.¹⁰ Yet given that there was considerable unanimity in the responses of the interviewees, there is strong evidence to support such a broad-brush approach.

This chapter briefly introduces the international environmental and developmental arena, then discusses the key aspects and policy challenges of climate change, examining both institutional and non-institutional pathways for influencing the international climate change negotiations. Finally, it assesses the degree to which developing countries are becoming disenfranchised.

Climate change and sustainable development governance

Sustainable development governance

Development and environmental issues are closely related. Access to food, water, shelter, health care, education and employment are closely linked to the state of the environment. The literature argues that one way to integrate the two concepts is through the notion of sustainable development. Achieving sustainable development calls for continuously making trade-offs between economic, social and environmental goals, where integration is not feasible. To achieve sustainable development at the local through to global levels, a good governance framework (which includes accountability, legitimacy, transparency, the rule of law, public participation)[11] and an intellectual ability to integrate environmental, economic and social parameters in decision-making are needed at national and international levels. At the national level, the lack of good governance is a serious challenge, and increasingly all domestic policy failures are being attributed to this lack. Santiso states that "In recent years, the strengthening of good governance in developing countries has become both an *objective* of and a condition for development assistance."[12]

At the same time, an examination of key features of the governance framework at the international level shows that an integrated approach to sustainable development appears impossible. Most authors agree that, at the international level, we do not have good governance or the rule of law.[13] Rather, nations negotiate with each other in an anarchic setting. This makes it difficult to address global issues in a systematic and structural manner, especially if addressing such issues is not in the direct interest of the most powerful countries. This observation is affirmed by theoretical projections from the realist and neo-realist schools of thought, and also from the structuralist school of thought.

Institutionalists, however, have argued that the challenge of dealing with environmental problems at the international level may be overcome by dividing issues into individual elements. Since power relations in specific issue areas may not necessarily correspond to structural global power relations, there may be room for cooperation.[14] However, if we accept that there is some truth in both what institutionalists argue and what realists predict, then any efforts at systemically linking issues to other elements and areas in the international context in order to achieve sustainable development will likely fail, even though there may be some windows of opportunity.[15] This implies that unless there is a major structural change in the global governance structure, policy approaches to sustainable development will tend to be in the form of issue-based governance in different forums.

Climate change – The problem

Climate change, ostensibly caused by the emissions of greenhouse gases, is a good case study because it encompasses many of the problems affecting the world today. Greenhouse gas emissions come from the energy, transport, agricultural and industrial sectors, i.e. almost all sectors of society. Three points can be made at the outset. First, the perception that greenhouse gas emissions are closely related to the economic growth of a country is strong and a dominant influence in both the developed and the developing world. This perception contrasts to earlier hopes that the climate change problem would be easier to address as countries became richer, because of the so-called inverted U curve – the environmental Kuznets curve argument, which states that beyond a certain amount of income per capita, environmental degradation should *decrease* as a country's wealth *increases*.[16] Recent research increasingly shows that the environmental Kuznets curve does not hold for global pollutants, nor does it hold for resource use in a society. Spangenberg argues that "The Environmental Kuznets Curve hypothesis narrows the view on the environment; following it would cause significant damages, environmentally as well as economically."[17] This means that reducing emissions is seen as a common challenge for all countries, but those countries with a technological edge and that can benefit from technological innovation[18] are more likely to be able to reduce emissions while increasing economic growth. This leads to the first inference, which is that the bulk of developing countries are unlikely to be in this category.

Second, the costs and benefits of climate change are inequitably distributed across the world.[19] The physical and economic impacts of the potential effects of climate change may be substantially higher in developing countries – many of which are small island or semi-arid states – than in the developed world.[20] However, the 2005 impacts of hurricanes Katrina, Rita and Wilma on the United States have suddenly focused considerable attention on the difficulties even developed countries may face in dealing with extreme weather events. But even so, these events have not led the United States to change its position categorically on climate change. In other words, from a political perspective the climate change problem faces the challenge of no longer being seen as a common problem and the debate may recede once more into a "winners versus losers" discussion.[21] This leads to the second inference. Although the driving factor behind the climate change regime thus far has been the developed world, they may soon wish to take the back seat, since it is very likely that it is the developing countries that will bear the brunt of the impacts.[22] They will do so by possibly setting the goals of the climate change regime at a level necessary to protect themselves, but not necessarily to protect the small island states or the coastal populations of low-lying developing countries.[23]

Third, whether one uses cost-benefit analysis or the participatory integrated assessment method, the results will tend to be skewed against the interests of the South. A cost-benefit approach will "price away" the South, while a participatory integrated assessment method may lead to a situation where the more powerful and influential stakeholders choose local benefits while paying lip service to global benefits.

Climate change negotiations

Let us then move to the negotiating arena. The climate change problem is being addressed within the framework of the UN Framework Convention on Climate Change. The convention, negotiated in 1992, entered into force in 1994 and since 1995 there have been annual meetings of the Conference of the Parties to discuss outcomes and negotiate future steps. The convention has two subsidiary bodies and these are now negotiating different elements of the climate change issue. In 1997 the Kyoto Protocol to the Climate Change Convention was adopted. The protocol entered into force on 16 February 2005, although the world's largest polluter, the United States, has decided not to ratify the agreement.

In the formal international negotiating arena, two groups, the developed world (Annex I) and the developing world (non-Annex I parties), are active. The developed world is formally divided into the rich and the not-so-rich countries (Annex II countries). Informally, it is divided into negotiating blocs – the European Union, the Eastern and Central European countries, the group of Japan, the United States, Switzerland, Canada, Norway and New Zealand (referred to as JUSCANNZ prior to the US withdrawal) and the rest. The developing countries are informally divided into the oil exporters (OPEC), the small island states (AOSIS) and the regional groupings.

Institutionalised pathways for influencing the climate negotiations

This section examines the ability of developing countries to influence the outcomes of international agreements through institutional pathways, as outlined by Green and Chambers in the introduction to this volume.

Proposing policies

To understand the degree of disenfranchisement, the first enquiry point is: are developing countries, in general, in a position to propose policies in time to influence the negotiating process?[24]

The ability to propose policies in the international arena is a function of one key factor: the ability of countries to develop a detailed and comprehensive negotiating mandate. The author maintains that the key bottleneck facing developing countries is the *hollow negotiating mandate*, the content of which is explained below.

Interviews reveal that developing countries face a number of challenges with complex environmental issues that are signalled primarily by the North. The first challenge is the problem of *ideological vacillation* and the *sustainability* dilemmas. Ideological vacillation refers to the fact that many developing countries have not yet internalised one particular ideology in their national system and they are still in the process of trying to understand what is best for them under different situations. Is the free-market approach most beneficial to their country? Or is some kind of mixed economy better? Is globalisation good for them? Without a thorough understanding of the implications of these questions – that is, without a concrete ideology to guide policy and develop a national negotiating position – many developing countries have fundamentally weak negotiating positions.

Flowing from the general problem of ideological vacillation is the specific problem of the sustainability dilemma. The sustainability dilemma refers to a combination of six fundamental dilemmas faced by developing countries in relation to global environmental issues, where answers are far from clear.

- The development dilemma, which refers to the question: "how does one modernise without Westernising?" This challenge is of particular relevance in relation to issues like climate change and sustainable development.
- The poverty dilemma includes issues such as: "how does one survive without squandering one's resources?" This question is of relevance in relation to the negotiations on the Convention on the International Trade in Endangered Species (CITES), the Clean Development Mech-

anism within the Climate Change Convention, the 1987 Basel Convention on the Transboundary Movement of Hazardous Wastes and the 1992 Convention on Biological Diversity. A corollary to the first question is: "how does one ask for help from the developed world without mortgaging one's future?"
- The privatisation dilemma asks how to empower the private sector to solve public problems. Although the mantra of privatisation is spreading throughout the world, and many developing countries are being encouraged to privatise, successful examples of this approach in the developed world are not numerous. Considerable evidence from the water sector does not suggest there are many reasons to be hopeful. Private sector participation in water management was expected to ensure that water services could be improved and would be provided at competitive prices. The initial evidence is that after privatisation, in most cases, the price of water went up and the poor now have less access than before.[25]
- The environmental space dilemma refers to the question: "how does one achieve environmental equity in an international regime without dealing with environmental equity issues at national level?" This is not only a serious dilemma in developing countries but also possibly reflects the US position. This dilemma plays a critical role in the negotiations on climate change and biodiversity and related domestic policy.
- The economic dilemma weighs issues of short- and long-term gain: "how does one serve short-term business and political interests without affecting long-term economic and environmental interests?"
- The negotiation dilemma asks how to combine the strengths of the G-77 without reducing the common negotiating position to the highest of the lowest common denominator positions.

A third key structural problem is how issues arrive on the agenda in the developing world. On issues signalled by the West, the agenda-building process in developing countries tends to take the foreign mobilisation model approach:[26] the subject reaches the domestic agenda via foreign policy. This means that the issue is often characterised by the following features. It is likely to be defined in alien terms – not as a domestic priority but as a competitor to domestic priorities. It is likely to have the features of a formal agenda item. It is unlikely to mobilise domestic grassroots organisations or to engage the attention of domestic industry since other social actors are less involved. As a result, the issue is unlikely to influence the political agenda unless there are political features that can be exploited. If the public cannot be motivated to take action, governments cannot be motivated to earmark funds for research and policy, and the issue will tend to remain a rhetorical agenda item.

If the issue is only a formal agenda item, then the chances that it will be discussed in the media in its full complexity are limited. Rather, there is far greater likelihood that the issue will be discussed in terms of its political and North-South challenges.

In terms of climate change, research shows that even if countries do establish a national climate change policy-making process, these tend to be more a matter of form than of strategy.[27] Therefore, although there may be cooperation among different parts of the government, such cooperation does not necessarily lead to structural change or integrated policies. In other words, simply imitating procedures in the West does not necessarily mean that the procedures and their goals are internalised and supported by different administrative levels.

Another key problem for developing countries is growing *structural imbalance in knowledge*, especially in relation to the climate change issue. The need for scientific research in the area of climate change is growing exponentially and has a high price tag. Developing countries have difficulty focusing research funds on issues of primary importance to their domestic agenda without taking on the complex issue of climate change. This is a consequence of a gap in resources. The result is a structural imbalance in scientific knowledge.

Since a large portion of research is undertaken by the developed world, there are gaps in the knowledge generated. There are gaps in terms of the substantive focus of the science, resulting in research that is sometimes less relevant to the developing world. There are also legitimacy gaps which arise because of the relatively lower capacity of the developing world to undertake scientific research, raising questions about whether or not the science is in fact consensual (see Chambers' discussion of this in chapter 4). Indeed, a lack of consensus about the social science of climate change may also arise from theoretical gaps – problems in terms of conflicting theoretical starting points and assumptions, and in extrapolation and interpretation. Finally, as Chambers discusses, there may also be an imbalance or gap between the representation of developing and developed country research in assessment panels, and in peer review control.[28]

The structural imbalance in negotiations has had a direct impact on climate negotiations. Instead of the negotiators being influenced by science generated domestically, they are often obliged to make assessments on the basis of a partial understanding of global science and its policy implications for their domestic agenda. As a result, the domestic articulation of interests tends to be more qualitative in nature, élitist and cast in diplomatic terms. This inevitably implies that the articulation of issue linkages tends to be in terms of all other development issues that developing countries are pushing on the international agenda, rather than in terms of concrete domestic policies.

Ideological vacillation, the sustainability dilemma, the roundabout way in which issues appear on the domestic policy agenda and the structural imbalance of knowledge have a cumulative and disadvantageous effect on the negotiating position and capabilities of developing country representatives. Together, these various phenomena add up to what the author terms the "hollow negotiating mandate": a bare skeleton of ideas that leans heavily on the national position in other issue areas, with limited legitimacy with respect to the scientific basis and the domestic buy-in for a country's negotiating position.

Responding to policy proposals

During the complex process of climate change negotiations there are several developed country proposals on the table simultaneously, which include how emissions should be calculated, carbon sinks defined and mechanisms elaborated. The incredible variety of issues that are on the table makes it difficult for the developing countries to come up with a clear response, even when they have ample time to prepare. For example, each change in the definition of carbon sinks – such as trees and grasses used to sequester carbon – will have implications for what actions a country must take to reduce its emissions. In turn, this will require extensive national research in relation to the issue of sinks within a domestic context. Answers to such questions cannot be whipped up in a few weeks or even a few months unless the country in question already has a long-standing research programme on climate change. As argued above, most developing countries have a structural imbalance in knowledge with the developed world.

One example of this structural imbalance can be seen in the 2001 Marrakesh Negotiations on Climate Change. There was a negotiating text that ran to 150 pages of complicated multidisciplinary text, and that required in-depth substantive knowledge to be able to understand (let along bargain about) the proposed measures. If developing countries do not possess the requisite knowledge and experience, as is often the case because of the structural imbalance described above, they are likely to oppose these new proposals simply on the basis of the assumption that they question the source of the proposal.

Voting/membership

In principle, developing countries individually have one vote each in the international negotiating process.[29] Together, in the climate change regime, the non-Annex I countries (i.e. developing countries) have 150 votes. Amendments can be made by consensus, and failing that, by a three-quarters majority of the parties present and voting:

> The Parties shall make every effort to reach agreement on any proposed amendment to the Convention by consensus. If all efforts at consensus have been exhausted, and no agreement reached, the amendment shall, as a last resort, be adopted by a three-fourths majority vote of the Parties present and voting at the meeting. The adopted amendment shall be communicated by the secretariat to the Depositary, who shall circulate it to all Parties for their acceptance.[30]

If voting were the common practice in the climate regime, developing countries would have considerably more leverage. At the present moment, consensus is the dominant form of decision-making within the FCCC; which clearly favours the more powerful countries. Even if voting were to become the common practice in the climate change regime, it is unlikely that developing countries would use their voting power to push some decisions through. This is because of their implicit fear that if they push the developed world too much, the developed world will withdraw completely from the regime and it would collapse.

There is also a human element in the negotiating process. Delegates must be given the floor during the negotiations, and the chairperson may be careful not to overlook the raised hand of a delegate from a prominent country (from the North or the South). Smaller, less prominent nations often do not enjoy the same privilege.

Reporting

Both the Framework Convention on Climate Change and the Kyoto Protocol have extensive reporting requirements. These include requirements to prepare national inventories of emissions of greenhouse gases and removals by sinks, and national communications on policies adopted by countries to deal with the problem of climate change. These types of reporting requirements are increasingly being used in a variety of different international treaties. However, they pose heavy demands on developing countries. The FCCC states that compliance with this requirement is dependent on the financial support received from Annex I countries, yet the resources available have not been adequate for some countries to undertake detailed analysis of the situation in their countries *vis-à-vis* emissions and adaptation. As argued in this chapter, the concern is not that many of these countries are in non-compliance, but rather they lack the resources and capability to formulate clear ideas about their contributions to climate change and the cost factors involved in mitigation and adaptation. This reinforces the inability to negotiate effectively and to propose constructive solutions.

The structural imbalance in negotiation

More broadly, the obstacles described above suggest a *structural imbalance in negotiation*. There are, in fact, additional non-institutional components to this imbalance, but this section will only discuss the institutional pathways that constitute this imbalance.

In terms of institutional pathways for influence, the structural imbalance in the negotiations means that in general developing countries have a limited influence on the agenda of the negotiations, except in removing items. This is directly related to their hollow negotiating mandate, where the negotiating position is poorly defined and leans heavily on other issues and priorities on the domestic agenda. The hollow negotiating mandate also implies that developing country representatives seldom prepare joint background papers. As such, when negotiating texts are interpreted through the course of the discussions, there are scarce opportunities to refer to the *travaux preparatoires* of developing countries.[31] This is an important way for countries to influence, indeed to draft, final texts, as well as to ensure that drafted texts are interpreted in the future in accordance with these preparatory documents when there is some room for such interpretation. However, this is often not an option available to developing countries because of their hollow negotiating mandate.

Although the rules of procedure should guarantee that developing countries are not disadvantaged during the negotiating process, the practice of actually preparing decisions on controversial issues in the corridors and in working groups has *de facto* disempowered developing countries. This is because non-plenary meetings are not subject to the UN rule of simultaneous translation, and as such the bulk of these meetings take place in English. Furthermore, many of these meetings actually take place simultaneously and often around the clock, putting huge burdens on the one- or two-person negotiating teams from these countries.

For example, the Ninth Conference of the Parties that took place over two weeks in 2003 was attended by over 5,000 participants. It was supposed to begin on 1 December, but in fact the preparatory meetings began three days before. Seventy topics were covered in the conference, 60 per cent of which needed specialised expertise. Of the 444 total hours of work during this conference, almost half the hours occurred after 5 pm. A student analysis of the statements showed that while 72 per cent of the statements of the South were defensive in nature, 73 per cent of Northern statements were constructive.[32]

The subject of the negotiations covers issues including finance, economics, hydrology, climatology, law, politics, physics, chemistry, meteorology, etc. It is easy to see that even without the language and time barriers, it is a great challenge to be an expert in all of the relevant issues.

All of these constraints have an influence on the outcome of the meetings, and developing countries tend to feel cheated by the final result. Even if a negotiated outcome represents the stated position of developing countries, since these positions are likely to be poorly developed because of the constraints that give rise to the hollow negotiating mandate, the final outcome is perceived as unfair. This is very important, since the sustainability of negotiation outcomes depends not only on the satisfaction of substantive and procedural interests but also on the satisfaction of psychological interests.[33]

Non-institutional pathways for influence

The non-institutionalised ways of influencing the climate change negotiations include the following elements.

Forming different organisational forms to increase leverage

Since 1964 developing countries have had the G-77 as a negotiating body within the United Nations. They also have a number of regional caucuses to represent their interests. The power of these bodies lies primarily in their success in opposing ideas coming from other parts of the world; they are far weaker in terms of suggesting new ideas. The lack of proposals coming from various negotiating blocs can be attributed to what the author terms "handicapped coalition-building power".

The handicapped coalition-building power

In order to build a strong coalition in the developing world, countries need to be able to come together and develop a strong strategy, supported by good science and political will, if not public support. However, when a number of different developing countries coalesce to discuss their position, they are faced with a difficult challenge: pooling together the contradictory and vacillating ideological frameworks and the sustainability dilemmas makes it challenging for negotiators to come to a common and constructive framework of ideas on which to base their negotiating position. Aggregating poor and inadequate science does not lead to better scientific insights; this is especially problematic since the G-77 level has no think-tank comparable to that of the OECD.

Further hindering efforts at strong coalition positions are apathy and helplessness. There is poor staying power which hampers intersessional work. In sum, the unification of abstract, diplomatic and qualitative interests implies that the policy content for the common G-77 position is largely rhetorical. Compounded by a lack of resources to meet and develop common positions, the result is that developing countries will be handicapped in terms of their ability to create and maintain strong negotiating blocs.

The handicapped negotiation power

The hollow mandate and the handicapped coalition power together add up to a handicapped negotiating power. The hollow mandate leads countries to adopt a "defensive strategy", where negotiators improvise, oppose proposals from the North rather than propose their own, vacillate from one ideological position to another, see issues holistically, feel cheated by the negotiation results and are vulnerable to side-payments.

The lack of good leadership also hurts developing countries' ability to influence the climate negotiations. As a result, the G-77 is highly susceptible to divide and rule through the use of the word "voluntary", side-payments and punishments in other fields. In addition, the fear among fast-industrialising countries that they will soon have to take serious, binding measures acts as an additional constraint to the group as a whole.

On occasion, developing countries may use a constructive strategy. There are many risks in such a strategy. For example, such strategies often suffer from a lack of legitimacy, since they have not been extensively discussed domestically. If these positions are articulated and negotiated poorly they may be picked apart by other negotiators and lead to a compromise text that scarcely resembles the original idea. One prime example is the Brazilian proposal on the Clean Development Fund. It was originally conceived as a way to channel fines paid by non-complying developed countries to developing countries, but through the process of negotiation was transformed into the Clean Development Mechanism which allows developed country investors to invest in developing countries in return for emission credits.

Ultimately, this handicapped negotiating power – the product of the elements discussed above – has severely hampered the ability of the South to participate effectively in solving modern environmental problems, as signalled by the North, including climate change. The potential outcomes of negotiations between such brittle, threadbare and defensive strategies of the South, when pitted against the realist constructive strategies of the Northern countries, are likely to be symbolic, controversial and/or forced decisions. To the limited extent that the other party has poorly articulated constructive strategies, the decisions will tend to be "non-decisions" or "decision-less" decisions, which have little impact on the implementation of policy.

Garnering media attention

In order to garner media attention effectively, countries need to have a combination of substance and procedural skills. At the international level, if a country is uncertain of its content and its argument it is not in a position to be proactive and hold press conferences with the media to gain its support for the national position. While most developed countries hold press conferences, individually (e.g. the United States and Japan) or within their formalised groups (e.g. the European Union), the developing countries are less forthcoming in holding such meetings. The small island states are sometimes more effective in getting press, but even so their influence on the international media remains marginal.

Lobbying/mobilising constituencies

There is limited use of lobbying during the formal sessions of the negotiations, but even less during intersessional discussions. This is largely due to the volume of meetings within international environmental policy-making: the handful of developing country negotiators who do cover climate change may simply get papered out of the process.

Increasingly disenfranchised

When the climate negotiations began in 1990, the author naively thought that developing countries would be able to catch up with the developed countries in terms of understanding the ramifications of the issue. However, as the years go by, it seems that they understand less and less the complexity of the problem, and with each new round of the negotiations there are new challenges to developing countries that further exacerbate existing ones. The result is that they are increasingly disenfranchised from international governance for sustainable development.

With sustainable development problems such as climate change, where costs and benefits are not evenly distributed, the lack of resources and institutional frameworks for constructing negotiating positions in developing countries makes it more difficult for them to protect their own interests at the international level.

Moreover, this trend is set to continue, if not worsen. The process of international environmental negotiation is only going to become more complex and challenging. The law on climate change is continuously being revised, and not just at discrete moments such as at the negotiation of the FCCC and the Kyoto Protocol.[34] Diplomats who think they can simply focus their energies on the moments during which the major negotiations are being held to protect their interests are mistaken. In order to identify and defend their interests effectively, countries will have to be continuously alert and participate in all the intersessional discussions as well as actively engage in the informal meetings in corridors and with friends of the chair.

What are the implications of developing countries' disenfranchisement for international law? If such trends continue, law will become less legitimate as procedural fairness is undermined. If instruments and mechanisms are adopted on an *ad hoc* basis and not on the basis of a consistent application of legal principles, as is now often the case, the risk of illegitimacy becomes even greater. All of these problems decrease opportunities for real environmental problem-solving, and consequently all countries lose. Indeed, the long-term success of international regimes and treaties for sustainable development, including climate change, will be hampered by the growing frustration of the South and the North.

The frustration of the South is because it is unable to prepare and negotiate effectively and hence unable to implement adequately its commitments under international agreements. This is further exacerbated by its perception that the *status quo* between countries is being maintained through the international problem-solving processes. It is evident from their negotiation strategies that states are behaving not as atomistic actors but are taking action in relation to other countries; i.e. their arguments are based on their analysis of how decisions will affect the relative positions of countries. Meanwhile, new precedents are being created that may take multilateral treaty design in the completely wrong direction. Failed processes are becoming institutionalised, and increasingly developing countries are being socialised into accepting positions that are not "possible" for them to accept. The normative function of law is being marginalised.

If the international system is to become more legitimate and more focused on solving problems, it needs to take cognisance of the challenges facing developing countries and accordingly work to facilitate and enhance their full participation in the process rather than their disenfranchisement. Even in the event that a few countries like China and India are able to make the leap forward as fast-developing countries, the rest of the developing countries will still continue to face serious challenges in the international negotiating arena.

Acknowledgements

This chapter was written as part of the project on "Intergovernmental and Private Environmental Regimes and Compatibility with Good Governance" financed by the Netherlands Organisation for Scientific Research (452-02-031).

Notes

1. South Commission (1990) *The Challenge to the South: The Report of the South Commission*, Oxford: Oxford University Press; Agarwal, Anil (1992) *For Earth's Sake: A Report from the Commission on Developing Countries and Global Change*, Ottawa: International Development Research Centre; Agarwal, Anil, Narain, Sunita and Sharma, Anju (1999) *Green Politics: Global Environmental Negotiations*, New Delhi: Centre for Science and Environment; Khor, Martin (2001) *Rethinking Globalization: Critical Issues and Policy Choices*, London and New York: Zed Books; De Rivero, Oswaldo (2001) *The Myth of Development*, London and New York: Zed Books; Gupta, Joyeeta (1997) *The Climate Change Convention and Developing Countries – From Conflict to Consensus?*, Dordrecht: Kluwer Academic Publishers; Gupta, Joyeeta (2001) *Our Simmering Planet: What to Do About Global Warming*, London: Zed Books; Gupta, Joyeeta (2001) "Legitimacy in the Real World: A Case Study of the Developing Countries, Non-Governmental Organisations and Climate Change", in Jean M. Coicaud and Veijo Heiskanen, eds, *The Legitimacy of International Organizations*, Tokyo: United Nations University Press, pp. 482–518.
2. Bhagwati, Jagdish (2004) *In Defence of Globalization*, Oxford: Oxford University Press.
3. Das, Gurcharan (2002) *India Unbound, The Social and Economic Revolution From Independence to the Global Information Age*, New York: Anchor Books.
4. Khor, Martin (2001) *Rethinking Globalization: Critical Issues and Policy Choices*, London and New York: Zed Books.
5. De Rivero, Oswaldo (2001) *The Myth of Development*, London and New York: Zed Books.
6. Banuri, Tariq (1996) "The South and the Governability of the Planet: A Question of Justice", in Jacques Theys, ed., *The Environment in the 21st Century: The Issues*, Vol. I, Paris: Themis.
7. Junne, Gerd (2001) "International Organizations in a Period of Globalization: New (Problems of) Legitimacy", in Jean M. Coicaud and Veijo Heiskanen, eds, *The Legitimacy of International Organizations*, Tokyo: United Nations University Press, pp. 198–220; Marks, Susan (2001) "Democracy and International Governance", in Jean M. Coicaud and Veijo Heiskanen, eds, *The Legitimacy of International Organizations*, Tokyo: United Nations University Press, pp. 47–69.
8. Gupta, 1997, note 1 above; Gupta, 2001, *Our Simmening Planet*, note 1 above; Gupta, 2001, "Legitimacy in the Real World", note 1 above.
9. The projects include "International Policies to Address the Greenhouse Effect", "Climate Change: Regime Development in the Context of Unequal Power Relations", "European Leadership on Climate Change", "An Asian Dilemma: Modernising the Electricity Sector in China and India", "Bridging Interest, Classification and Technology Gaps in the Climate Change Regime" and the current "Intergovernmental and Pri-

vate International Regimes and Compatibility with Good Governance", financed by various Dutch research programmes and the European Commission.
10. Various authors have focused on how the classification of developing countries in current negotiations is based on poor criteria and have developed criteria for improved classification of these countries and suggested tailor-made solutions for them. See Faure, M; Gupta, J. and Nentjes, A., eds (2003) *Climate Change and the Kyoto Protocol: The Role of Institutions and Instruments to Control Global Change*, Cheltenham: Edward Elgar; Van Ierland, E., Gupta, J. and Kok, M., eds (2003) *Issues in International Climate Policy: Theory and Policy*, Cheltenham: Edward Elgar.
11. See, for example, Doornbos, Martin (2001) " 'Good Governance': The Rise and Decline of a Policy Metaphor?", *Journal of Development Studies* 37(6): 93–108; Woods, Ngaire (1999) "Good Governance in International Organizations", *Global Governance* 5: 39–62; Ginther, Konrad and JIM De Waart, Paul (1995) "Sustainable Development as a Matter of Good Governance: An Introductory View", in Konrad Ginther, Eric Denters and Paul JIM De Waart, eds, *Sustainable Development and Good Governance*, Dordrecht: Kluwer Academic Publishers, pp. 1–14; EC (Commission of the European Communities) Communication from the Commission to the Council, the European Parliament and the European Economic and Social Committee: Governance and Development, Brussels, 20 October 2003 COM(2003) 615 final; UNDP, *Governance for Sustainable Human Development*, available from http://magnet.undp.org/policy/chapter1.htm. (1997).
12. Santiso, C. (2001) "Good Governance and Aid Effectiveness: The World Bank and Conditionality", *Georgetown Public Policy Review* 7(1): 1–22.
13. See, for example, Correll, Hans (2001) "The Visible College of International Law: 'Towards the Rule of Law in International Relations' ", *American Society of International Law Proceedings* 95: 262–270; Koskenniemi, Martti (1990) "The Politics of International Law", *European Journal of International Law* 11(1): 4–32.
14. E.g. Junne, Gerd (1992) "Beyond Regime Theory", *Acta Politica* 27(1): 9–28.
15. Hisschemöller, Mathijs and Gupta, Joyeeta (1999) "Problem-solving through International Environmental Agreements: The Issue of Regime Effectiveness", *International Political Science Review* 20(2): 153–176.
16. The environment Kuznets curve hypothesis states that as countries become richer they will cause more environmental pollution, but beyond a point they will also invest more in environmental protection and so economic growth may not necessarily be accompanied by corresponding increases in pollution.
17. Spangenberg, Jochem H. (2001) "The Environment Kuznets Curve: A Methodological Artefact?", *Population and Environment* 23(2): 189.
18. The S curve of technological innovation refers to the way in which technological innovations develop in society.
19. See, for example, the reports of the Intergovernmental Panel on Climate Change, available from www.ipcc.ch.
20. For example, climate change is likely to have major impacts on the water cycle, and consequently people's access to water and food, in developing countries. It is likely to influence health in these countries by increasing the occurrence of vector-borne diseases. Furthermore, the threat of sea-level rise and melting glaciers can affect infrastructure and the lives of people in low-lying regions and on river banks.
21. In the early 1990s there was speculation about who would be winners of climate change and who would be losers. This discussion was apparently politically laid to rest with the adoption of the UN Framework Convention on Climate Change. However, ever since the realisation in the mid-1990s that measures to deal with climate change can be sub-

stantial, countries have been reverting to a discussion of possible winners and losers in this discussion.
22. This is evident in the way the developed countries are taking small incremental measures, if at all, to deal with climate change, and the current Kyoto Protocol goals are unlikely to make more than a marginal difference to the rising emissions. Discussion on the long-term target of the climate change regime are stagnant, and the few discussions that are occurring are not taking into account that even an eventual stabilisation at 550 ppm CO_2 equivalent concentrations is unlikely to protect the small island states from rising sea levels, melting glaciers, coral reef bleaching, increased temperatures and changed rainfall patterns.
23. For example, the long-term target in the FCCC is expressed in qualitative but not in quantitative terms. At the international level there is very little discussion about how this long-term target should be articulated, and even scientists are wary of undertaking such an exercise because the impacts of climate change will be different in different parts of the world and will be experienced differently because of different vulnerabilities. Meanwhile the European Union has tentatively decided that global temperatures should not rise beyond 2°C from pre-industrial levels. This, however, may be a higher target than many developing countries would have liked, since the target is based on protecting a relatively less vulnerable society from the worst impacts of climate change.
24. Gupta, 1997, note 1 above; Gupta, Joyeeta (2000) "North-South Aspects of the Climate Change Issue: Towards a Negotiating Theory and Strategy for Developing Countries", *International Journal of Sustainable Development* 3(2): 115–135; Gupta, 2001, "Legitimacy in the Real World", note 1 above; Gupta, 2001, *Our Simmering Planet*, note 1 above.
25. In France customer fees went up by 150 per cent; in the United Kingdom they went up by 106 per cent in six years (1989–1995); in India this has led to households paying up to 25 per cent of their income on water; see Barlow, Maude and Clarke, Tony (2002) *Blue Gold: The Battle Against Corporate Theft of the World's Water*, London: Earthscan, p. 90; Petrella, Ricardo (2001) *The Water Manifesto: Arguments for a World Water Contract*, London: Zed Books, p. 73. In Buenos Aires the water rates went up by 13.5 per cent in the first year after privatisation. In Chile Suez asked for a 35 per cent profit. In Johannesburg after Suez took over the water it became unsafe, inaccessible and unaffordable to many, leading to disconnections and cholera infections; Shiva, Vandana (2002) *Water Wars: Privatisation, Pollution, and Profit*, Boston, MA: South End Press, p. 91. In the United Kingdom the prices went up so much that in 1997 a special windfall tax was levied and water companies had to pay £1.6 billion in 1998 and 1999.
26. After Cobb, Roger W., Ross, J. K. and Ross, M. H. (1976) "Agenda Building as a Comparative Political Process", *American Political Science Review* 70: 126–138.
27. Gupta, 1997, note 1 above; Gupta, 2000, note 24 above.
28. Gupta, Joyeeta (2001) "Effectiveness of Air Pollution Treaties: The Role of Knowledge, Power and Participation", in Matthijs Hisschemöller, Jerry Ravetz, Rob Hoppe and William Dunn, eds, *Knowledge, Power and Participation, Policy Studies Annual*, New Brunswick: Transaction Publishers, pp. 145–174; Kandlikar, Milind and Sagar, Ambuj (1999) "Climate Change Research and Analysis in India: An Integrated Assessment of a North-South Divide", *Global Environmental Change* 9: 119–138.
29. UN Framework Convention on Climate Change (1992) 31 I.L.M. 1992, Article 18.
30. Ibid., Article 15.
31. The rules of interpretation of negotiated text calls on countries first to interpret the text in accordance with its ordinary meaning and finally on the basis of the *travaux preparatoires*. In most cases, since developing countries often have not prepared background documents during the negotiations, there is little to represent their interest.
32. Holleman, Anne, et al. (2004) "Defensive by Default: The South's Strategy for Climate

Change", paper for the completion of a course on negotiation and conflict resolution (manuscript on file with author), unpublished.
33. Priscoli, Jerome D. (2002) *Participation, Consensus Building and Conflict Management and Training Course*, Paris: UNESCO/IHP/WWAP; IHP-VI/Technical Documents in Hydrology/PCCP Series No. 22.
34. Jutta, Brunnée (2002) "COPing with Consent: Law-making Under Multilateral Environmental Agreements", *Leiden Journal of International Law* 15: 1–53.

2

In tension: Enfranchising initiatives in the face of aggressive marginalisation

John W. Foster

Introduction

This chapter examines the role of non-governmental organisations (NGOs) in various international debates on systemic and structural issues which affect sustainable development policy. It focuses on two theatres, one regional and one multilateral, in which civil society organisations engage with governments and with representatives of the private sector.

Given the significance in the past decade of international trade, investment and intellectual property agreements, the first theatre is that of the inter-American regional negotiations in these areas. In particular, the chapter focuses on the activities, successes and failures of the Hemispheric Social Alliance (HSA), a network of labour-based, environmental, peasant and indigenous networks, mobilised to participate in discussions about globalisation taking place within the negotiations of the Free Trade of the Americas Agreement and the broader *"cumbre"* of Summit of the Americas process.

Development financing and the international institutions which shape policy continue to define many of the limits of sustainable development. The second theatre examined in this chapter is that of the UN Financing for Development process (FfD) (for a full discussion of this process see Herman, chapter 7). In the case of the FfD, the NGO actors include the International NGO Facilitating Group, the New Rules coalition and a number of other alliances, individual organisations and networks.

This chapters examines the role of NGOs in debates about globalisation by looking at these two specific examples. More broadly, it discusses the impact of globalisation on the NGO sector, which has been marginalised due to a ceding of national sovereignty to the international system; offers some suggestions for future enfranchisement of NGOs in global governance; and finally comments on the need for a broader global governance agenda in order to ensure more meaningful engagement of NGOs.

Given the confusion and overlap in the many discussions and definitions of NGOs, it is appropriate that this chapter begin with a brief treatment of who, exactly, these actors are. In considering the place of NGOs in the context of the problem of enfranchisement, this chapter takes a pragmatic approach. Given that much of the terrain is populated by a shifting spectrum of organisations, in the case of the FfD it focuses on those "organisational particles" of NGOs which tend to be found in the halls of the United Nations, its various bodies and agencies and/or periodic events relating to the governance of international financial institutions. To distinguish them from the broader constituencies of civil society organisations, of which they are essentially a subset, the chapter simply asks "do they have a mass base"? Are they a movement? Thus, from an organisational point of view, the International Confederation of Free Trade Unions (ICFTU) is a social organisation and not an NGO. Oxfam, Greenpeace and a Ugandan women's centre are NGOs.

In the case of the HSA, the constituency at a regional level includes a few region-wide organisations, like the regional trade union body of the ICFTU, ORIT (Organización Regional Interamericana de Trabajadores), but is primarily defined by the membership of national-level coalitions which vary considerably in coverage and strength.

It should be noted that in many cases of international policy-making for sustainable development, the non-governmental players include coalitions that span a whole series of sectoral definitions. Within the United Nations these actors have traditionally been identified by their so-called "consultative status", which arises from the way they are accredited to the United Nations. However, the great diversity of actors covered in this description shows that this nomenclature is no longer sufficiently descriptive. Even the term "civil society organisations" is a rather plastic one, representing varieties of bodies which are hardly monolithic in purpose or form.

For all of these reasons, this chapter, for purposes of further mapping the terrain of NGOs, has narrowed the purview significantly. It draws upon the approach of Jan Aart Scholte of Warwick University, who approaches global civil society in the context of the ongoing evolution of global governance and global rule-making, defining it essentially as those bodies engaged in the debate and often struggle over the *rules*.[1] Thus a sports association or gun-owners' club may on occasion be engaged in global civil society when the debate focuses on international standards for tests for "doping" or transborder transport of personal weapons.

The ceding of sovereignty: An overall problematique

The creation of the World Trade Organization (WTO) and its associated agreements, as well as the further development of regional trade organisations like the North American Free Trade Area (NAFTA) and the ill-fated attempt at a Multilateral Agreement on Investment, have catalysed a series of threats to the ability of governments and multilateral governmental bodies to pursue sustainable development adequately. In a number of cases and sectors, the ability of national and subnational democratic jurisdictions to regulate for sustainability, to govern the nature of investment and resource use in their areas, has been limited by the ceding of sovereignty to transnational trade, investment and intellectual property regimes. The result of this ceding of sovereignty is tantamount to the disenfranchisement of electorates in general and the marginalisation of specific groups of organised civil society, including environmental, labour, peasant, indigenous and other associations and unions.

The development of the WTO, its components like the regime on Trade-Related Aspects of Intellectual Property Rights (TRIPS) and coincident developments of regional trade and investment pacts represent perhaps the most publicly known terrain of battle between those who feel disenfranchised and the aggressively advancing claims of relatively opaque institutions and their clients. There are many other examples, some of which will be examined later on in this chapter.

Much attention has been devoted to the procedural aspects of the relationship between civil society and these trade and investment negotiating processes, agreements, implementation and supervision. Despite the attention, relatively modest change has occurred. Such change as has occurred has been largely due to "shocks to the system", either as a result of developing country coalescence, popular pressure – including e-mobilisation, demonstrations and direct action – or a combination of the two. The collapse of the proposed Multilateral Agreement on Investment (MAI), the blockage of "fast-track" negotiating authority in the US Congress, the collapse of the Seattle Ministerial and frustration of the Cancun Ministerial are well-known "moments" where civil society has managed to slow the process of this ceding of sovereignty, or what the author also calls "aggressive marginalisation".

Although a good deal of debate in various quarters focuses on trade, arguably investment and investment provisions are even more important. While the global MAI fell apart, investment provisions of a similar character are inserted in bilateral and regional accords continually. Perhaps most egregious, from the point of view of many civil society organisations, was the creation of the "investor-state" mechanism in the NAFTA regional agreement, permitting corporations to sue host states for damages from alleged "expropriation" injuring present or even future returns.

These developments represent a rapid extension of regimes that extend and deepen the reach of commercial law and procedures. In this respect they have a marginalising effect on existing human rights, environmental and labour agreements. They have a wide-ranging and, apparently, irreversible effect on national sovereignty and on policy autonomy of governments. In this respect, they can threaten constitutionally protected legislative "space" and reduce the autonomy of national and subnational democratic processes and accountability.[2] They may have a significant "chill" effect on future democratic policy choice.

Further, despite broad claims in preambular portions of the mandate, the WTO was constructed outside a direct relationship with the United Nations and outside the framework of the hard-fought and extensive treaty-based norms on human rights, environmental protections and labour standards which find their home in the United Nations and its Charter.

In procedural terms, the trade and investment negotiations and the WTO itself are characterised, in general, by exclusive processes and secrecy. They privilege certain participants (government technocrats, trade and investment lawyers and corporate representatives) and marginalise others (parliamentarians, civil society organisations, the general public and, to some extent, the press).

In recent years even the physical meetings of these bodies have become increasingly difficult to access, convening at isolated and highly defended locales. The Cancun WTO Ministerial took place on what is essentially an island, with a carefully and fully defended perimeter. The most recent Summit of the Americas occurred in the colonial fortress city of Quebec with tens of thousands of police and security. Similarly, the most recent FTAA Ministerial occurred behind aggressive police lines in Miami. Both resulted in confrontations with popular mobilisations, arrests and violence.

These practices and the ensuing aggressive marginalisation have elicited a strong negative and multisectoral reaction among some parliamentarians, writers and cultural figures, civil society organisations (CSOs) and social movements and some NGOs. The response has been focused on the active disenfranchisement of national policy-making through the ceding of sovereignty; the opaque and secretive procedures characteristic of trade and investment negotiations; the preferential access accorded some actors, and coincident marginalisation of others; and the isolation of these processes from the broader forums, norms and Charter accountability of the United Nations. With respect to the final factor contributing to disenfranchisement, as Willetts puts it, the WTO "stands out as a deviant organisation in many ways. It is not a UN specialised agency. It does not have a normal policy making structure. It does not have any formal engagement with non-governmental organisations, beyond public relations outreach."[3]

Indeed, these characteristics raise the question of whether, in fact, *it is the United Nations itself that is disenfranchised*.[4] As the WTO asserts the pre-eminence of trade and investment negotiations and accords, and the Bretton Woods institutions (BWIs) coalesce through policies which encourage and support coherence with WTO rules, the "space" for effective debate on economic governance on the part of the United Nations or agencies like UNCTAD is more and more restricted. The relative lack of transparency in the WTO and other regional and bilateral trade/investment negotiations together with their increasingly complex, multi-layered and intrusive nature marginalise those not directly participating or consulted (largely the private sector).

The agents of this institutional disenfranchisement are governments which prioritise, or simply permit, the rapid extension of mandate on the part of trade ministers and their officials, the WTO itself from its foundational delinking from the UN system and the participating governments which connived in what can be viewed as a violation of their Charter commitments. The implications of this disenfranchisement for NGOs and the broader CSO universe are manifold and at the base of skirmishes, battles and ongoing alienation.

The WTO is embodied in a continuing organisation, a secretariat and a decade's history of (much-debated) procedures and practices. The expanding range of specific agreements – TRIMs, TRIPs, GATS, etc. – together with the variety of regional trade and investment agreements and the plethora of bilateral negotiations present a complex and often rapidly moving challenge for those concerned about their direction and potential impact. Nevertheless, CSOs have shown considerable gains in their capacity to challenge and, in cases like the Cancun Ministerial, have forced modifications in the inter-state and corporate agenda.[5] The following section will turn to specific examples of civil society's response, as illustrated by the HSA campaign against the Free Trade Area of the Americas (FTAA).

The FTAA: A regional agreement with global implications

The civil society and NGO response to the proposed FTAA involves regional rather than global institutions, and has been embodied in cross-sectoral rather than simple NGO alliances. Nonetheless, it is relevant to the project of this volume in that it represents forms of disenfranchisement in other trade and investment negotiations at the global level.

The negotiating modalities for the FTAA are one of three overlapping and linked hemispheric processes which engage all but one of the countries (Cuba) of the Americas. The trade negotiations exist alongside the periodic Summits of the Americas and parallel to the continuing processes of the Organization of American States. The latter organisation, taking several pages from the experience of the UN Economic and Social Council, has developed rubrics for legitimising and regularising liaison with NGOs in the Americas. Neither the summit process nor the FTAA negotiating process has ventured nearly as far.[6]

Among CSOs there are two streams of response to the FTAA discussions to be noted, which generally may be described as "insider" and "outsider". The first group of networks represents organisations receiving assistance from major institutional and official funders (US foundations and the US government, among others). This group emphasises dialogue with negotiators and has undertaken consultative processes with broader groups of NGOs and other social forces, such as those mobilised by Participa (based in Chile) and FOCAL (a Canadian government-supported research centre) prior to the Quebec Summit of the Americas. This "insider" group of networks has emphasised an iterative response to the official agenda, with the development of proposals for extension or amendment thereof. In some cases members of these insider NGO groups serve on national delegations, offering input and legitimacy to state negotiating positions.

The second group represents some popular mass movements (in labour, farm and indigenous sectors), critical research, environmental, human rights and development assistance NGOs, women's organisations and national coalitions or platforms organised either against the preceding NAFTA or for engagement with the FTAA process. Key organisations, like the Reseau Quebecois sur la integration continentale (RQIC), Common Frontiers (English Canada), Alliance for Responsible Trade (ART) in the United States and the Red mexicana al frente de libre comercio (RMALC) in Mexico, were joined by labour-based, environmental, peasant and indigenous networks in such countries as Brazil, Bolivia, Ecuador and a number in Central America. Organised in the HSA, this group of networks has sought policy engagement but also challenged national governments and resisted the overall negotiating project. The HSA has developed several successive examples of a comprehensive alternative project for the Americas.

Institutionalised pathways

Focusing on the trade and investment negotiations, which have been distended due to inter-state disagreement and the shifting balance of forces in the WTO and trade and investment discussions globally, it is clear that there are fundamental problems at the level of *institutionalised pathways*. Specifically, although institutionalised pathways provided ways to participate, this should be distinguished from the ability to influence these negotiations, which was not always possible. To illustrate this point, the FTAA negotiators undertook two initiatives with regard to civil society input, creating a civil society committee composed of national representatives to consider what might be done, and establishing a "mail-box" which would receive comments, proposals and critiques. At a national level practice varied extensively, from totally exclusive to briefings and consultations at a ministerial or subministerial level. Both initiatives were greeted with significant scepticism on the part of the HSA and its members, and somewhat greater interest on the part of the "insider" networks. A recent official evaluation of consultative experience in Canada elicited the response from the leading anti-FTAA coalition that information provision was still inadequate, consultation on agenda lacking, official response in detail to CSO submissions absent and evidence of suggestions and proposals being taken on board non-existent.

Policies and proposals

The preparation of studies, critiques or alternative proposals was initially hampered by the obscurity of the official process. Negotiating texts and national official proposals were secret. Secrecy makes it extremely difficult to undertake effective lobbying or public education. In the case of the NAFTA negotiations, civil society groups used the relatively porous official channels of the US Congress to elicit information on negotiations that was blocked officially in Mexico and Canada. Civil society coalitions of all stripes, dealing with the FTAA negotiations and the Summit of the Americas, demanded they be made public and succeeded in eliciting a response. Prior to the Quebec Summit of the Americas, a commitment was made to release a draft text. This, in turn, led to further demands which would make such a release useful; for example, timeliness and inclusion of country-specific identification of proposed amendments, additions or deletions. These issues remain.

Nevertheless the HSA continues to revise and renew *Alternatives for the Americas*.[7] Three of its North American precursors have published a joint work on *Lessons from NAFTA*[8] and constituent or allied groups continue specialised work on issues like intellectual property.

Voting, membership and procedural rights

At least one constituency – the private sector – has a recognised ongoing forum and relationship with the official process. The business forum often meets parallel to and close to the official sessions. Messages from one to the other are normal. Neither CSO grouping has anything like voting, membership or procedural rights. Consultative sessions involving the "insider" group and some members of the "outsider" group have, on occasions like the Quebec Summit, been organised at the initiative of host governments.

At the 1999 trade ministers' meeting in Toronto, Canada, the Canadian government agreed to facilitate a meeting of the CSOs adjacent to the official sessions and the business forum; to encourage and participate in a session where more than 20 of the ministers met for a morning session with approximately 200 civil society representatives to hear their questions and proposals and respond in some measure; and to provide some funding to support these activities. This type of initiative has not been repeated with the HSA. Attempts on both sides to reach agreement to meet at a high level at the Quebec Summit failed due to issues presented by the high-security approach of the organisers. CSO representatives refused to cross the militarised cordon, officials refused to come outside it and agreement could not be reached on a neutral mid-point.

By 2003 the balance had shifted extensively. At a macro level, the election of new governments in Brazil and Argentina and a sympathetic government in Venezuela altered the play of interests, marginalising Mexico to some extent as a leading advocate of integration and parrying US ambitions from time to time. With regard to civil society the shift empowered, relatively, social forces allied in the HSA.

At the 2003 Trinidad negotiating meeting, Brazil included civil society representatives in its delegation, rupturing, to some extent, the tissue of secrecy and the traditional power relations in negotiations. The Canadians, previously posing as leaders toward transparency and curtseying in the direction of civil society, protested against the initiative. Another frontier had been traversed.

Reporting

While the lack of transparency makes systematic monitoring of governmental proposals and positions difficult, NGOs have contributed extensively to the overall movement by critical study of which negotiating texts become available through a so-called technical team of the HSA. Given that some NGO personnel also double as governmental advisers, the level of analysis and detail possible is considerable. Further, some NGOs have provided detailed sectoral analysis, as for example the extensive studies on intellectual property agreements from the Quaker UN Centre, and the ongoing critiques of the same accords by Medecins Sans Frontiers. Further, NGOs and NGO research centres, including the Institute for Policy Studies (United States), Development GAP (United States), KAIROS (Canada), trade union researchers and allied academics in Quebec, Mexico and the United States with similar sources throughout Latin America, have provided detailed analysis of the experience and effects of previous relevant agreements, including *Lessons from NAFTA*. Despite this continuing and growing commentary and the alternative policy proposals based upon it, occasions for serious debate with government policy-makers are few, although some national parliamentary bodies have taken note. The institutionalised pathways for influence therefore remain limited.

Non-institutional pathways

Because the HSA is not a strictly NGO alliance, and because in countries like Brazil and Bolivia it can connect with significant broad-based social movements, it has had some success in effecting influence through non-institutional pathways. Further, the single government excluded from the FTAA process, Cuba, has sponsored large annual conferences for actors throughout the hemisphere to assist them in planning strategies and deepening organisational links.

The HSA has organised a hemispheric campaign against the FTAA in dozens of countries, with varying impact. In some countries, like Brazil, this involved a non-governmental plebiscite with millions of participants. In others it has involved conferences, demonstrations and media campaigns. The HSA has also worked in league with the World Social Forum to extend its social base and linkages with other mass movements and NGOs, including, for example, lawyers' groups concerned with the legal implications of the trade and investment proposals. In addition, the HSA also sponsored a forum of ideas and proposals adjacent to the Quebec Summit of the Americas.

Direct action, including the more than 60,000 who marched against the Quebec Summit, the thousands who tested the perimeter of the Miami Ministerial and a variety of national engagements, has been a significant dimension in CSO strategies. Despite continued advocacy by a diminishing number of governments (the Canadian negotiators continued to press for the FTAA in 2005, and the Caribbean governments wrote collectively to the Brazilian and US co-chairs regarding restarting the process), the FTAA appeared to be a dead letter as hemispheric chief executives gathered for the 2005 Summit in Mar del Plata, Argentina. A largely opaque and exclusive negotiating process, dominated by "true believers" in neoliberal doctrine, quite impermeable to alternate approaches, had failed its sponsors. Its characteristics have been representative of a number of other international trade, investment and intellectual property negotiations. Unlike many other regional negotiating processes, the FTAA elicited a sufficiently large civil society reaction that this response, combined with powerful political factors in MERCOSUR, Venezuela and a number of other countries, stymied the ambitions of the United States and Canada.

Engaging financial resources and institutions: Systemic issues for enfranchising NGOs

The history and accomplishments of the Monterrey Financing for Development (FfD) process are evaluated by Herman in this volume. The process is an extremely important one to consider from the perspective of NGOs, as it embodies a case where efforts were made to amplify institutionalised pathways as well as to engage a more comprehensive group of institutional players (and their national ministerial sponsors) in the overall process.

Institutionalised pathways

Early in the FfD preparatory process, a parallel CSO (largely NGO) process was initiated by Mexican host groups. This process embodied two overlapping structures, a Mexican host committee which encompassed a wide variety of Mexican NGOs, with a significant proportion of its base coming from women's organisations and the RMALC, which included independent labour, environmental and human rights organisations. This host committee created an International Support Committee (ISC) composed of representatives from Northern and Southern NGOs chosen at caucus meetings of NGOs during the New York preparatory process. Unlike the 2005 Millennium+5 Summit session of the General Assembly, the preparatory process for FfD included facilities for the participation of non-governmental "stakeholders" from both civil society and the private sector. The ISC and the Mexican host committee prepared the Global Civil Society Forum prior to the Monterrey conference, assisted in organising civil society presence at the conference and developed (see below) a process for nominating participants in the various preliminary and conference roundtable processes.

Voting/membership

In terms of simple access to the meetings, the rules of the FfD were fairly permissive. As noted in Herman's chapter, the United Nations used its existing consultative-status framework on the NGO side and engaged business participants in spite of a lack of equivalent institutional framework or precedent.[9] Further, building on prior UN global conference experience, the credentials for NGO participation in Monterrey were extended to a broader range of groups, and were quite simple in application. (The issue of access to US or host-country visas for some Southern participants was more daunting than that of access to the United Nations or the FfD process itself – a noteworthy obstacle to participation.)

An additional important factor was the work of UN staff in the Department of Economic and Social Affairs (DESA) in engaging with NGOs, not only through the able facilitation of the contact point, but on the part of the staff and lead functionaries as a whole. The establishment and maintenance of open lines of communication and provision of relatively timely information established trust levels that smoothed potentially difficult relationships.

Although difficult and time-consuming to access, the United Nations, through the FfD process, provided some limited funding to the NGO process, and the UN's Non-Governmental Liaison Service facilitated the participation of a number of Southern NGO participants. As mentioned earlier, some governments provided access to meetings by building on previous global conference experience and including NGO or other CSO members in their national delegations. Others, reversing previous good practice, did not.

Concern regarding security and potential clashes with security forces preoccupied NGO organisers, and an initiative was taken to engage the state governor (later Federal economy minister), who responded relatively positively and made a point of attending one of the NGO forum plenary sessions with members of his staff. Although trust levels were probably fairly marginal, the face-to-face meeting and the attendance in person probably defused potential confrontation.

Opportunities for proposing policies

As noted, the FfD preparation embodied several innovations in the official process, and these implied active NGO representative participation. But how was such participation to be assured? The Mexican host NGO committee and its sister ISC took on this task. These bodies developed criteria for soliciting nominations (including gender, region, sector, demonstrated interest/experience in the issues, etc.). A broad "call" was undertaken via electronic and paper channels.

Although the process resulted in a high level of engagement, factors such as more time and money would have enhanced the process and reduced strain. Given that the process was relatively new, both the UN staff and NGO committee members would have benefited from more time to clarify fundamental issues, including how to evaluate the quality of the NGO proposals, whether proposals were subject to debate, whether suggested participants were nominations or appointments and how to gauge the relative power of the DESA staff or bureau to negate or modify the work of the NGO committee. Time lines were tight, particularly given the increased difficulty and time-consuming nature of obtaining visas and travel tickets for many Southern nominees.

With respect to funding, the NGO committee had virtually none, living on anticipation and e-mail. The tiny staff capacity of the two NGO bodies was exploited radically, and telephone or in-person meetings were restricted, with decision-making often based on piggy-backing on other events and requiring a high level of trust. In the end, criteria were applied, decisions were taken and more than 80 participants were selected for proposal to roundtable seats. Anticipated difficulties with competing or transcending DESA nominees erupted, but to a lesser extent than feared.

A further and instrumental role played by the NGO committee was preparation of the participants in the roundtables, which were an important component of civil society's overall input. The Global CSO Forum, in which most but not all of the potential presenters to the roundtables participated, resulted in a declaration which provided an overall orientation to NGO participation in the conference, with a clear critical commentary on the pre-existent conference declaration. The NGO committee drew the more than 80 presenters together, organising them in roundtable-specific caucuses. The caucuses then worked to share policy priorities and coordinate agendas for presentation and, in some cases, for mutual support. This process, although last minute and under considerable pressure of fatigue and linguistic and other differences, contributed to a common agenda for a number of the roundtables and an exercise in mutual reinforcement.

Responding to proposals

Although the preparatory period for Monterrey provided opportunity for NGO and private sector input through the hearings held early in the process and for the usual lobbying and side events during preparatory meetings, the finalisation of the agreed official conference declaration caught some NGOs by surprise. A number had calculated that, as in several prior global conferences, there would remain space for debate and advocacy at the event itself, which was not the case. There would be no further debate on the text; no square brackets going into Monterrey! This process aspect, as well as the balance of content in the actual document, contributed to a sharply critical stance by the Global CSO Forum and in many of the press comments made by members of the Mexican NGO host committee and the ISC.

The FfD conference did, however, provide some avenues for continuing the debate, dubbed "staying engaged", which many of the NGOs who participated in Monterrey pursued. The Mexican NGO host committee and the ISC worked to ensure NGO representation in the roundtables provided at the high-level meeting of the UN Economic and Social Council, the BWIs and the WTO that followed Monterrey in 2002. Utilising the broader caucus of NGOs present at that time in New York, the committees closed business and sought support for a new mandate for the International Facilitating Committee on Financing for Development or IFG. This new group included a number of representatives of key sectoral organisations, such as women, religious, labour, social and development research organisations, and developed a strategy to open up its membership with an eye to regional representation. The IFG has since acted as an informal interlocutor with the FfD office that emerged within DESA, continuing to nominate participants for CSO hearings and for the 2003 General Assembly informal session and the 2004 high-level meeting with ECOSOC, the BWIs, the WTO and UNCTAD.

Reporting

Monitoring state actions and follow-up to ECOSOC and General Assembly dialogues is limited by two main factors: one having origins within the international system, the other within NGOs in general. In terms of international policy-making, the way sessions are recorded and records kept in the UN system makes it very difficult for the untrained observer to ascertain whether and to what extent any NGO proposals or critical advisories have been taken on board. If one of the marks of successful policy consultation is that the parties can identify what impact they have had, the FfD follow-up process still has a good distance to go. As noted earlier, the major limitation of NGO participation and influence was the lack of resources to assure dedicated staff time, monitoring and reporting. This is a fundamental obstacle, with considerable consequence.

Non-institutional pathways

The Mexican host NGOs and social movements were most successful in affecting press and media coverage of both the NGO global forum and

NGO points of view on the official Monterrey conference. The terrain, at least for the national press and radio, was fertile given the number and variety of Mexican media outlets. The Mexican NGOs secured the services of an NGO with considerable experience in working with the domestic press. However, it is worth noting that internationally press coverage was much less successful.

The press coverage successfully raised questions about the negative social and economic effects of globalisation. More importantly, the arrival of a large international presence in Monterrey was used by local social organisations to sound alarm and give visibility to the tragic and violent deaths of dozens of women employed in *maquiladora* plants on the *frontera norte* of the state of Nueva Leon. There were attempts by Mexican anti-globalisation forces to mobilise various constituencies in a parallel series of seminars and assemblies and street demonstrations in the city centre and near the conference. There were also attempts to maintain contact between NGOs inside the perimeter of the conference and those organising outside to explore the benefits of coordinated action. By and large, the forces involved were too small or dispersed and the difficulties of transperimeter communication too great to achieve anything comparable, for instance, to the sizeable and high-impact popular mobilisations that occurred around the Cancun WTO Ministerial in 2003. An additional factor affecting the use of non-institutional pathways to exercise influence was the relatively conservative political atmosphere in Monterrey, and the surrounding state of Nueva Leon. Moreover, the distance from Mexico City made it less likely that constituencies with a base there would be able to make the journey.

Prospects

"Yes, we can *speak* now, but is anyone *listening*?"
John Clark, project director, Cardoso High Level Panel

A number of NGOs and NGO networks such as the ecumenical and Cooperation Internationale pour le Developpement et la Solidarité (CIDSE) religious networks, the Social Watch, the Third World Network and allied social movements – labour, women – took advantage of the openings offered by the FfD process to elaborate their detailed critique of the dominant "consensus", whether "Washington" or "Monterrey",[10] and various aspects of neo-liberal approaches to development. Both World Bank and IMF representatives attended the Global CSO Forum as resource persons and observers. High-level representatives of the BWIs and WTO, along with government ministers, encountered NGO input in detail in the roundtables at the conference. These encounters, at a less elegant level, have continued in an annual follow-up ECOSOC meeting and in biennial General Assembly meetings. Nevertheless, as Herman points out in chapter 7, the gravitational pull to Washington not only for finance ministers but for finance-debt-aid-oriented NGOs remains, and the WTO and trade ministers remain relatively in splendid self-imposed isolation in Geneva, seeking ever more isolated locales for ministerial conclaves.

Elements of mutual interest and support continue to exist for a mechanism or forum which provides opportunity for review and discussion of macroeconomic policies and their social and developmental consequences, and for the exploration of alternative general and specific approaches. The United Nations, through the FfD process and related civil society events, provided at least a "teaser" of what that forum or mechanism might be.

A number of iterative enhancements of occasions like the ECOSOC/BWIs/WTO/UNCTAD high-level sessions and the biennial General Assembly sessions could be developed. The timing of events (before rather than after World Bank/IMF meetings), the time devoted to events (more than one afternoon or one day), the full participation at a high level of the WTO, some measure of accountability reporting and enhanced facilitation and specific reporting could all contribute to more meaningful meetings. At the same time the leadership of one or more countries in ensuring higher-level participation and active advocacy by NGOs in capitals might create greater interest.

Finally, the meaning and effectiveness of such comprehensive meetings ultimately depend on the perceived, practical and legal relationship of the associated institutions. Ultimately, only a change in the mandate of the WTO and its legal relationship with the United Nations and the enhancement of the mandates of the BWIs will permit comprehensive reviews at the United Nations to have decisive effect on the direction and practices of these organisations. In the meantime, as the preparatory process for the FfD indicates, bringing about deeper operative collaboration between staff and between country executive directors and UN missions is not impossible. Leadership and persistence, as well as an occasion or focus for engagement, are all essential.

Civil society and the global governance agenda

"Hence the paradox – that while the *substance* of politics has become globalized, the *process* of politics has not. Its principal institutions – elections, political parties and parliaments – remain firmly rooted at the national level."[11]

Despite the fact that many NGOs engage at times with issues of global governance, and that the number of them is growing, relatively few have, until recently, made global governance central to their mandate or priorities. There is evidence that this is changing. In part this shift may be a result of positive experience in creating new agreements and institutions (see below). Yet it is also a reaction to the increasingly intrusive impacts and implications of the trade and investment regimes.

A number of new initiatives wrestling with various aspects of global governance have emerged since the turn of the millennium. Some – including the Helsinki Process, the World Commission on the Social Dimensions of Globalization, the Eminent Persons Panel on Threats, Challenges and Change, and Reform of the International System – have been initiated by governments or global institutions. Others – the International Facilitating Committee on FfD, UBUNTU, the Finnish Network Institute for Global Democratization, the Forum International de Montreal, the World Civil Society Conference, the "Blue Mountain group", the NGLS initiative on the future of the multilateral system, the ECOSOC Reform project of UNA-USA – have origins among NGOs and global networks.[12] One of the most thoughtful recent studies, commissioned from a leading NGO representative, was sponsored by the German foundation Friedrich Ebert Stiftung.[13] This volume will also contribute to the debate. On a broader CSO level it can be argued that one of the main purposes and potential impacts of the World Social Forum and its various regional offshoots is the reform or reinvention of global governance.

The report of the Commission on Global Governance – *Our Global Neighbourhood* – anticipated a process leading toward a world conference on governance, and made an extensive series of proposals to that end.[14] Yet no UN conference on global governance has developed in the decade following *Our Global Neighbourhood*. While eminent persons and high-level panels produce mounting piles of reports and recommendations, they are often initiated without NGO input and are inconsistent in terms of engaging NGOs and CSOs. They frequently lack clear follow-up strategies and support. For example, the then Canadian Prime Minister, Paul Martin, actively encouraged an informal expanded leaders process – the so-called G-20 – but this has many of the same weaknesses of other clubs of the "invited".

At the initiative of Secretary-General Annan, the United Nations has undertaken to engage the global private sector through initiatives such as the Global Compact or visits to Davos retreats. However, the United Nations has not developed an effective strategy for relating to the World Social Forum, which is a public relations failure and a substantive tragedy. NGOs, national governmental and academic initiatives on the future of global governance will undoubtedly continue, but lacking a focus, or a strategic process or occasion (a world conference or a series of General Assembly or ECOSOC-sponsored sessions, for example), this is a very one-sided and potentially cynicism-producing affair.

Cardoso and after

The report of the high-level panel on the relations of the United Nations and civil society has the potential to advance the discussion of the role of NGOs in particular and enfranchisement of CSOs in general. Its comprehensive survey of existing practices, together with its consultations with various actors, provide useful background for a variety of research initiatives.

Where is the Cardoso Panel likely to lead?[15] The Cardoso Panel report released in June 2004, was put before the General Assembly along with a report on implementation by the Secretary-General. The General Assembly, despite some initiatives from Brazil and other delegations, has not to date taken action on the Cardoso Report, and it was not integrated into the process for the Millennium+5 Summit session in September 2005.[16]

Cardoso Panel member Birgitta Dahl outlined the challenges the panel had faced and sketched the orientation of its recommendations. She noted that the panel argues for three paradigm shifts.
- From an institutional focus and culture which is essentially inter-state to a much more inclusive and flexible approach emphasising multistakeholder, inter-constituency and *networking* initiatives, extending well beyond the UN's history as a convening forum.
- A greater focus on country-level alliances and coalitions responsible for implementing the Millennium Development Goals and much else, with UN country-level facilitation. The objective is to "get things done".
- Addressing "democratic deficits", for example reversing the perceived marginalisation of parliaments and moving beyond the dominance of foreign relations in the executive power within states. The panel will attempt to find a way to engage parliamentarians more directly in the United Nations, to give them a voice.

In overall terms, the panel's report takes an approach that emphasises *inclusion*, which focuses on accessibility and transparency in global governance, with clearer roles for civil society and easier access for citizens in general. Opening the United Nations to greater recognition of and response to *global public opinion* is a logical consequence of this approach.

To implement such an approach will require opening the UN's major formal structures, and those processes which attract both high-level participation and informal exchanges, roundtables, hearings and other initiatives (see FfD). The panel has heard a good deal about global policy networks, and implementation of the report will mean trying to transform the United Nations into one node in these networks. Indeed, the emphasis on *partnerships* in order to respond effectively to global challenges is one proposed step to implement this new approach and develop a new role for the United Nations. The proving ground for new partnerships is likely to be efforts to achieve the Millennium Development Goals, yet the United Nations should be seen as a body which promotes and catalyses new partnerships in all aspects of its work.

As Dahl noted, the panel responds to what it perceives as a global "democratic deficit" and recommends strengthening the global role of parliamentarians by establishing the equivalent of global "parliamentary committees" on key global challenges.[17] To these ends, the report proposes some organisational changes, aiming to establish a cross-institutional entry point and accreditation procedure lodged with the General Assembly. It seeks a specific high-level office under the Secretary-General to coordinate UN relations not only with CSOs but with parliamentarians, business and others. It also recommends this sort of strengthened liaison role at country level, stimulating and enabling multisectoral dialogue. Although the release of the report should be an occasion for close scrutiny and active response by CSOs seeking to engage with the United Nations, the report, like others of its kind, will have little impact unless taken up by interested constituencies and finding some lead UN agencies and support in some key national ministries. Since many CSOs with a variety of mandates want an expanded say in UN bodies, the recommendations of the Cardoso Panel provide an occasion which should not be missed – to engage allies in considering ways to enhance engagement with civil society in policy, decision-making, implementation and evaluation.

A global inter-parliamentary committee focused on conflict prevention, on the global HIV/AIDS challenge or on environmental crises may be one way of translating the general proposals of the panel into a useful mechanism for advancing the civil society conflict prevention agenda. In addition, *partnership* can be an important element in responding to global challenges of many types. However, it must be noted that there is a great deal of ambiguity and "looseness" in much of the discussion of partnership in UN circles. As Ann Zammitt points out in her useful and wide-ranging study of UN-business partnerships, "if a common approach to partnerships does exist, it seems to be 'anything goes'". For example, there is little evidence to show that progress has been made on finding "a common understanding for the scope and modalities of partnerships to be developed as part of the outcomes of the World Summit on Sustainable Development".[18]

Clarity about the different nature of various types of "partner" organisations and their objectives, interests and resources is essential. Clarity of the relative power of different partners is as important in UN relations as in gender relations. Zammitt argues that the current variety of UN-business partnerships is unlikely to make a significant contribution to development and may actually "be counterproductive". She puts the emphasis on the transcendence of appropriate *development* objectives and promotes a strategy of clear social and economic goals and a development-centred economic framework within which partnerships may be defined.[19] Groups seeking to develop new partnership arrangements with the United Nations for economic or social policy purposes should benefit from Zammitt's emphasis on the development context, the need for clarity in roles and expectations and her detailing of the diverse ways in which one sector – private business – has exercised extensive influence in diverse aspects of the UN family.

In terms of other proposed mechanisms, the report avoids responding directly to calls for a global people's assembly or an ongoing global civil society forum. It does favour continued sparing use of world conference formats for global agenda-setting. While understanding and sharing many of the reservations they might cite regarding a global parliament or people's assembly, the author would argue for consideration of options both of a parliamentary assembly and an advisory civil society forum. The first might be a significant step toward enhanced transparency and legitimacy of global governance. The second could provide a forum for coalescence of civil society priorities and pressure, and for the advancement of civil society contributions to the reform of global governance.

In lieu of such initiatives, we are likely to see a multiplication of networks, so-called "global policy networks" or "global problem-solving networks", producing high-quality, specialised and oft-ignored reports with an unclear mandate arising from some or other institutional invitation but lacking broad popular connection. Finally, the Cardoso Panel Report (in Proposal 29) suggests leadership by the Secretary-General in his capacity as chairman of the UN system coordination mechanism. It suggests that he "encourage all agencies, including the Bretton Woods institutions, to enhance their engagement with civil society and other actors and to cooperate with one another across the system to promote this aim, with periodic progress reviews". This proposal is suggestive. If the Secretary-General were to initiate such encouragement, he would be well advised to seek the opinion of diverse civil society sources, to review issues that transcend organisational boundaries or come into conflict among the agencies concerned and to engage civil society in both proposals for further enhancement and evaluation of progress.

Conclusion

Neera Chandhoke, in her consideration of the "limits" of global civil society, reminds us that the "three sector" – state, market, civil society – mode of analysis may be based on a false assumption regarding the discrete nature of the three categories. She urges an approach that keeps constantly in mind the diverse power relations, and cautions against thinking which concludes that civil society actors, including NGOs, offer a clear alternative to present governance approaches and are autonomous of either states or markets.[20] For example, to consider the advocacy agenda for 2005 of Oxfam International without considering the relatively high-level access it has to the Blair-Brown government would be inadequate. Similarly, to consider the action strategy of Greenpeace without reference to the marketing potential of pictures of bludgeoned seals in certain European constituencies would be inadequate. The transcendent explanation of stasis and frustration is probably not about the limitations and particularities of real NGOs and CSOs but about the posture and agenda of the superpower and its effects on its allies and satraps, and its effective direct and indirect "chill" effect on the perception of opportunities by all actors. These cautions may have much to do with why no global governance forum has yet emerged. However, the experience of the past decade in alliance-building for new agreements and institutions may indicate that the current stalemate may be broken. Besides a potential "critical mass" among NGO and CSO actors, the key ingredient may be the creation of what Jens Martens calls "pacesetter coalitions of like-minded governments".[21] For that to occur requires at least one government to take the initiative in the following.

- Encourage the Secretary-General to initiate a process of consultation, involving CSO representatives from diverse sectors and regions, with relevant UN agencies, the BWIs and, if possible, with the WTO on how to enhance engagement with civil society across the institutions and, in particular, how to address with CSOs those issues which transcend the boundaries of individual institutions or which provoke inter-institutional confusion or conflict.
- Encourage the creation of a panel of inquiry by the Secretary-General, including experts and civil society representatives in such fields as human rights, labour and the environment, to consider mechanisms whereby the precedence of human rights, environmental and other normative treaties and regimes can be assured in contrast to the claims of trade, investment and intellectual property accords.
- Encourage cross-agency comparative evaluation of new formats and

procedures for engaging CSOs in official processes (such as hearings, multi-stakeholder encounters, roundtables, field visits, etc.).
- Urge the maintenance of sustained financial support and relative autonomy for such experienced agencies in NGO liaison as the UN NGLS.

Notes

1. Scholte, Jan Aart (2000) *Globalization: A Critical Introduction*, London: Macmillan.
2. Clarkson, Steven (2002) *Uncle Sam and Us: Globalization, Neoconservatism and the Canadian State*, Toronto: University of Toronto Press.
3. While this chapter does not examine the WTO and disenfranchisement as a whole, specific suggestions as to how the WTO might enhance its day-to-day relations with NGOs are outlined in Willetts, Peter (2002) "Civil Society Networks in Global Governance: Remedying the World Trade Organization's Deviance from Global Norms", paper presented at the Colloquium on International Governance, Palais des Nations, Geneva, 20 September, unpublished.
4. See Herman, this volume.
5. See Gray, this volume.
6. Shamsie, Yasmine (2003) *Mutual Misgivings, Civil Society Inclusion in the Americas*, Ottawa: North-South Institute.
7. Hemispheric Social Alliance (2002) *Alternatives for the Americas*, available at www.cptech.org/ip/ftaa/FTAAAlternative2003E.pdf.
8. Hemispheric Social Alliance (2003) *Lessons from NAFTA: The High Cost of "Free" Trade*, available from www.art-us.org/docs/high%20cost%20of%20free%20trade.pdf.
9. The issue of whether there are clear "rules of the game" regarding business access to UN meetings and processes, equivalent for example to the resolutions which define civil society access to ECOSOC, continues to preoccupy a number of NGOs. See, for example, Global Policy Forum (2004) *Joint Civil Society Statement on the Global Compact and Corporate Accountability*, July, available from www.globalpolicy.org.
10. One wag – the author – was quoted in the local press as typifying the result as "the Washington Consensus in a sombrero".
11. United Nations (2004) *We the Peoples: Civil Society, the United Nations and Global Governance. Report of the Panel of Eminent Persons on United Nations-Civil Society Relations*, A/58/817, p. 8.
12. For a brief overview discussion of governance issues and proposals see Foster, John W. and Wells, Pera (2005) *We the peoples ... 2005, Mobilizing for Change, Messages from Civil Society*, Ottawa: NSI-INS, pp. 72–79; Foster, John W. (2004) *Links for Life: Opportunities for More Effective Civil Society Engagement with the UN System*, Utrecht: European Centre for Conflict Prevention; UBUNTU Secretariat and Foster, John W. (2004) *Proposals to Reform the System of International Institutions: Future Scenarios*. Barcelona: Ad Hoc Secretariat of the UBUNTU Forum. The following websites should be consulted for current commentary and proposals: www.un-ngls.org, www.wfuna.org, www.helsinkiprocess.fi, www.wfm.org, www.nigd.org, www.fimcivilsociety.org, www.globalpolicy.org.
13. Martens, Jens (2003) *The Future of Multilateralism after Monterrey and Johannesburg*, Berlin: Friedrich Ebert Stiftung.
14. Commission on Global Governance (1995) *Our Global Neighbourhood*, Oxford and New York: Oxford University Press.

15. The author benefited from conversations with panel secretariat chief John Clark, and with Birgitta Dahl, panel member and former speaker of the Swedish Parliament, who was both a plenary speaker and working session resource person at the Dublin Conference, 31 March–April 2, 2004.
16. United Nations, 2004, note 11 above; United Nations (2004) *Report of the Secretary-General on the Implementation of the Report of the Panel of Eminent Persons on United Nations-Civil Society Relations*, A/59/354.
17. Dahl, note 15 above.
18. Zammitt, Ann (2003) *Development at Risk: Rethinking UN-Business Partnerships*, Geneva: South Centre/UNRISD.
19. Ibid.
20. Chandhoke, Neera (2002) "The Limits of Global Civil Society", in Marlies Glasins, Many Kaldor and Helmut Anheier, eds, *Global Civil Society 2002*, Oxford and New York: Oxford University Press.
21. Martens, note 13 above.

3
Business-society interaction towards sustainable development – Corporate social responsibility: The road ahead

Mikoto Usui

Introduction

Agenda 21 distinguishes "business and industry" from other "major groups of non-governmental stakeholders".[1] The term is used interchangeably with "business", "industry" or "the private sector". While there is no unique official definition of the term, its common-sense interpretation includes multinational corporations (MNCs) and large private enterprises; small and medium-sized firms, venture businesses, cooperatives and micro-businesses; and business-supported NGOs as distinguished from non-business NGOs (the latter being called "civil society organisations" (CSOs) hereafter to avoid confusion). As for (MNCs), it should be noted that the collapse of the Soviet Union and expansion of the European Union have given rise to a phenomenal growth in relatively small MNCs with less than 250 employees (or even fewer in the case of service companies), with their headquarters based in countries other than the United States. Now the estimated total number of MNCs is about 63,000, with 821,000 subsidiaries spread all over the world. In total these MNCs employ 90 million people (of whom 20 million are in developing countries), and their total production accounts for a quarter of the world's GDP.[2] The second subcategory is only partly woven into MNCs' supply chains, while the rest may be seen, rather, as subsumed into "civil society" (along with "workers and trade unions"). The last subcategory includes various not-for-profit associations, research institutes, advocacy networks, professional service organisations and philanthropic foundations which are based on memberships drawn predominantly (though not exclusively) from business communities.[3]

Thus "business" is no more monolithic than "civil society". This chapter is essentially intended to grapple with the dynamics of business-society relationships characterising the current "reflexive" phase of modernisation and globalisation. Its title, "business-society interaction", is meant to locate business in the political realm as an agency for change alongside CSOs. This may surprise most NGO scholars, since they usually conceptualise business (or the economy) outside the realm of civil society. Indeed, business and civil society operate according to different logics. In the conventional structuralist perspective, business is seen as a private economic power that dominates the state-society relationship, while CSOs are viewed as a critical countervailing force against business and state. Now, amidst the deepening of economic globalisation and the widening of anti-globalisation sentiment, the challenge of reintegrating *business* into *society* has become one of the most contentious public policy issues of the twenty-first century. Business has begun to respond, first rather passively but recently more positively, to the burgeoning buzz of "corporate citizenship" or "corporate social responsibility" (CSR). This chapter tries to capture the dynamics of business-society interaction in that perspective, focusing on the latest developments related to the rule books for corporate responsibility and accountability.

Many other chapters in this volume focus primarily on formal intergovernmental conference diplomacy (or what the editors call "institutional pathways") with a view to exploring how to enhance the voice and influence of civil society and/or developing countries in multilateral policymaking. In contrast, this chapter will focus on non-institutional and what are termed quasi-institutional pathways that are of particular importance for non-state actors. These quasi-institutional pathways are consistent with the project of this volume, which is to promote the engagement and influence of a diverse set of actors from both developed and developing countries.

In the context of institutional bargaining, "public diplomacy" has gained prevalence by engaging a myriad of non-state actors and unfolding along increasingly widened and multilayered pathways. In this context, "institution" matters in the broadest sense of the term, signifying the way humans structure their interactions in society, be they local, national or global. Both formal rules (such as constitutions, laws and public regulations) and informal rules (behavioural norms, customs and self-imposed codes of conduct) are equally important, and are being enforced at three different levels: first-party (voluntary self-enforcement), second-party (confronting and conflating engagement among concerned parties), and third-party enforcement (by governments implementing the terms of formal agreements). In fact, even though corporate citizenship circles declare that CSR has been shifting from the margins to the mainstream of corporate governance, the CSR-related guidelines and codes remain largely in the category of informal rules, and are left to voluntary self-enforcement. While the corporate wall of voluntarism remains quite firm, a growing space seems to be emerging for second-party enforcement, if not third-party enforcement, since civil society is pressuring for deeper institutionalisation of CSR with more formal, legally binding rules for corporate conduct.

The subtle combination of "confronting" and "conflating" the engagement between business and CSO leaders has been poorly studied. The author has attempted to show elsewhere that formal conference diplomacy at the global level has seldom engaged the two camps in face-to-face negotiations to solve problems, but rather has tended to leave them in sharp positional confrontation.[4] Most typically, business leaders accord priority to "concrete actions and deliverable results other than process and procedures", while CSO activists keep calling for "a legally binding framework for corporate accountability and liability".[5] The "Type II outcome" was an attempt to respond to these two different voices. Officially introduced in the World Summit for Sustainable Development (WSSD) process, Type II outcomes consist of voluntary proactive multi-stakeholder partnerships/initiatives; a supposedly business-friendly institutional innovation. Nevertheless, the result of Type II arrangements appears to be fraught with difficulties. Currently there are two parallel showcases administered in a mutually isolated manner: one official registry with the UN Commission for Sustainable Development (CSD), the other a portal comprising business-led and business-oriented partnerships maintained by a business-affiliated non-profit institution.[6]

The Global Compact, a historic experiment in learning and action on corporate citizenship and UN-business partnership launched in 2001, is another example of the difficulties in confronting and conflating business and civil society engagement. UN Secretary-General Kofi Annan had to counterbalance the Global Compact with another civil-society-focused initiative, the Panel of Eminent Persons on United Nations–Civil Society Relations, launched in 2003. The conflicting but potentially coinciding agenda for change is perhaps most evidenced by the simultaneous staging of the World "Social" Forum in parallel to the World "Economic" Forum which is now in its sixth year.

These macro politicisation games need not worry us too much, since they may well be considered a variant of "tacit" bargaining or a way of navigating "dialectical" interaction among contradictory forces. They may not have immediate direct effects on state policies, but hopefully they will in time help the stakeholders seek new space for creative change, reconstructing their relationships, norms, roles and rules in the long run.

In fact, the confrontational postures of the Davos Man versus the Porto Alegre Protester seem to subside as we move down towards more pragmatic business-society confluence at intermediate and local levels. This is the case where both business and civil society stakeholders are enticed by opportunities for engaging each other for mutual gains through joint problem-solving activities. The remainder of this chapter focuses on the quasi-institutional developments associated with the CSR movement and various forms of codes for corporate conduct. These include so-called "multi-stakeholder" codes that are privately agreed without direct governmental backing, as well as voluntary codes backed by formal intergovernmental processes. Surprisingly, sustainability-oriented reflexive corporate governance is becoming increasingly receptive to the world's "poverty alleviation" agenda, as witnessed at the World Economic Forum's annual meeting 2005.[7] There is also an emergent international discourse coalition advocating for a deeper institutionalisation of corporate responsibility and accountability at multilateral level, with greater attention to developing countries' participation and their priority concerns.

Corporate social responsibility and related international codes

Originally (during the 1970s) CSR focused on social "obligation" to satisfy shareholder interests and legal requirements *plus* "philanthropy". Subsequently it has embraced an additional thematic framework of social "responsibility", which implies accommodating demands from a broader range of stakeholders, including labour, consumers, suppliers, local communities and governments. Changing societal expectations have led to a growing attention to "socially responsible investment" (SRI), i.e. the fiduciary case for CSR that engages institutional investors. The alleged positive link between corporate sustainability and financial performance does not so much reflect a robust cause-and-effect relationship as the tendency of leading corporations to embrace the notion of CSR deeper in their mainstream business strategy. Today, CSR overlaps considerably with other concepts in flux, such as corporate citizenship, corporate sustainability, corporate responsibility, business ethics, business in society and ethical corporations.

CSR is more broadly defined than "corporate governance" and "business ethics". In terms of "social" responsibility there are at least seven categories of stakeholders or azimuths: owners/shareholders/potential investors; managers (especially CEOs and the board of directors); employees (including trade unions); customers (demand chains) and consumers; business partners and contractors/suppliers (and their work conditions); the natural environment; and the communities within which an enterprise operates, including local neighbourhood community, local CSOs, local autonomies and national governments (and sometimes even foreign partners' countries in which it does business).[8]

The notion of corporate governance, as addressed by the OECD Guidelines on Corporate Governance (1999), concentrates on the first two of the seven stakeholders – the rights of shareholders, the equitable treatment of shareholders, disclosure and transparency and the board's responsibilities. The discussion on "good corporate governance" is occasionally extended to address ethical and broader stakeholder issues. "Business ethics" is also a corporation's intramural matter, covering four of the seven stakeholders: managers, investors, customers and employees. Ethics refers to the principles which guide behaviour (and sometimes involves specific situations in which ethical controversy arises). Social responsibility encompasses good ethics both within and beyond the corporation's walls.

During the 1980s and 1990s the responsibility for regulating MNC conduct shifted from the governmental "command and control" approach towards corporations' voluntary "self-regulation". More recently, emphasis has been on "co-regulation" in CSR, involving two or more stakeholders in the design and implementation of norms and standards. The outcomes are more or less internationally accredited voluntary standards and certification schemes. In sectors where only weak or fragmentary international regimes exist (such as forestry and tourism), there is a plethora of initiatives that are not many steps removed from the gimmicks of intra-industrial oligopolistic competition. Critics dismiss them as instances of "the fox guarding the hen house".[9] Where sustainability-conscious CSOs are actively involved in local conservation activities, business-community partnerships for building locality-specific standards and labelling schemes can stimulate locally adapted innovation and competition that help hitherto marginalised local business and non-business actors. However, the proliferation of localised schemes tends to reduce confidence on the part of international producers and consumers, and thus offers little tangible (market) benefits to operators themselves. Such a situation would call for public policy initiatives in building an internationally credible regulatory framework in which to re-embed the dispersed local schemes.[10] All the same, it is important to have global schemes built on multiple local realities, with due attention to the needs and traditions of developing countries.

In fact, quite a few codes and schemes of cross-border significance exist that have evolved out of partnerships between reputable MNCs and

CSOs. Commonly cited examples include the Forestry Stewardship Council (FSC, since 1993), developed originally by the partnering of WWF-UK and B&Q (wood products dealer); the Marine Stewardship Council, born from Unilever-WWF cooperation (MSC, since 1995); and the Global Reporting Initiative (GRI, since 2000), which was triggered by Royal Dutch Shell in cooperation with the Coalition for Environmentally Responsible Economies (CERES) and the UN Environment Programme (UNEP). These private schemes are often likened to global "soft conventions", but not all stakeholders agree with them. Perceived lack of equity in their governance structures and operation has contributed to a continued proliferation of more locally adapted schemes.

Table 3.1 gives a list of selected major "multi-stakeholder" codes of international significance. Category A (voluntary multi-stakeholder codes developed without direct governmental backing) includes general cross-industrial codes and initiatives (such as AA1000, the GRI and the Global Compact) as well as industry-specific codes (such as the CCC, FLA, FSC and MSC). The table includes, under Category B, the CSO-relevant voluntary codes that are derived from intergovernmental processes (especially the United Nations, the OCED and the European Union).[11]

A corporate code of ethics, or code of conduct, is typically a set of principles that state the moral obligations of the company in relation to the general public or stakeholders. Such codes have grown in prominence, particularly in the United States and the United Kingdom. Other European countries, as well as South Africa, Brazil, India, etc., have also become actively involved in developing ethical guidelines for corporations. In Europe initiatives have come mainly from trade unions, employers' associations and the European Union. The substance of ethical codes relates typically to matters such as child labour, discrimination, working hours, minimum wages, social benefit payment, safety and health in the workplace, subcontractor conditions, human rights and environmental considerations. But there is currently no universally accepted standard for codes of ethics.

The Caux Roundtable, founded in 1986 by Frederick Philips (former president of Philips Electronics) and Oliver Giscard d'Estang (vice-chairman of the business school INSEAD), is an international forum for business leaders from the United States, Europe and Japan committed to energising the role of business in reducing social and economic threats to world peace and stability. The Caux Principles (see table 3.1) include the so-called "stakeholder principles" which outline how a company should behave in relation to customers, employees, owners/investors, suppliers, competitors and communities.

The self-motivated collaborative arrangements between major corporations and sustainability-oriented CSOs are based on rational motiva-

Table 3.1 International codes related to corporate social responsibility

Voluntary "multi-stakeholder" codes	Near created	Web address
Cross-sectoral		
Caux Roundtable	1994	www.cauxroundtable.org
ISO 14001	1995	www.iso.org
Social Accountability 8000 (SA8000)	1999	www.sa-intl.org
AccountAbility 1000 (AA1000)	1999	www.acountability.org.uk
Global Reporting Initiative	1999	www.globalreporting.org
Global Alliance for Workers and Communities	1999	www.theglobalalliance.org
Workers Rights Consortium (WRC)	2000	www.workersrights.org
ISO Framework for ISO Standard on Corporate Social Responsibility	2001 (proposal)	www.bsdglobal.com/issues/csr_standard.asp
Publish What You Pay Campaign	2002	www.publishwhatyoupay.org
Sector specific		
Forest Stewardship Council (FSC)	1993	www.fsc.org
Marine Stewardship Council (MSC)	1997	www.msc.org
Fair Labor Association (FLA)	1998 (garments and sports shoes)	www.fairlabor.org
Ethical Trading Initiative	1998 (food, beverage and garments)	www.ethicaltrade.org
Clean Clothes Campaign (CCC)	1998	www.cleanclothes.org
Worldwide Responsible Apparel Production (WRAP)	2000	www.wrapparel.org
Framework Agreements between specific multinational corporations and international trade secretaries	1998–	
• IFBWW (building and wood products		
• ITGLF (textiles, garments and leather)		
• IUF (food, hotels and catering)		
Kimberley Process Certification Scheme (KPCS)	2003 (conflict diamonds)	www.Kimberleyprocess.com

UN and other intergovernmental initiatives

UN Universal Declaration of Human Rights	1948	www.un.org/Overview/rights.html
UN Centre on Transnational Corporation, Draft Code of Conduct for Transnational Corporations	1977	www.multinationalguidelines.org
ILO Tripartite Declaration of Principles Concerning Multinational Enterprises and Social Policy	1977	www.ilo.org/public/english/stsndards/norm
OECD Principles of Corporate Governance	1999/rev. 2004	www.oecd.org
OECD Convention on Combating the Bribery of Foreign Public Officials in International Business Transactions	1999	www.oecd.org
OECD Guidelines for Multinational Enterprises	1976/latest rev. 2000	www.oecd.org
UN Global Compact	2000	www.unglobalcompact.org
EC Green Paper on Corporate Responsibility	2004	www.bsdglobal.com/issues/eu_green_paper.asp
EU Multistakeholder Forum	2002	www.eurosif.org/eupol-mshf-work.shtml
World Commission on the Social Dimension of Globalization	2002	www.ilo.org/public/english/wcsdg/policy/index.htm
UN Sub-Commission on Human Rights' Draft Norms on the Responsibilities of Transnational Corporations and Other Business Enterprises with Regard to Human Rights	2003	www.unchr.ch/Huridocda

tions. Often CSOs, disenchanted with government policies, seek to gain greater leverage through business links with government. Many mainstream CSOs of today, which started small and focused on problems seen as symptoms of market failures, have grown into major international institutions. They continue to invest heavily in their networks to work on increasingly complex, multidimensional agendas. Even well-established advocacy CSOs need to create problem-solving and concrete action programmes, in order to earn a high degree of legitimacy and become truly influential players. Such action programmes should preferably include solutions that are deliverable through markets. Partnering with credible business corporations would be particularly important in gaining more funds and technical and managerial resources for leveraging change. Such partnerships would prove more crucial now, as traditional sources of NGO funding are increasingly squeezed.[12] From the perspective of business corporations, major motivations for teaming up with CSOs include to avoid negative public confrontations, take advantage of CSOs' credibility with the public and establish new visions concerning social issues and priorities. Needless to say, a partnership is not a merger of the partners' respective mainstream operations. It is customary to externalise the outcome of the collaborative engagement as a non-profit third-party organisation as the agreement enters its implementation and maintenance phases. The listing of CSR-related international codes in table 3.1 includes UN and other intergovernmental initiatives. A World Bank-sponsored recent survey asked managers of large MNCs which of these instruments were the most "influential" on their practice. Out of the total 107 respondents, 46 per cent cited the ISO 14000 series, 36 per cent the GRI and 33 per cent the UN Global Compact.[13]

The OECD Guidelines for Multinational Enterprises (or MNEs, used here interchangeably with MNCs) were initiated as early as in 1976, and subsequently reviewed in 1979, 1982, 1984, 1991 and 1998. The latest revision, in 2000, adopted an unusually extensive multi-stakeholder approach. The views of business, labour and civil society were represented by the two advisory bodies to the OECD, BIAC (Business and Industry Advisory Council) and TUAC (Trade Union Advisory Council), and ANPED (the Northern Alliance for Sustainability based in the Netherlands). Each group organised and presented a common position to the negotiators and OECD staff, and the latter posted these groups' comments and each negotiation draft on a website. Through this internet exposure, many other major CSOs gave comments on and influenced the guidelines, including World Wildlife Fund, Amnesty International, Friends of the Earth and Tradecraft Exchange. The 1998 review involved a few developing countries (Argentina, Brazil and Chile) as observer nations to deal with some of the new labour-related issues. In spite of these procedural refinements in the drafting process, the guidelines' language has remained rather unclear on implementation, leaving much to the discretion of individual governments and MNEs. The reports provided by the OECD on the status of implementation of the "national contact points" – supposedly an important innovation of the new revision – show that the process is not working as effectively as anticipated.

With respect to new multi-stakeholder approaches, the World Summit on the Information Society (WSIS) deserves particular mention, although its final outcome is not listed in table 3.1. The WSIS Phase I (Geneva, 2003) adopted a carefully programmed multi-stakeholder approach to its preparatory process. Business was represented through the CCBI (the Coordinated Committee of Business Interlocutors in which the International chamber of commerce (ICC) plays a leading role), and civil society by a great diversity of groups, networks and movements[14] which participated in six regional caucuses and several thematic caucuses and working groups. These efforts would appear to be a whole-hearted attempt at operationalising deliberative democracy in formal multilateral conference diplomacy. However, it should be noted that business groups and civil society groups still tended to work separately in these processes. The WSIS Phase II (2005) is to formulate an action plan for implementing the general principles, norms and guidelines adopted by WSIS I, including technically sophisticated issues such as internet governance, as well as concrete regulatory measures including options of self-regulation, coordination and cooperation. Although the preparatory process for Phase II is also set in a multi-stakeholder environment, it remains to be seen whether the process will effectively increase the influence of civil society actors and developing country participants in this traditionally business-dominated high-tech domain.

With respect to the UN Global Compact, the conflict between business and society was accentuated rather than abated during the process of its formulation. Representatives of the international business community had a number of informal meetings with UN Secretary-General Kofi Annan's "good office", while civil society caucuses were set aside. The latter's suspicion of UN-business "complicity" led to a call for a "Citizens' Compact" to push for a legally binding framework to govern the behaviour of global corporations. Now, the Global Compact Advisory Council includes several resourceful international NGOs such as Oxfam International, Amnesty International, Human Rights Watch, etc. These members seem to serve not as a leader but rather as a sort of intramural watchdog. The Advisory Council's weakest point may be that it remains without formal links to any state governments. The claim for a Citizens' Compact has subsequently been rewarded by the establishment of the Panel of Eminent Persons on UN-Civil Society Relations (chaired by

Fernando Enrique Cardoso). Curiously enough, the first report of this high-level panel[15] remains reticent on the role of business as a key constituency for global governance. It makes only passing remarks about the need to strengthen the Global Compact's capacity for enhancing corporate responsibility and engaging with local small firms and microbusinesses.

Regulatory implications of stakeholder engagement

One of the key drivers for mainstreaming CSR is the fear of becoming a target of the powerful campaigns of vigilant consumers, media and activist CSOs. They would indeed comprise an important impact on the business discipline of risk management. In such a defensive context, "mainstreaming" may imply just a "bolt-on", rather than "built in" to corporate strategy. Some scholars regard partnerships as "momentary coincidences" of the different interests and visions of stakeholders/partners that shape shared activities and do not automatically engender a well-shared common long-term goal among them.[16] In spite of the optimistic rhetoric to the contrary, partnerships are ephemeral in nature and may disappear when one party's interests are better served by other means.

Fortunately, multi-stakeholder engagement is not a one-shot affair. The power of civil society to influence business derives from a combination of sticks and carrots. It seems that the "sticks" are swung more often in the form of politics of confrontation in arenas for macro institutional bargaining, and the "carrots" more often in the form of proactive partnerships with business for jointly solving specific shared problems at local levels. But CSOs' sticks are swung at every level, and most effectively through their "watchdog" function, triggering "naming and shaming" pressure and even litigation against corporate (and state) breaches of prevalent norms and standards.

The effectiveness of these sticks should not be underestimated. Evolutionary theories of law and institution, which have emerged during the past two decades, attest to how the power of ethical norms derives from human capacity for moral emotions, which is as fundamental as human capacity for language.[17] Moral sentiments such as shame, disdain and indignation can serve as social-sanctions-based incentives for compliance with prevailing norms. Expressions of praise and admiration, as well as reputation-enhancing gossip, can serve as positive inducements. Thus multi-stakeholder codes, voluntary as they are, involve an element of "civil regulation". They mobilise, both in their formative phase and in the subsequent implementation phase, CSO watchdog activities, shareholder activism, ethical training programmes and sustainability-oriented advisory and consulting services. Complaints-based actions for dispute settlement also constitute an important dimension of civil regulation. Given the proliferation of voluntary multi-stakeholder codes, the complexity of the tasks related to monitoring, reporting, audit and certification makes it difficult to reconcile, consolidate or standardise those procedures among different codes. As a result, "complaints-based systems" have come to attract increasing attention. They focus on how to address abuses of corporate power and breaches of agreed standards rather than how to monitor and overhaul a broad array of corporate practices.

For example, the Workers Rights Consortium (WRC) is essentially a complaint-based system; its investigative procedures become operational in response to specific complaints lodged. Watchdog NGOs, such as Corporate Watch, Greenpeace, Friends of the Earth and the International Baby Food Action Network, adopt "naming and shaming" tactics which let civil society actors "confront" rather than "engage" business corporations.

NAFTA has side agreements concerning labour and environmental affairs that provide some scope for complaining about corporations. The UN Human Rights Commission has long utilised complaints-based mechanisms for dealing officially with cases of violation. Its sub-commission has contemplated establishing a "special rapporteur" to deal with cases of MNCs contradicting the set of "Norms on the Responsibilities of Transnational Corporations and Other Business Enterprises with Regard to Human Rights". The draft "norms", adopted by the subcommission in August 2003, propose to see MNCs' "sphere of influence", in the context of supporting human rights, broadly enough to cover the economic, social and cultural rights of their subsidiaries, agents, suppliers and buyers as well as the local communities in which they operate. Although the "norms" have no legal standing as yet, the Commission decided, in April 2004, to have the Office of the High Commissioner on Human Rights (OHCHR) conduct further study and multi-stakeholder consultations with governments, businesses and NGOs. In response to the OHCHR report[18] it requested, as of April 2005, the Secretary-General to appoint his "Special Representative" on the question of human rights and business with a view to identifying and clarifying "universal standards of corporate responsibility and accountability" in regards to human rights. The Special Representative will liaise closely with the Special Adviser to the Secretary-General for the Global Compact and endeavour to reflect more effectively the views of states and stakeholders from developing countries.[19]

The 2000 revision of the OECD Guidelines for MNCs has tried to strengthen the role of "national contact points" (NCPs), which handle complaints and (at least) initiate discussions between the parties in case of disputes. According to the 2004 *Annual Report of the National Contact Points*, 27 NCPs are governmental departments (single or multiple) and 11 NCPs are either tripartite or quadripartite. A number of countries use advisory committees or permanent consultative bodies whose members include non-governmental partners. The "specific instances" procedure of the guidelines allows for case-specific exploration of ethical issues encountered in concrete business situations. Many such specific instances have been brought up by trade unions and NGOs from non-OECD countries where OECD-based businesses have subsidiaries. The annual report acknowledges the importance of considering the voices of non-OECD actors and of providing international forums in which they can voice their concerns and gain experience with international procedures.[20]

The UN Global Compact is unique in that it does not provide a detailed code book, but consists of a series of nested networks that involve the Secretary-General's office and five supporting UN agencies (the UNDP, UNEP, UNHCR, ILO and UNIDO), business corporations participating from both developed and developing countries, trade unions and some CSOs. The Compact has so far been lenient about monitoring and penalising non-compliant signatories. Its governance does not include national governments, even though some governments (e.g. France and the United Kingdom) give active moral support to the Compact. Critics warn that its legitimacy may be fatally belittled unless an institutional facility is provided for watchdog NGOs and trade unions to bring to public attention serious breaches of the agreed principles.[21]

Towards deeper institutionalisation of corporate responsibility: An overview of various stakeholders' preferences

The current CSR discourse is divided into two extremist corners: one corner favouring a market-based nurturing approach, and the other stressing the need for new international rules of the game. On the one hand, the international business community holds on to the principle of "self-regulation" or voluntarism, giving a higher priority to "concrete solutions and deliverable results rather than process and procedures".[22] On the other, activist CSOs make vociferous calls for "legally binding" frameworks or conventions for corporate accountability and liability.

As noted previously, support for MNC codes of conduct came mainly from developing country governments during the 1970s. It culminated in the UN "Draft Code of Conduct for Transnational Corporations" (sponsored by the UN Centre on Transnational Corporations and negotiated in the UN Commission on Transnational Corporations) and the ILO "Tripartite Declaration of Principles concerning Multinational Enterprises and Social Policy". But the 1980s witnessed the faltering of confrontational politics between MNCs and developing host countries amid the "lost development decade" which followed from the unprecedented scale of debt crisis. In the 1990s, in the wake of discussions about sustainable development, support for MNC codes began to emerge – mainly from OECD countries, environmental and development NGOs, international trade unions and business-supported sustainability research and advocacy organisations. At the same time, and in contrast to before, developing country governments now seem more strongly interested in attracting foreign direct investment. They vehemently oppose inclusion of social and environmental clauses in the WTO rule books, and criticise Northern eco-labels and social labels which might lead to increased non-tariff barriers to their exports.

Now, in between these two ends of the spectrum, we find a broad middle region where the possibilities are explored more or less seriously for further "mainstreaming" of CSR in individual companies' corporate governance and for consolidation or standardisation of proliferating voluntary codes. The key question, in the language of Sabapathy and Zadek,[23] is whether CSR can become a "Mecca" pathway for change, rewarded by the market with the help of effective public policy and legislation, or whether it will remain at best an "oasis" for a not insignificant but limited number of leading companies willing to deliver greater social and environmental responsibility. Before looking into post-Johannesburg developments, it is important to examine how this landscape resonates in the preferences of several types of major stakeholders – large corporations, small businesses, trade unions and consumers' organisations in developed and developing countries.

Large corporations and sustainability consultants

Large corporations, particularly those having international supply chains for branded products and/or which are directly involved in overseas operations, have been the main target of CSOs' watchdog campaigns and have been prompted to build partnerships with major international CSOs to negotiate for internationally significant multi-stakeholder codes. Such MNCs find it in their own interest to sponsor stricter international codes for levelling the playing field, provided that the codes relate to specific sectors in which they are confident of their technological advantage. Such leading corporations tend to look for the "Stiglerian threshold"[24] – a public regulatory initiative that would promise an opportunity for earning quasi-monopoly rents on their technological advantages. A growing number of CSR-advocating consulting professions are interested in stimulating a larger cohort of "quiet business leaders" who are not yet renowned but potentially ready to innovate to reconcile the dynamic interests of business and society.[25] They seem to be less interested in promoting a minimalist version of CSR codes for the benefit of laggards and stragglers.

Small businesses and trade unions

Small and medium-sized enterprises (SMEs) are less visible to the public and are likely to resist the introduction of even a minimalist version of codes of conduct *domestically*. However, SMEs in developed economies tend to welcome, out of a protectionist motive, higher labour and environmental standards being adopted *overseas*, particularly by Southern exporters whose cheap labour threatens their security. Northern workers (trade unions), too, would be pleased to see Southern producers subjected to stricter labour standards. But they generally seem to regard corporate voluntary codes as an inferior means of securing labour rights to collective bargaining.

MNC codes of conduct can have a negative effect on marginalised workers in the South. For instance, an elimination of child labour in sports-goods-producing factories would lead to the shift of production from micro-businesses employing women and children towards larger factories that employ mostly male workers. So it would be naïve to expect that human rights and child labour codes alone could meet the priorities of Southern workers in general.

The International Confederation of Free Trade Unions (ICFTU)[26] tries to ensure that corporations respect workers' rights in every part of the world. The ICFTU works in partnership with global union federations (comprising 11 industry-specific unions) to assist workers from national unions in uniting at the international level for bargaining with particular global enterprises. Several international trade secretariats (e.g. for the textile, wood product and hotel, catering and allied industries) have negotiated "framework agreements" with specific MNCs. For example, the International Federation of Building and Wood Workers (IFBWW) has managed to develop framework agreements with IKEA, Farber Castell, Hochtief, Ballast Nedam and Skanska, which ensure the full recognition of labour union rights and effective implementation of all the related core ILO conventions.[27]

It should be noted here that Southern CSOs do not necessarily share the same interests as their Northern counterparts. They often stand against measures that might imply a non-tariff barrier to their countries' exports, and are suspicious of implications of the codes developed jointly by Northern businesses and NGOs. Southern NGOs generally accord higher priority to the task of augmenting the capacity and role of labour unions, which they wish to see include women, home-workers and informal sector workers as well.

Consumers

The last, but not the least important, category of stakeholder is consumers. Consumers are individualised in their daily decision-making. The proportion of "green consumers" is still not much larger than 5–10 per cent, even in developed countries. In earlier decades organised consumer movements were preoccupied with product- or producer-specific matters of safety, performance, pricing and redress. Today their expanded international networks are evolving a broader concern with "co-regulatory" approaches to corporate responsibility and accountability. Consumers International (CI), a worldwide non-profit federation of consumer unions,[28] has recently become active in campaigning for corporate accountability, as witnessed in the special event on the World Consumer Rights Day 2001, entitled "Corporate Citizenship in the Global Market". CI has since embarked on a new project, "Rapid Alert System for Unethical Business Behaviour", which proposes to pair up consumer groups in both home and host countries of MNCs to investigate cases of double standards and unethical conduct.[29]

Although CI's activism on CSR matters is generally kept within measure, it has secured an important watchdog position in the Codex Alimentarius Commission, and also an active observatory position in the International Organization for Standardization (ISO) through its Consumer Policy Council (COPOLCO) and Committee on Developing Country Matters (DEVCO). Now, the agenda of "sustainable consumption" heightens consumers' awareness not only of producers' obligations and consumers' rights, but also of consumers' own obligations or initiative-taking in matters such as promotion of the Sustainable Shopping Basket and the Environmental Product Declaration. It is anticipated that these new dimensions will lead to enhanced exchange between consumer organisations and business actors in order to inform and influence the latter's policies and practices.

The above discussion illustrates the variety of positions and preferences prevailing among different types of stakeholders of CSR. Since it is not very easy to locate a politically robust anchoring point between the two ends of the CSR spectrum, the project of promoting deeper institutionalisation of CSR is a challenging one.

Post-WSSD developments

In Johannesburg, Friends of the Earth International (FoEI) led a coalition of some 70 environmental NGOs from both developed and developing countries campaigning for "an effective, legally binding international framework to deliver corporate accountability". At one stage a broad coalition of governments from the European Union and many G-77 countries loomed with an attempt to respond positively to the FoEI-led call. Faced with vehement resistance by the United States and others, the outcome was just to include a clause for "active promotion of corporate accountability" in the Plan of Implementation. But some people hoped even that might become a new point of departure for building stronger binding standards for global corporations.[30]

The eleventh meeting of the UN Commission on Sustainable Development, held in 2003, made no explicit mention of CSR in its "Multi-Year Programme of Work" (although it might be taken up later as one of the cross-sectoral issues). Meanwhile, however, various new initiatives have continued to emerge at both at the market- and the rules-oriented ends of the CSR spectrum. Those sympathetic with the rules-oriented approach within the UN-associated policy research community system, such as the UN Research Institute of Social Development (UNRISD), raised their voices calling for a new "post-CSR agenda" – that is, an urge to re-conceptualise CSR as a means of "development cooperation" and to reshape the role of UN institutions in promoting the corporate accountability movement. The UNRISD-organised international conference with that theme (17–18 November 2003) was followed by a joint publication with the South Centre, entitled *Development Risk: Rethinking UN-Business Partnerships*. This activism, although judicial in its intention, had a typical shortcoming in that its point-blank emphasis on the need for "deeper structural and institutional change to limit corporate power"[31] was left without any prescriptive detail.

On the other hand, various kinds of finer-grained initiatives have been emerging from the market-oriented corner or, better to say, in the middle region lying between the two extremist positions. For example, the Nordic Partnership has urged governments and IGOs to take the lead in breaking the current stakeholder deadlock by giving clearer signals about provision of appropriate market incentives that would make both business and CSOs more actively involved in the development of new national and regional frameworks. CSOs are urged to keep their role as watchdogs so as not to lose their integrity and legitimacy, but to be more innovative in working in partnership with businesses and governments (instead of depending on their initial funding fuelled by public anger and business guilt).[32]

The ISO-COPOLCO began deliberating in 2001 on the desirability and feasibility of ISO CSR standards. Its interim report suggested that, in order not to be drowned in the confusing sea of variable quality initiatives, ISO standards should focus on processes and systems for operationalising individual firms' CSR commitments in measurable and verifiable terms. The suggested approach is to constitute a "third generation" of ISO management systems that is fully compatible with ISO 9000 and 14000, but includes techniques for stakeholder engagement and public reporting.[33] The matter was deliberated by an Advisory Group on Social Responsibility (from early 2003), and then in international workshops in Prague and Stockholm (May and June 2004) which brought together business experts, consumers, labour unions and governmental and inter-governmental agencies. The three-year process has led to the ISO's official decision (June 2004) to establish a new working group that answers direct to the ISO Technical Management Board. Its Social Responsibility Working Group has adopted a twin leadership system that links developing and developed country members and facilitates participation by experts from developing countries, consumer associations and other NGOs.

The CSR Minister of the UK government, which is known for development of CSR legislation that is more stringent than the voluntary EU standards, announced a draft "International Strategic Framework" of CSR in 2004. That framework was intended to "mainstream CSR in all the UK government departments, and also multilaterally through international organisations".[34] After a year-long consultation with national and international stakeholders, its outcome seems (for the time being) to have concluded by establishing "the UK government Gateway to Corporate Social Responsibility" (a specialised governmental website on CSR news accessible to everybody) and a new CSR Academy which provides "master-classes" and "regional CSR road-shows" for high-ranking corporate professionals, as well as "seminars" for SME owners/managers.[35] The website's section on "Policy and Legislation – International" now gives only a guarded statement about the desirability of globally agreed and well-targeted CSR minimum standards, and affirms the need for learning further from experiences in different countries and the perspectives of different stakeholders.

Boundary areas of legislation: Company laws and trade laws

As shown in table 3.1, there already exist quite a few inter-governmentally endorsed CSR-related codes, partly overlapping and partly complementing one another, but none is legally binding. It is not clear yet which avenue would be more promising than others for international policy intervention, mutual recognition, fine-grained coordination, consolidation of existing numerous initiatives or else development of an additional set of codes aimed to deliver specific international objectives that are unmet by existing initiatives. To sort out and consolidate elements of existing codes into a legally binding instrument is likely to prove a difficult task even at national level, and still more so in the multilateral context.

Leaving aside the question of political feasibility, at least three slippery problems must be overcome in order to command a clearer perspective on what an international regime on corporate accountability should look like. First, many "boundary" areas of legislation need to be cleared up, especially company laws and trade laws that directly or indirectly bear upon corporate responsibility and accountability. Second, it is important to take into account the considerable variation of priority issues, institutional cultures and legal systems that bear upon corporate responsibility. Third, a new multilateral mechanism must reflect priority concerns and needs of developing countries.

As for the first quandary, we need carefully to take account of the existing and emerging legislation about business transparency in order to make meaningful progress through the difficult boundary areas lying between government, business and civil society responsibilities. It is because voluntary approaches to CSR are readily embedded in such a legal context that social and environmental reporting and institutional investment are more or less readily framed by company laws relating to misrepresentation or false advertising.[36]

Also, interactions between the CSR agenda and other realms of international policy offer an important area for further study. For example, international norms of corporate governance, formally embraced by the OECD Principles of Corporate Governance (1999), are now upgraded by its latest (2004) revision. The revision makes strong references to the value of a broad spectrum of stakeholders and attempts to enhance shareholders' rights in such a way as to affect the responsibilities of institutional investors and rating agencies as well. The Kimberley Process Certification Scheme may be cited as an innovative way of addressing the boundary areas that link an inter-governmentally agreed framework of national control on trade in rough diamonds to industry self-regulation. Another issue area is the "foreign direct liability" claim. It increases possible litigation risks at the frontiers of corporate responsibility, because the claim is intended to hold parent companies responsible for the liabilities of producers and retailers operating elsewhere in the supply chain.

CSR carries a dimension of international trade law. Voluntary labelling and certification schemes as well as labour rights norms can have potential negative impacts on market access and WTO compatibility. This is not merely an area of legal uncertainty, but a source of trade tension between developed and developing countries, as well as among developing countries themselves. For example, the World Bank-hosted international conference on "Public Policy for Corporate Responsibility" (2003) featured an intense debate about the predicted impact of the termination (in 2004) of the Multi-Fibre Arrangement. In the face of intensified price competition from China, countries such as Cambodia, Thailand and El Salvador felt the need to adopt credible international CSR standards as a source of possible non-cost competitive advantage. Meanwhile, however, China has established its own Global Compact Learning Forum Center (as of April 2003) to help advance the domestic tenets of corporate citizenship. Also, the China Business Council for Sustainable Development, which brings together both national and foreign companies in China, has become the forty-eighth member of the WBCSD (as of January 2004).

Here, it might be tempting to argue in favour of a minimalist version of CSR legislation that would help level the playing field for all Southern corporations, even in remote locations in China, India or Africa. But that alone would not dissolve the North-South divide at all. Besides, a minimalist version designed to "pull" laggards and stragglers would not entice the large corporations at the leading edge of green competition, sometimes called "quiet business leaders".[37] Such business leaders would rather look for the "Stiglerian threshold" – the kind of regulatory proposal that promises an opportunity for earning quasi-monopoly rents on their new technologies and products.

When it comes to effective regulation, there is simply no substitute for stronger national action.[38] The implementation of the OECD Guidelines for MNEs can and should be facilitated to a considerable extent by individual governments' policies on NCPs before they are subjected to the first serious six-year review (expected in 2006). Similarly, further deepening of the UN Global Compact (GC) and the Global Reporting Initiative (GRI) is likely to require national-level policy initiatives that heed local legal and institutional idiosyncrasies in individual countries. In parallel, continued refinements of multilateral initiatives would help advance inter-country policy coordination from mere mutual recognition towards collective adjustment for levelling the playing field at an ever higher level. For example, France passed a "new economic regulations law" in 2001 – a completely overhauled domestic corporate law that mandates annual corporate reporting on the triple bottom-line performances by 2004. It has no provision for specific indicators, auditing requirements and sanctions for non-compliance, nor for French companies' reporting on their overseas operations and on their environmental performances.

Nevertheless, French institutional investors seem to trust that French companies will be creative enough to utilise the GRI and other international guidelines to make up such gaps in the new economic regulations law.[39]

Further enfranchisement of developing country stakeholders

Developing countries need to be brought to the centre of multilateral discussion on the matter of institutionalisation of CSR. We need to evaluate how existing CSR initiatives fall short of their priority concerns and assess what additional initiatives are likely to meet their needs. But, as discussed in an earlier section on different stakeholders' preferences, there are good reasons to anticipate that not many Southern governments are very enthusiastic about this. As a result, unprepared diplomats from developing countries might be easily ensnared by critical media that all too often denounce CSR as being underpinned by Western values and adorning the prerogative of MNCs exploiting the poor in developing countries. Besides, it would be difficult for them to build well-informed coalitions in multilateral diplomacy because the variation in legal and institutional systems is much greater between different developing countries than between the OECD countries.

For instance, Kingsway Fund Management, a Hong Kong-based socially responsible investment (SRI) firm, has recently evaluated corporate performances in eight East Asian countries (other than Japan) by using its own SRI screening methodology that distinguishes the measures of responsibility (corporate governance, community development and gender equality) from those of sustainability (energy management, pollution emissions and resource management). The result reveals sharp differences in cultural norms and government policies. Korea and Singapore, for example, rank first and second, respectively, in terms of the sustainability scale, while ranking last and seventh in terms of the responsibility scale. In contrast, Malaysia and Thailand rank fourth and sixth, respectively, in sustainability while first and second in responsibility. Such an insight, however, should not be abused to help ultra-nationalists defend the *status quo* by over-blowing cultural dimensions of comparative national features.

The author would argue that CSR issues are by and large universal in nature and not culturally based. Decisive governmental action would be needed to improve disclosure and enforcement standards in countries where many firms are still run by families. Since the Asian financial crisis, governments in the region have stepped up their efforts to improve the level of corporate governance. According to PricewaterhouseCoopers,

Malaysia today is even ahead of the United States in corporate governance as far as the Kuala Lumpur Stock Exchange listing requirements are concerned; the Thai National Board which monitors corporate governance is now chaired by the Prime Minister; and the Republic of Korea requires one-third of a corporate board to be independent directors even though the influence of political patronage and family controlled *Chaebols* has not much diminished yet.[40] In contrast, the African continent still suffers from endemic government corruption and incompetence as well as the lack of basic infrastructures.

The World Bank (jointly with the International Finance Corporation) has recently published the results of a survey on how CSR issues influenced MNCs' investment and sourcing decisions and how developing country governments could create a more attractive foreign investment environment from the CSR perspective.[41] It recommends that host country governments develop stronger CSR laws and enforcement systems at home, invite MNCs with advanced CSR systems into partnerships contributing to development objectives and engage local civil and religious institutions more effectively in building an enabling CSR environment. Parallel to this study, the World Bank has established an exploratory project, "CSR Practice", which provides policy advice and technical assistance in country- and industry-specific contexts and seeks to identify specific issues of priority concern to the developing country governments with which the Bank works.[42]

The UNDP launched the initiative "Growing Sustainable Business in Least Developed Countries" at a high-level roundtable during the WSSD. Its activities are guided by the GC principles (now including the tenth principle of anti-corruption), as well as by the goals of NEPAD (New Partnership for Africa's Development) in the case of Africa. The GC has created national networks in an increasing number of developing countries that serve as platforms for MNCs, domestic firms (including SMEs) and non-profit organisations to work with governments to promote CSR and develop partnership projects. The number of signatories to the GC now seems to exceed 1,800. As of February 2005, more than 40 local (national) GC networks exist that are devoted to the task of adapting universal values into local language and culture, encouraging "communications on progress" and promoting partnership projects to scale up good practices toward reaching the Millennium Development Goals.[43]

The GC Advisory Council recommended (in July 2003) establishing a task force that addresses issues such as non-performing participating companies and the abuse of the GC logo. Some people hope that, as the GC gains depth and momentum, it may promote convergence with CSR codes and initiatives. It should be borne in mind, however, that the Global Compact is meant to be essentially an open network system. John G. Ruggie warned that the critics of the GC on the anti-globalisation front all too often addressed what it was not: a regulatory arrangement.[44] The joint editors of *Learning to Talk* (2004) reiterate that the GC is primarily a "convening platform to bring together disparate actors across the community in ways that have not been attempted previously". They would thus wish to see the GC "remain aloof from the traditional hierarchic regulatory mechanisms in order to retain its ability to raise the level of conversation to the humanisation of globalisation".[45]

Conclusions

This chapter attempts to locate both business and civil society actors in the political realm as a binary change agency endeavouring to find space for creative change in the context of contradictory structures. The thematic focus is on one of the most contentious public policy issues of today: how to reintegrate business into society and where the ongoing corporate citizenship movement is leading. The subtle mix of confrontation and conflation strategies in the CSR debate extends beyond the stark juxtaposition of enfranchised versus disenfranchised actors. Instead, CSR can be understood broadly as a tacit form of reflexive institutional bargaining of dialectic significance.

The post-Rio decade witnessed a high-paced proliferation of CSR-related codes, including private co-regulatory initiatives involving direct business-CSO engagement as well as norms and guidelines updated through inter-governmental processes. Even the latter processes have come increasingly to make efforts to operationalise the principle of inclusion or multi-stakeholder engagement for collective decision-making.

In examining regulatory implications of stakeholder engagement, the effectiveness of CSOs' influence through their "watchdog" function, "naming and shaming" and litigation against corporate breach of prevalent norms underpins the evolutionary theories of law and institution which have gained currency during the past decade or two. Given the proliferation of voluntary multi-stakeholder codes and the complexity of the tasks related to monitoring, reporting, audit and certification, it proves difficult to reconcile or standardise those procedures among the existing different codes. As a result, "complaint-based systems" have come to be incorporated in many of the codes of international significance. However, the UN Global Compact remains unique, not only in that it is not intended to evolve any regulatory code books, but also in that it remains lenient about monitoring and penalising non-compliant signatories.

The CSR discourse continues to be divided into two extreme ends: one favouring a market-based nurturing approach, and the other calling for some new legally binding global regulatory instruments. In between the two, we find a broad middle region where the possibilities are explored for further "mainstreaming" of CSR in corporate governance and consolidation or standardisation of proliferating voluntary codes. CSO activists continue to push the international business community to break its resilient wall of voluntarism, while, unfortunately, their claim is typically enshrined on the perceived systemic malfunctioning of the world economic structure, failing to give a sensible prescription as to how to go about it. Different categories of stakeholders (such as SMEs, trade unions and consumers' organisations, as well as developing countries' governments and NGOs) have different perspectives on that sort of claim. And the balance between regulation, self-regulation and co-regulation varies among different countries and seems to be shifting in time.

After all, when it comes to effective regulation there is no substitute for stronger national action. Much progress may be made towards deeper institutionalisation of CSR through national public policies. Great care should be exercised to clear through many difficult boundary areas of legislation now present in existing and emerging company laws and trade laws. Differences in institutional cultures and government policies are generally greater among developing countries than among the OECD countries, but exaggerating such differences would only please the ultra-nationalists advocating the *status quo*.

There have been some interesting developments in post-WSSD years looking for some stable anchoring points between the market- and the rules-based approaches. Examples include the ISO initiative towards international CSR standards, the accelerated extension of Global Compact local networks to SMEs in developing countries, the French and the UK governments' domestic initiatives for further streamlining of CSR, and certain new programmes of multilateral institutions such as the World Bank, the UNDP and the OECD. They all stress the importance of multi-stakeholder engagement for democratic decision-making and further enfranchisement of developing country stakeholders in multilateral policy discourse.

Notes

1. The other eight categories identified in Section III of Agenda 21 are farmers, women, youth, indigenous people and their communities, local authorities, workers and their trade unions, the scientific and technological community and "NGOs" (other than business-supported non-profit organisations).
2. Gabel, M. and Bruner, H. (2003) *Globalinc*, New York: The New Press.

3. This definition is compatible with the one given in United Nations (2002) *Building Partnerships: Cooperation between the United Nations System and the Private Sector*, New York: United Nations, Appendix I.
4. Usui, Mikoto (2003) "Sustainable Development Diplomacy in the Private Business Sector: An Integrative Perspective on Game Change Strategies at Multiple Levels", *International Negotiation* 8(2): 267–310; Usui, Mikoto (2004) "The Private Business Sector in Global Environmental Diplomacy" in N. Kanie and P. M. Haas, eds, *Emerging Forces in Global Environmental Governance*, New York and Tokyo: United Nations University Press.
5. Quoted from UN General Assembly, *Dialogue Paper by Non-governmental Organizations* (A/CONF.199/PC/18/Add.4) and *Dialogue Paper by Business and Industry* (A/CONF.199/PC/18/Add.7), both being Addenda to Note by the Secretary- General for PrepCom IV for the WSSD, 27 May–7 June 2002.
6. On the one hand, the official UN registry of Type II partnerships/initiatives for sustainable development is administered by the CSD secretariat (available at www.un.org/esa/sustdev/partnerships). Since 2004 the "Partnerships Fair" has been organised annually as a side event for the CSD sessions. On the other hand, the showcase of business-led partnerships/initiatives adopting business-oriented approaches was administered and posted separately until late 2002 by Business Action for Sustainable Development (BASD) (a coalition of the International Chamber of Commerce (ICC) and the World Business Council for Sustainable Development (WBCSD) formed to orchestrate the business community's participation in the WSSD). The BASD showcase has recently been followed up and renovated by a new portal (www.partnershipscentral.org) administered by a newly created business-supported Center for Advancement of Sustainable Development Partnerships (CASDP: www.casdp.org). It seems, however, that the work of the CASDP has made little progress during recent years.
7. In January 2005 the United Nations unveiled a package of fairly concrete measures to combat poverty: UNDP, *Investing in Development: A Practical Plan to Achieve the Millennium Development Goals* (prepared by a Jeffrey Sachs-led blue-ribbon team of 265 development experts). Apparently that resonated well in Davos on 23–30 January. Some 700 participants, assembled in the interactive session called "Global Town Hall", engaged in an electronically assisted fast-cycle delphi-type dialogue process, and selected six out of over a dozen "tough issues" to be placed at the top of the global agenda for the year. "Poverty" and "equitable globalisation" ranked first and second (see www.weforum.org). Wider representation for democratic decision-making was stressed in conjunction with equitable globalisation, and greater leadership, transparency and accountability for multilateral institutions for global governance.
8. This definition of CSR, as distinguished from corporate governance and business ethics, owes to Hopkins, Michael (2003) *The Planetary Bargain: Corporate Social Responsibility Matters*, London and Sterling, VA: Earthscan Publications, especially chapters 1 and 3.
9. For example, the proliferation of would-be sustainability-oriented timber certification schemes can be explained by the fact that forest-exploiting MNCs usually work under short-term permits with little incentive for longer-term planning and have to compete fiercely to acquire new, as well as renewed, permits. Many of the certification schemes of local significance tend to serve the purpose of disenfranchising potential new entrants by differentiating thresholds for "good practices".
10. The workshop on principles for certification of ecotourism and sustainable tourism, held in New York in November 2000, adopted a recommendation by consensus to develop a global "Sustainable Tourism Stewardship Council". (see, for example, Bass, Steve, Font, Xavier and Danielson, Luke (2001) "Standards and Certification: A Leap Forward or a

Step Back for Sustainable Development?", in IIED, *The Future Is Now*, Vol. 2, pp. 21–32, available from www.iied.org/pubs/pdf/full/9110IIED.pdf.
11. These are extracted from various documents: particularly Utting, Peter (2002) "Regulating Business via Multistakeholder Initiatives: A Preliminary Assessment", in UN-NGLS Development Dossier, *Voluntary Approaches to Corporate Responsibility* (Section II), pp. 61–130 (available from www.un-ngls.org); Leipziger, Deborah (2003) *Corporate Responsibility Code Book*, Sheffield: Greenleaf Publishing; Calder, F. and Culverwell, M. (2004) *Following-Up the World Summit on Sustainable Development Commitments on Corporate Social Responsibility: Interim Report*, London: Royal Institute of International Affairs, especially annex 1.
12. SustainAbility's project on the twenty-first century NGO identifies several CSO pressure-building waves. The first wave peaked during 1969–1973 and was followed by a down-wave through the late 1980s. The second wave peaked in 1988–1991 and also was followed by another down-wave. The third wave began to build from 1999 with the "battle of Seattle", but the twenty-first century NGOs will have to muster new agendas and approaches with the advent of the third down-wave and in preparation for the fourth wave by focusing on the triple bottom-line accountability not just of business and government but of NGOs themselves. See SustainAbility (2003) *The 21st Century NGO: The Market for Change*, London: SustainAbility, available at www.sustainability.com/publications/.
13. Based on Berman, J. E. and Webb, T. (2003) *Race to the Top: Attracting and Enabling Global Sustainable Business – Business Survey Report*, Washington, DC: World Bank and IFC.
14. Civil society groups included professional and grassroots NGOs, the trade union movement, the scientific and academic community, indigenous people's think-tanks, parliamentarians, local autonomies, gender advocates and philanthropic organisations.
15. United Nations (2004) *We the Peoples: Civil Society, the United Nations and Global Governance*, A/58/817.
16. Zadek, S., ed. (2001) *Endearing Myth, Enduring Truths: Partnerships between Business, Civil Society Organizations and Government*, Washington, DC: Business Partnership for Development, reprinted as a chapter in S. Zadek and P. Raynard, eds (2004) *Tomorrow's History*, Sheffield: Greenleaf Publishing.
17. These points are stressed by Mackenzie, C. (2004) "Moral Sanctions: Ethical Norms as a Solution to Corporate Governance Problem", *Journal of Corporate Citizenship*, 15(Autumn): 49–61. The relevant literature includes Trivers, R. (1985) *Social Evolution*, Menlo Park, CA: Benjamin/Cummings; Frank, R. (1988) *Passions Within Reason*, New York: W. W. Norton; Frank, R. (2004) *What Price The Moral High Ground?*, Princeton, NJ: Princeton University Press.
18. OHCHR (2005) *Report of the Office of the High Commissioner for Human Rights on the Responsibilities of Transnational Corporations and Related Business Enterprises* (E/CN.4/2005/91).
19. Human Rights Resolution 2005/69 (adopted at the Commission's fifty-ninth meeting on 20 April 2005). The Secretary-General has appointed Professor John Ruggie of Harvard University as his Special Representative, and he is expected to report back to the Commission at its sixty-second meeting. Even prior to this formal development, some existing UN Special Rapporteurs (such as those dealing with Sudan and the Right to Food) have been prompted to look into the human rights-related aspects of MNCs' activities.
20. OECD/Directorate for Financial and Enterprise Affairs (2004) *OECD Guidelines for Multilateral Enterprises: 2004 Annual Report of the National Contact Points*, 14–15 June, Report by the Chair, available at www.oecd.org/documents.
21. Bendell, Jem (2004) "Flags of Inconvenience? The Global Compact and the Future of

the United Nations", Nottingham University Business School/International Centre for Corporate Social Responsibility Research Paper Series ISSN 1479-5124, available at www.globalpolicy.org/reform/indexbiz.htm. This article discusses the pitfalls of the Global Compact at length and proposes a "new agenda for the Global Compact".
22. UN General Assembly (2002) *Dialogue Paper by Business and Industry*, – Addendum 7 to Note by the Secretary-General for "multi-stakeholder dialogue" segment of the fourth session of the CSD acting as the preparatory committee for the WSSD, PrepCom IV, 27 May–7 June (A/CONF.199/PC/18/Add.7), Para. 2.
23. Sabapathy, J. and Zadek, S. (2004) "Responsibility Competitiveness", in *Accountability Forum* 1, Sheffield: Greenleaf Publishing and AccountAbility.
24. The "Stiglerian threshold" and its implication for issue division in regime design are discussed at some length in Usui (2003) note 4 above, especially pp. 296–297 and Usui (2004) note 4 above, especially pp. 244–247.
25. For example, the "Whistling in the Dark" project of the University of Nijmegen, School of Management attempts to go beyond well-established names in the European CSR discourse to identify such "quiet business leaders", who are less well known but have established innovative ways of reconciling dynamic interests of business and society (see www.corporateresponsibility.nl/).
26. The IICFTU was set up in 1949 and now has 233 affiliated labour organisations in 152 countries, with a total membership of some 150 million.
27. Examples of the international trade secretariats having industry-specific framework agreements with MNCs include the IFBWW (International Federation of Building and Wood Workers), the ITGLF (International Textile, Garments and Leather Workers Federation) and the IUF (International Union of Food, Agricultural, Hotel, Restaurant, Catering, Tobacco and Allied Workers Associations).
28. CI is a global professional NGO that directly represents now more than 270 consumer unions in 120 countries (nearly three-quarters of which are developing countries).
29. See www.consumersinternational.org/document_store/Doc169.html.
30. Bigg, Tom (2003) "The WSSD: Was It Worthwhile?" *IIED Working Paper*, available at www.iied.org.
31. The UNRISD programme on Technology, Business and Society/Business Responsibility for Sustainable Development (see www.unrisd.org); Zammitt, Ann (2003) *Development at Risk: Rethinking UN-Business Partnerships*, Geneva: South Centre and UNRISD.
32. The Nordic Partnerships (2003) *Executive Brief 2003: Balancing Corporate and Society Goals*, December, available at www.nordicpartnerships.org.
33. Report to ISO COPOLCO on *Desirability and Feasibility of ISO CSR Standards*, submitted to the ISO COPOLCO meeting in Trinidad and Tobago in June 2002 (see www.iso.org/iso/en/prods-services/otherpubs/).
34. *Corporate Social Responsibility – A Draft International Framework*, March 2004, available from www.dti.gov.uk/sustainability/.
35. www.csr.gov.uk/ and www.csracademy.org.uk/.
36. Ward, Halina (2003) *Legal Issues in Corporate Citizenship*, London: IIED.
37. See note 25 above.
38. Ruggie, J. G. (2002) "The Theory and Practice of Learning Networks: Corporate Social Responsibility and the Global Compact", *Journal of Corporate Citizenship* 5: 32.
39. *Ethical Corporation Newsdesk*, 28 March 2002, available at see www.ethicalcorp.com/.
40. Roche, Julian (2002) "Is Asia Arid Territory for Good Corporate Governance", *Ethical Corporation, Special Features: Analysis*, available at see www.ethicalcorp.com.
41. Berman and Webb, see note 13 above.
42. www.worldbank.org/privatesector/csr/prac_work_prog.htm. The CSR Practice project focused on footwear in Viet Nam, oil in Angola, mining in the Philippines and light manufacturing and tourism in El Salvador.

43. According to the latest *Global Compact Network News* (Issue 4, February 2005, available at www. unglobalcompact. org), the Swiss government has provided funding to support country networks in low-income countries for their start-up investments; the Bulgarian network is paying heed to enhancement of microfinance facilities for local communities, and the first GC South Asian Regional Conclave (March 2005) includes a session on "eradicating poverty through profits" by addressing the bottom of the pyramid of the world market.
44. Ruggie, note 38 above.
45. McIntosh, M., Waddock, S. and Kell, G., eds. (2004) *Learning to Talk: Corporate Citizenship and the Development of the UN Global Compact*, Sheffield: Greenleaf Publishing, p. 26. This edition assembles both critical and positive views about the Global Compact.

4
Developing country scientists and decision-making: An institutional perspective of issues and barriers

W. Bradnee Chambers

Introduction

The reservoir of human knowledge and technological advancement has developed significantly in the last 100 years. Yet despite these advancements, the last century has just marked the most rapid decline in the earth's environmental quality in human history, and we face major problems such as global climate change, persistent organic pollutants, ozone depletion and major losses of biodiversity. Perhaps the true "tragedy of the commons" is this seeming paradox of how humankind has used knowledge to advance society, yet ignored other knowledge so vital to solving problems that concern the very existence of the planet.[1]

Scientific knowledge and scientists now play a critical role in sustainable development governance and multilateralism more broadly. However, institutional theories of international governance have given only limited consideration to the role of scientists and knowledge in policy-making. Much more emphasis has been placed on understanding conflict, the role of power and, more recently, international organisations. But because of the complexity and uncertainty involved in environmental governance, scientific knowledge is an important component of interstate relations and merits closer examination. Scientists have become important actors in the creation of international environmental policy – creating the knowledge that provides the basis for policy action, in particular through scientific assessments such as the Millennium Ecosystem Assessment (MA) and the Global Environment Outlook (GEO). But which scientists are creating this knowledge? And does the unequal representation between developed and developing countries in this area have an impact on the knowledge presented, and therefore the decisions taken?

This chapter will examine the institutional pathways available to scientists from developing counties, as well as their capacity to make use of them. It starts with a discussion of scientific knowledge and its role in international decision-making, followed by an examination of institutional pathways linking scientific knowledge and policy-making, in particular social networks and scientific assessments. The issue of consensual knowledge and its legitimacy is then discussed, followed by an overview of barriers to participation of developing country scientists in research and policy-making. The chapter concludes by recommending changes to the present "scientific assessment" model to incorporate more fully the participation and input of scientists from developing nations.

Institutional pathways for scientists in policy-making

What is "scientific knowledge" and what is its role in international decision-making?

There are considerable challenges in incorporating new knowledge into decision-making. Knowledge from past experiences may show a strong causal effect on the present problem, but new knowledge does not enjoy this advantage. Thus, in order to understand scientific knowledge in the context of environmental decision-making, another dimension to the learning process must be added. Ernst Haas defines learning by policy-makers as the ability and willingness to incorporate consensual knowledge into the definition of interests that motivate international behaviour.[2]

Haas' definition identifies consensual knowledge as a prerequisite to learning, implying that there may be reluctance on the part of policy-makers to employ new knowledge that is not consensual. This can be problematic for new scientific knowledge, as consensus and the human experience tend to reinforce and support an existing baseline of knowledge, which may become entrenched by norms, laws or even religion. New knowledge challenges this entrenchment, but before old knowledge gives way to the new it must go through a consensus-building process. Consensual knowledge can simply be understood as what is widely accepted by society as being true. More specifically, Ernst Haas defines consensual knowledge as "a body of beliefs about cause-effect and means-ends relationships among variables (activities, aspirations, values, demands) that is widely accepted by relevant actors, irrespective of the absolute or final truth of these beliefs".[3] However, as Robert Rothstein has observed, the delineation of who comprises relevant actors greatly affects the ability to build consensus. In a group of like-minded technical or scientific experts, consensus may be easier to reach than between national ministries or across cultural and national boundaries. In the G-77, for instance, Rothstein states that consensus may be merely a sum of all demands impervious to knowledge and learning.[4]

The consensus process may also involve the politicisation of knowledge in order to justify existing ideologies or to protect political and economic self-interest. For instance, in the lead-up to the UN Framework Convention on Climate Change (FCCC) Third Session of the Conference of the Parties, national governments such as Australia, one of the world's leading coal producers, and members of the US Senate, who believed that any emission reduction would cost American jobs, played on the uncertainties of the climate change science as a strategy to reduce the possible emission commitments. Similarly, interest groups such as the Climate Change Coalition – a business, industry and labour lobby – spent over $13 million in the United States on a national advertising campaign that stressed the lack of evidence and uncertainty of the climate change phenomenon.

Building consensual knowledge on environmental issues may be particularly daunting given the long time spans of ecosystem change, combined with heavy uncertainty. Normally, if new knowledge is applied to solve a problem and provides a successful solution, it then becomes more accepted as consensual. If, however, the result from the application of the knowledge proves to be unsatisfactory, the problem is re-analysed by assessing the use of previous knowledge, and a new solution or new knowledge is applied. This trial-and-error process is a natural way of managing uncertainty. However, many environmental problems deal with time spans that are so long that this type of process is rendered less effective. For instance, climate change involves emissions that if curbed or abated now would not show results until 50 years later. Under these circumstances building consensus on environmental issues involves much more speculation and thus may be more vulnerable to critics.

In the modern context of international environmental governance, ensuring that scientific knowledge is used in policy-making depends largely on saliency, the relevancy of the information; credibility, that the information deserves to be believed; and legitimacy, that the information was created based on a fair process that involved the participation of actors perceived to be unbiased by the user of the information.[5]

To summarise the above discussion, the employment of scientific knowledge in policy-making requires certain prerequisite factors such as incentive and motivation for policy-makers to learn or acquire new knowledge. It also demonstrates the importance of consensus-building, which can lead to a better environment for scientific knowledge to become more acceptable to policy-makers. Institutions in this regard play a crucial role in providing mechanisms and incentives that can operationalise knowledge and mobilise scientists. The following section of the chapter turns to how social institutions such as social networks, epistemic communities and scientific assessment work in this capacity.

Institutional pathways bridging scientific knowledge and international policy-making

While cognitive, cultural and socio-communicative variables at the actor level are also considerations in the use of knowledge to develop policy, only institutional factors are considered here. Robert Keohane defines institutions as "persistent and connected sets of rules, formal and informal, that prescribe behavioural roles, constrain activity and shape expectations".[6] Institutions are important for decision-making because they can internalise ideas, which can then be implemented more effectively by the operational support of the institution. For instance, the concept of sustainable development that emerged from the 1987 Brundtland Report has now become firmly implanted in the *modus operandi* of most UN organisations. Development assistance by the UN Development Programme looks to programmes hinged on sustainable development practices. Similarly, the World Bank has made loans conditional upon environmental impact assessment, and the environmental treaties negotiated at Rio (the FCCC and the UN Convention to Combat Desertification and Convention on Biological Diversity) contain clauses that have expanded the idea of environmental protection to the more encompassing idea of sustainable development.

Judith Goldstein takes this argument one step further and believes that institutions do more than support knowledge but actually firmly embed knowledge or ideas by legal mechanisms in inter-governmental organisations.[7] This can be seen in the WTO for instance, whose consistent rulings such as in the *Turtle Shrimp Case* or the *Thai Cigarettes Case* continue to dictate that technical barriers to trade put in place to restrict foreign products according to their production processes are protectionist and violate WTO member disciplines. Consequently, policy-makers of states that are members of these institutions are persuaded and influenced by the institutional policy directions or knowledge, and in some cases even constrained by the legal mechanism of the institution itself.

The level of institutional influence on policy varies from institution to institution. In the case of informal networks, the institutional embeddedness of knowledge is less pronounced and knowledge is bound only by very loose norms, shared beliefs and principles. In the case of more formal arrangements with strong ties the production of scientific information is directly influenced by the "norms and procedures setting research priorities, targeting resources, conducting experiments, assuring quality control and disseminating results.[8] The following sections describe the basic institutions normally associated with linking scientific knowledge and international policy-making.

Social networks

Social networks are a "set of social relations or social ties among a set of actors (and the actors themselves thus linked)".[9] Social networks theory focuses on the connections among individuals, dependencies, advice and scientific élites.[10] The relationships are defined as either strong, organised formal connections or weak informal ties; or as Malone and Edgerton have put it, "friendships versus acquaintances".[11]

One type of social network that has been commonly associated with environmental policy formulation is Peter Haas' "epistemic communities". Peter Haas defines these communities as "networks of professionals with recognised expertise and competence in a particular domain or issue-area".[12] He acknowledges "that systemic conditions and domestic pressures impose constraints on state behaviour", but argues that the ways that states define their interests and choose appropriate policy options is influenced by the "manner in which the problems are understood by policy makers or are represented by those to whom they turn for advice under conditions of uncertainty".[13] He believes that within the theoretical context of regimes the significance of the effects they may have on the transformative process has been neglected. In terms of his case study on the Mediterranean Action Plan, Haas showed that in the face of technical uncertainty and because of the lack of technical expertise at the national decision-making level, a group of scientific experts (i.e. ecologists, biologists) were consulted. As these new actors became involved, their advice gradually began to carry greater weight. They first became accepted authorities on the matter, which both empowered them and gradually legitimised their advice. Once firmly established as experts, national governments began to reflect this advice in their policy decisions. Haas' study identified epistemic communities as a new actor in regime analysis. More important, however, is the way he illustrates how knowledge and technical expertise can affect inter-state policy formulation and coordination.

Peter Haas argues that the epistemic community not only offers expert advice, but also proactively advocates specific policies for governments to adopt. At the international level, the influence of the epistemic community is a source of concern for those fundamentally worried about maintaining the status of sovereignty. As Lawrence Susskind has argued, "it would mean that an ad hoc group of mostly appointed bureaucrats, no different than any other coalition of non-elected actors, had achieved disproportionate influence over crucial global decisions".[14]

Epistemic communities, although an important contribution to institutional literature, are only one model for the role scientific and expert knowledge is playing in recent environmental regimes. For example, Peter Haas' work deals very little with the characteristics of these networks or how they come into existence. Indeed, some of the networks that Haas describes are actually much stronger collaborative arrangements between governments, and have become synonymous with managing environmental problems through more formally constituted institutional arrangements, such as scientific assessments.

Scientific assessments

Scientific assessments are formally organised groups which foster strong ties among individual scientists so that they can work collaboratively to synthesise existing scientific knowledge into information that can be readily used for policy applications. According to Siebenhuner, "scientific assessments could be understood as social processes which help to translate expert knowledge into policy-related forms of knowledge that exert some form of influence on actual decision-making processes".[15] The best known assessment is the Intergovernmental Panel on Climate Change (IPCC), but major assessments have been carried out on a wide variety of environmental topics and problems in the last 40 years.

Scientific assessments have become important not only because they can deal more economically with costly research at the international level through, for example, economies of scale or pooling resources, but also because they can be considered a type of pre-negotiation stage. During scientific assessments, states can assess the levels of dissent and build scientific consensus in a less politicised forum.[16] This approach is consistent with functionalist theorists like David Mitrany, who argued that transnational linkages in technical areas might lead to international integration and cooperation. Mitrany observed that governmental tasks had become significantly technical and non-political, requiring highly specialised personnel. The culmination of the same effects in other countries contributed to the emergence of issues at the international level that were more technical, and thus better addressed by technicians rather than politicians. As a result, Mitrany postulated "that the growth in importance of technical issues in the twentieth century is said to have made necessary the creation of frameworks for international cooperation".[17]

Participation, legitimacy and developing nations: How consensual is "consensual knowledge"?

Thus, to be applied to environmental policy-making, scientific knowledge must be agreed upon, or to some extent consensual. One of the often-cited barriers in terms of acceptance of knowledge in developing nations is the degree of participation that developing countries have had in generating that knowledge. If the participation of developing nation scientists is low, it is argued that the knowledge may not be truly consensual, and therefore can be viewed as less legitimate. This raises the following questions: is the knowledge currently used in environmental decision-making truly consensual? Or is the lack of developing country participation having an effect on the outcome and results of the assessments itself? If so, then what are these effects?

The standard view on these questions is that there is a direct correlation between participation of scientists and the extent to which knowledge is accepted by policy-makers.[18] In the 1990s such concerns were highly debated when designing and operating the IPCC. In 1990 the IPCC set up a special committee to examine how to strengthen the participation of developing nations in its activities. More recent assessments such as the Millennium Ecosystem Assessment (MA) have learned from the IPCC experience and have gone to great lengths to include developing country scientists. Moreover, the MA has followed some of the conclusions from the IPCC Special Committee and revised its rules of procedure, requiring that each working group contain one member from a developing country and one from a developed country. Special travel funds and quotas are also set up in many assessments to increase developing country participation.

On the surface the correlation between legitimacy and participation of scientists seems intuitive, but when examined closely certain questions emerge. Successful assessments have learned that institutional embeddedness – "the degree to which scientific assessment processes are circumscribed by the organisation using the assessment to inform or validate its policy decisions" – is a crucial point for the saliency and usefulness of the assessment.[19] A Harvard-based research study on the influence of scientific assessments on policy-making suggests that "higher levels of autonomy and less involvement [of policy-makers] may impede the transmission of scientific knowledge to policy makers".[20]

Thus, participation can be defined in many ways, and there are no guarantees that simply involving developing country scientists will necessarily increase the legitimacy and saliency of assessments. In fact, there are arguments that scientific knowledge is not as widely depended upon in developing nations for policy formulation as it is in developed countries.[21] This would seem to suggest that although participation is important for striking a balance of perspectives and prioritising the right issues (as will be discussed further below), it may be less critical for legitimacy and influence in developing nations so long as measures are in place for peer review and the involvement of policy-makers within the assessment process itself. For example, a recent case study conducted by Frank Biermann on India's participation in scientific assessments seems to suggest that the participation of its scientists in the ozone, climate change and biodiversity assessments did not ensure the acceptance and influence of the results by decision-makers in their policy formulation.[22] Participation, however, also has indirect benefits that can lead to furthering environmental policy formulation. Generally involving more developing countries in assessments has an overall effect of empowering scientists and increasing the scope of the issues addressed. Scientific assessments often have publicity and outreach capabilities behind them designed to reach multiple parts of society, either by directly engaging policy-makers, civil society or business in the assessments[23] or by using press officers to generate media attention with the public at large. This widespread dissemination can raise interest in the results of assessments and can promote stakeholders to seek out scientists for further explanations, advice or applications for their own needs.[24] Ultimately, this can provide an opportunity for scientists to increase their visibility and may impact positively on the chances of finding funding for furthering their research. Indirectly, greater awareness of the outputs of assessments could encourage policy-makers in developing countries to use scientific advice more readily and engage with scientists more actively, which currently tends not to be the case. According to Farell, Van Deveer and Jager, assessments bring more actors into the issue's domain, thereby increasing awareness, and through the exposure more people engaged in scientific research or activity promote the themes of the assessment.[25] Therefore from the standpoint of participation there is a positive impact on promoting awareness while forming a better information foundation for policy formulation. Also, according to Mitchell et al., by engaging scientists in developing countries, for example, assessments can "demonstrate implications of global assessments to national and sub-national actors".[26]

An additional question about the parity of Northern and Southern participation is whether the under-representation of developing country scientists in assessments or scientific social networks has an impact on the research agenda of the assessment or on the very nature of the assessment itself. Are there institutional barriers to setting up more Southern-driven assessments, generating scientific cooperation or creating epistemic communities? Are the current assessments that are undertaken the ones developing countries actually want or need? In 1991 Agarwal and

Narain put this question in simple terms: "if issues like climate change have to put [sic] on the agenda, then it is equally important to put environmental problems like desertification, land and water degradation [...] on the global agenda".[27]

A cursory analysis of the various assessments that have been conducted over the last couple of decades does not seem to suggest that the areas that have been addressed have been overly focused on green issues. For example, there have been three Global Environment Outlook (GEO) assessments that have taken a national, subregional, regional and global approach and cover a range of issues such as the atmosphere, biodiversity, coastal and marine areas, disasters, forests, fresh water, land, socio-economic and urban issues and two assessments on water (Global Environmental Monitoring System/Water Programme 1978 and Global International Waters Assessment, 1999–2003).[28] And while there have been major assessments on biodiversity (Global Biodiversity Assessment, 1995), ozone (Ozone Assessment, 1988–present) and climate change (IPCC, 1988–present) that have been criticised for not addressing developing country interests, these assessments have in recent years had a much stronger focus on developing country priorities. The MA, one of the most recent assessments at the global scale, is the first integrated assessment that has taken a cross-cutting approach (land, water, biodiversity, climate etc.) and has framed these issues with human well-being, including poverty reduction. The Third Assessment of the IPCC has had major sections on developing country impacts and there have been special reports on land use, regional impacts and technology transfer.

The thematic focus of assessments such as the IPCC and the importance of developing countries issues in the MA, however, have not occurred without the continued insistence and prodding of developing countries. As such, the progress that has been made must continue to be guarded against prevailing Northern agendas, as has been the case in the past. Since assessments tend to be both demanded and paid for by Northern interests, it is only natural that their influence will be, to a certain degree, focused on questions of importance to the North. Therefore it is only through the continued involvement of developing country scientists and policy-makers in the assessments that we can be assured that their interests and priorities are accepted.

Barriers to participation for scientists from developing countries

Agenda 21 and the Johannesburg Plan of Implementation (JPOI) have recognised the importance of science and technology for sustainable de-

velopment. The JPOI in particular points out the need to promote and improve science-based decision-making for the protection of the environment.[29] It also singles out the need to "assist developing countries, through international cooperation, in enhancing their capacity in their efforts to address issues pertaining to environmental protection, including in their formulation and implementation of policies for environmental management", specifically in particular areas:
- environmental monitoring, assessment models, accurate databases and integrated information systems;
- satellite technologies for quality data collection;
- science education and research and development activities necessary for effective science and technology policy-making;
- mechanisms for providing better communication between policy-makers and the scientific community related to the implementation of Agenda 21;
- networks for science and education for sustainable development, at all levels, with the aim of sharing knowledge, experience and best practices and building scientific capacities, particularly in developing countries;
- information and communication technologies including better access to information and communications;
- publicly funded research and development entities to engage in strategic alliances for the purpose of enhancing research and development to achieve cleaner production and product technologies, through, *inter alia*, the mobilisation from all sources of adequate financial and technical resources, including new and additional resources, and encouraging the transfer and diffusion of those technologies, in particular to developing countries.

But addressing the gaps that exist in developing countries is not an easy task. Historically, investment in science and technology and strengthening science capacity has generally been much lower in developing countries,[30] particularly in sub-Saharan Africa and small island states.[31] Scientific assessments have attempted to address some of these problems and have supported capacity-building programmes within the assessments themselves. The MA, for example, has launched a fellowship programme "to enhance the capacity of individual biophysical and social scientists to carry out ecosystem assessments". Targeting young scientists at early stages of their careers, the fellowships allow the scholars to attend author meetings and become lead authors. The IPCC has provided internal funds for these purposes, but analysis has suggested that these types of add-ons to existing research programmes are limited as they only provide short-term support and do not guarantee that knowledge or technology is diffused. This seems to suggest that although these types of programmes are important, a longer-term targeted commitment to assisting developing countries to conduct assessments is needed.

Table 4.1 Researchers in developing countries

Region	Region researchers per million population
Africa	70[a]
Middle East	130
India	130
Asia (remainder)	340
Latin America	550
Europe	1,990
North America	2,640
Japan	4,380

Source: UNDP (2003) *Human Development Report 2003: Millennium Development Goals: A Compact among Nations to End Human Poverty*, New York: Oxford University Press.
a. South Africa has 992 researchers per million persons

Women's participation in higher education generally, and science more specifically, is also a problem in developing countries. Despite the fact that women have made significant gains in higher education enrolment in most regions of the world (in some regions women's enrolment now equals or surpasses that of men), the poorest countries of the world continue to show little improvement, having the lowest enrolment of women in universities. In addition, there are significantly lower numbers of women than men pursuing science careers in developing countries.

Various reasons exist for the low entry level of women into scientific study and careers in developing countries, including cultural attitudes and gender stereotyping, the relatively lower number of girls who receive basic education, difficulties in balancing scientific careers with households and family responsibilities and the tendency of scientific communities in developing countries to be resilient to change. The women who do become scientists face further obstacles, and "are notably absent from leadership roles and positions of responsibility in institutions concerned with science policy and administration".[32] Recent articles concerning the role of women in negotiations and policy-making on climate change have been critical of the levels of participation of women.[33] Although women are considered among the most vulnerable in developing countries, and it is widely believed that climate change will have the most serious effects on the most vulnerable sectors of society, there is relatively little gender-specific research done on climate change.

Few references to gender are made at FCCC Conferences or Meetings of the Parties and there are no references to gender in the text of the Kyoto Protocol or the FCCC. Recently some attention has been paid to gender at the Seventh Session of the Conference of the Parties (COP), such as the issue of women's participation in FCCC bodies, and the Secretariat was requested "to maintain information on the gender composition of each body with elective posts established under the Convention and the Kyoto Protocol, and to bring this information to the attention of the Parties" whenever vacancies occur.[34] However, information is not readily available on the gender composition of assessments such as the IPCC and MA, and until this becomes available speculation is sure to be made that lack of attention to gender issues in assessments may be directly linked to the lack of participation of women and the opportunity to raise gender-specific concerns.

Traditional knowledge and assessments

"Traditional knowledge is seen as wise, non-exploitative and sustainable."[35] Most local communities possess specialised knowledge that is highly useful for managing natural resources in ways that have led to the long-term maintenance and integrity of their environment. Bridging this knowledge with modern scientific assessments could improve the practical application of new technologies and science at the local level. The MA is the first global assessment to use traditional knowledge, and in this regard is breaking new ground. Most assessments until this point had policies that did not permit so-called "grey literature" or non-peer-reviewed findings to be used. The IPCC eventually changed its practices, recently easing the restrictions on grey material in 1999, since it needed to take better consideration of traditional knowledge in mitigation and adaptation activities.

Traditional knowledge is an important component of the MA, as the results of the global assessment are checked against nested regional and local assessments. So, while ecosystem change and biodiversity loss and their solutions are of global concern, the subglobal dimensions are important because they act as local tests of global results. This issue of scale is also important because it takes into account the difference in space and time between the global and the local. As the director of the MA, Walter Reid, has stated, "in light of this multi-scale nature of both the issues involved and the decisions being made, early in the exploration of the idea for the MA it became clear that a strictly 'global' assessment would be insufficient".[36] Not only does traditional knowledge help address the scientific issues of scale, it has an important political function: legitimacy. The MA is meant to appeal to multiple stakeholders, including local and indigenous groups. As Reid notes, given "the level of suspicion and distrust of 'global' processes by local communities [it] is unlikely that a global assessment of ecosystems would be seen as legitimate by a local community of indigenous people in the Andes or a village in South Africa if the process excluded their own local knowledge concerning their ecosystems".[37]

The challenge for the MA and future assessments looking to integrate traditional knowledge will be twofold. First, there are methodological and epistemological hurdles that have to be overcome: how can a global assessment use traditional knowledge and incorporate it with technologically derived knowledge?[38] The second challenge will be to address adequately issues of participation and legitimacy. Indigenous groups have found solidarity internationally from a common experience of oppression and exploitation. This experience has created an air of suspicion and caution when dealing with ownership and development-related issues. Their knowledge in particular has been a topic of intense focus in recent years over cases of exploitation and unlawful commercialisation with no benefits returning to the knowledge holders. Thus sharing their knowledge with scientific assessments will understandably raise suspicions and questions of the political nature of the assessment and the intended use of the knowledge. The challenge for the MA is to remain apolitical and to ensure that the knowledge is used in a way that respects the rights and traditions of the local people. This of course will be difficult as scientific assessments are meant to influence multiple stakeholders, including the very stakeholders that have power over indigenous groups and which have been responsible for their exploitation.

Conclusion

Scientific knowledge is a key element in successful governance of environmental and sustainable development issues and problems. Knowledge is a complex concept that is derived from many sources and influences, but in policy-making consensual knowledge is of central importance and can be defined as what is widely accepted by society as being true. In the context of international environmental governance, studies have shown that ensuring the use of scientific knowledge in policy-making will depend largely on the saliency, credibility and legitimacy of knowledge.

The significance of scientific knowledge in international decision-making places scientists as key actors in environmental and sustainable development governance. The role of scientists, however, is often determined by the institutional pathways that organise their participation in the international decision-making process. Deciding who participates and how they participate will have an effect on the level of acceptance and influence the knowledge can have on decision-making. But participation is not straightforward. Participation of scientists from developing nations in scientific assessments is a necessary but not sufficient requirement to ensure the influence and acceptance of the scientific information produced.

In addition, and more importantly, involving developing countries in scientific assessments will lead to a more balanced approach in the analysis of issues in the assessments and decisions concerning agendas within the assessments. Though a cursory analysis does not demonstrate that global assessments thus far have been overly directed at environmental priorities of developed countries, there should be more emphasis on assessments that are connected to Southern problems and linked with poverty reduction. Setting the agenda in this direction, however, will be difficult because assessments, as large financial undertakings, are usually financed by the North which results in a reflection of their interests as priority issues.

Participation can also create indirect benefits that can empower scientists and lead to furthering environmental policy formulation. The dissemination of the results of scientific assessments often plays a role in raising the profile of assessments and interest in the issues addressed, and can prompt decision-makers to seek the advice of scientists. Concurrent effects may include increasing scientists' visibility and reputation, broadening the range of actors in the issue's domain and increasing the attention of national and subnational actors to global priorities.

Participation of developing country scientists in assessments and other institutional pathways that link them with the policy-making process is challenged by certain barriers to their entry. Scientific capacity is by far the largest problem, and although the importance of scientists in sustainable development governance has been recognised by important legal agreements such as Agenda 21 and the JPOI, a lack of focused assistance from the North to engage developing nation scientists effectively into processes such as assessments that are linked to decision-making remains. Contributions linked to ongoing programmes are important, but longer-term targeted commitments to assist developing countries to conduct assessments are also needed. In particular, the under-representation of women in science and in processes that are linked to decision-making must be tackled as a priority.

This chapter has also discussed the link between scientific assessments and traditional knowledge. Traditional knowledge, though not considered scientific according to standard Western definitions, plays an important role in providing practical information that can assist assessments to bridge the scales between the local and the global. Because local and indigenous groups are key actors in ecosystem management, their participation is also important for legitimacy and acceptance of the assessment.

Based on the analysis of this chapter there seems to be a number of measures that could be taken either to strengthen the role of developing

country scientists individually or to improve the institutional processes by which they contribute to international decision-making.
- Target graduate-level curriculum development on assessments in developing country universities and work to integrate more content in course modules related to environmental science and policy studies or develop stand-alone graduate degrees on assessment and environmental policy-making. Rich materials on environmental assessments including conceptual frameworks, modelling, scenario-building and policy studies now exist and could form a basis for this curriculum development.
- Future assessments should have dedicated capacity development programmes on scientific assessments. Existing programmes such as travel and participation grants could form the practical part of a programme, but a more holistic sustained approach is required.
- Many policy-makers do not know how to use scientific knowledge in decision-making, which results in many of the assessments' outputs being unused. Traditionally, capacity-building efforts around assessments have targeted the assessors instead of the users. Therefore capacity development programmes for policy-makers on how to use science, understand risk and uncertainty and ultimately how to apply assessments in their work is one way of ensuring the utility of the assessments and informing decision-making.
- Many of the barriers to involving women in assessments are deep-seated perceptions and culturally based resilience that will take long periods to overcome. While this requires continued efforts such as education and awareness-raising, interim positive measures should be sought for greater participation of women, including transparency of gender composition in assessments, institutional policies for the involvement of women and participation grants targeting women.
- Institutions play an important role in regime formation and negotiation. Given the levels of uncertainty and therefore the ability to politicise knowledge, progress will only be made if a common understanding of knowledge is formally agreed. In this regard assessments like the IPCC have played an important role in focusing negotiations and moving debates forward based on accepted information. But assessments remain *ad hoc* and require greater formalisation of institutional mechanisms for bridging international decision-making and science (after all, design does matter) and there is much more scope for integration of needs (i.e. MEAs). These goals could be achieved through better centralisation of assessment processes and a stronger coordination role played by UNEP.
- Scientists are increasingly being required to participate as diplomats, negotiators and policy-makers without the appropriate background or

formal training. While technical training is important for policy users, training for scientists from developing countries is required to give them the skills to be successful at policy-making.
• Traditional knowledge can play an important role in scientific networks and assessments, but to date there has been limited work on how the two bodies of knowledge can be integrated. More research and study is required to formalise the relationship and make the two bodies of knowledge integrated and functionally applicable for decision-making.

Notes

1. Although the tragedy of the commons can be traced back to English philosopher David Hume, Garret Hardin popularised the metaphor in a 1968 essay entitled "The Tragedy of the Commons." The tragedy refers to a scenario where herdsmen have access to graze their cattle freely on an open pasture; no problem exists as long as the capacity of the pasture is not overloaded. However, the inherent logic of the herdsmen is to increase their cattle to sell for short-term profit, which leads to environmental degradation. See Hardin, Garret (1977) "The Tragedy of the Commons", G. Hardin and J. Baden, eds, *Managing the Commons*, San Francisco: W. H. Freeman, pp. 16–30; Hume, David (1888) *A Treatise of Human Nature*, edited by L. A. Selby-Bigge, Oxford: Clarendon Press.
2. Ernst Haas' guidelines for a panel at the APSA meeting in Chicago, September 1983, cited in Rothstein, Robert L. (1984) "Consensual Knowledge and International Collaboration: Some Lessons from the Commodity Negotiations is Power", *International Organization* 38(4): 736.
3. Ibid.
4. Ibid.
5. Mitchell, Ronald, Clark, William C., Cash, David and Dickson, Nancy, eds, (2006) *Global Environmental Assessments: Information and Influence*, Cambridge, MA: MIT Press.
6. Keohane, Robert (1990) "Multilateralism: An Agenda for Research", *International Journal* 45(Autumn): 732.
7. Goldstein, Judith (1994) *Ideas, Interests and American Trade Policy*, Ithaca and London: Cornell University Press.
8. Mitchell et al., note 5 above.
9. Emirbayer, Mustafa and Goodwin, Jeff (1994) "Network Analysis Culture and of the Problem of Agency", *American Journal of Sociology* 99(6): 1448.
10. Burt, Ronald (1994) "Stratification and Prestige among Elite Experts in Methodological Mathematical Sociology", *Social Networks* 1: 105–158.
11. Malone, Elisabeth and Edgerton, Sylvia (2001) "The Strength of Weak Ties: The Influence of Horizontal Research Ties on National Environmental Policies", in *Proceedings of the 2001 Berlin Conference on the Human Dimension of Global Environmental Change*, p. 1.
12. Haas, Peter M. (1992) "Introduction: Epistemic Communities and International Policy Coordination", *International Organization* 46(1): 3.
13. Ibid., p. 2.
14. Susskind, Lawrence (1994) *Environmental Diplomacy*, Oxford: Oxford University Press, p. 74.

15. Siebenhuner, B. (2002) "How Do Scientific Assessments Learn? Part 1: Conceptual Framework and Case Study of the IPPC", *Environmental Science and Policy* 5: 411–420.
16. Robert Keohane has argued international regimes thus allow governments to take advantage of potential economies of scale. Once the regime has been established, the marginal cost of dealing with each additional issue will be lower than it would be without a regime. See Keohane, R. (1984) *After Hegemony: Cooperation and Discord in the World in World Political Economy*, Princeton, NJ: Princeton University Press, p. 90.
17. Dougherty, James E. and Pfaltzgraff, Robert L. Jr (1990) *Contending Theories of International Relations*, New York: HarperCollins, p. 432.
18. See for example, Steinburg, James and Mazarr, Michael (2004) *Developing Country Participation in Transnational Decision-making: Lessons for IT Governance*, available from www.markle.org/downloadable_assets/lessons_it_governance.pdf.
19. Mitchell et al., note 5 above.
20. Ibid.
21. Kandlikar, Milind and Ambuj, Sagar (1999) "Climate Change Research and Analysis in India. An Integrated Assessment of a South-North Divide", *Global Environmental Change* 9(2): 119–138.
22. Biermann, Frank (1999) "Big Science, Small Impacts in the South? The Influence of International Environmental Information Institutions on Policy-Making in India", ENRP Discussion Paper E-99-12, Kennedy School of Government, Harvard University, available from http://environment.harvard.edu/gea, p. 26.
23. For instance the MA has created a board that is made up of representatives of multiple sectors including business, government, indigenous groups, civil society and international organisations.
24. Haas, note 12 above.
25. Farrell, A., Van Deveer, S. D. and Jager, J. (2001) "Environmental Assessments: Four Under-appreciated Elements of Design", *Global Environmental Change* 11(4): 311–333.
26. Mitchell et al., note 5 above, p. 16.
27. Agarwal, Anil and Narain, Sunita (1991) *Global Warming in an Unequal World. A Case of Environmental Colonialism*, New Delhi: Centre for Science and Environment.
28. See http://science.unep.org/Mandate.asp for the most recent list of assessments done in the last 15 years.
29. UN Document, Johannesburg Plan of Implementation, A/CONF.199/20, para 109.
30. UK Parliamentary Office on Science and Technology, Postnote: Scientific Capacity in Developing Countries, March 2004, No. 216, p. 2.
31. Wijesekera, R. (2002) *Pedestrians on the Highways of Global Science*, Committee on Science and Technology in Developing Countries, Occasional Paper No. 7, International Council for Science.
32. Hassan, Farkhonda (2000) "Islamic Women in Science", *Science* 290(5489): 55–56.
33. See Skutsch, Margaret (2002) "Protocols, Treaties, and Action: The Climate Change Process Viewed through Gender Spectacles", *Gender and Development* 10(2): 30–39; Villagrasa, Delia (2002) "Kyoto Protocol Negotiations: Reflections on the Role of Women", *Gender and Development* 10(2): 21–29 and 40–44; Denton, Fatma (2002) "Climate Change Vulnerability, Impacts and Adaptation: Why Does Gender Matter?", *Gender and Development* 10(2); 10–20.
34. "Improving the participation of women in the representation of Parties in bodies established under the United Nations Framework Convention on Climate Change and the Kyoto Protocol", FCCC/CP/2001/L.22, November 2002.
35. Nadkarni, Manoj and Chauhan, Malavika (2004) "Assessments and Empowerment", paper presented at Bridging Scales and Epistemologies – Linking Local, Knowledge

and Global Science in Multi-Scale Assessments Conference, Alexandria, Egypt, 17–20 March, unpublished.
36. Reid, Walter (2004) "Bridging Scales and Epistemologies in the Millennium Ecosystem Assessment", paper presented at Bridging Scales and Epistemologies – Linking Local, Knowledge and Global Science in Multi-Scale Assessments Conference, Alexandria, Egypt, 17–20 March, unpublished.
37. Ibid.
38. Ibid.

5
The legacy of Deskaheh: Decolonising indigenous participation in sustainable development governance

Leanne Simpson

Introduction

Indigenous nations have been engaged in international governance since time immemorial. In the times prior to contact with colonising powers, indigenous national governments engaged in a variety of political relations with other indigenous national governments: negotiating treaties, political alliances and trade agreements amongst other issues. Since the inception of the United Nations, indigenous political and spiritual leaders have also been active in participating in the activities of the United Nations and its affiliated bodies as avenues to address the occupation of their lands, colonialism, genocide, human rights abuses and environmental degradation. In 1924 Cayuga Chief Deskaheh travelled to Geneva attempting to represent the Six Nations of the Haudenosaunee Confederacy at the League of Nations. Travelling on a passport authorised by the Six Nations, Deskaheh wanted to petition the League of Nations to explain that the Canadian government had no jurisdiction over their country. The treaty that his nation had signed with King George III acknowledged their nationhood and guaranteed a spot at the League of Nations. After spending over a year in Geneva, his requests were seriously considered by some of the delegates, including Japan and the Netherlands which sponsored him to address the League. Canada and Great Britain, however, pressured the Secretariat to inform Deskaheh that his nation would not be allowed as a petitioner before the plenary session, and he was ultimately denied even a seat in the gallery as an observer.[1] The majority of the international community failed to recognise Haudenosaunee sovereignty, but Deskaheh's persistence and sense of justice are a legacy for contemporary indigenous peoples demanding to have their rights recognised by the international community.

Chief Deskaheh was not the only indigenous leader to demand access to the League of Nations in the 1920s. In 1924 T. W. Ratana, a Maori religious leader, travelled to England to meet with King George V after New Zealand broke the Treaty of Waitangi, a treaty which guaranteed the Maori ownership of their lands. He was denied access to the King, so he sent part of his delegation to the League of Nations in Geneva, where they were also denied access and recognition. Thus began the long road indigenous nations have travelled to gain access, influence and recognition at the United Nations. The experiences of Chief Deskaheh and the Ratana delegation are not unique, nor are they the relics of another era. Indigenous peoples from all over the world repeat the same efforts and practise the persistence demonstrated by Deskaheh and Ratana in attempting to participate in, receive acknowledgement and ultimately achieve justice from the global governing structures of the world community.

In contemporary times indigenous peoples face the same denial of national sovereignty as did Deskaheh and Ratana, and they are repeatedly denied access to UN decision-making bodies. When they are allowed to participate, it is most often as observers, stakeholders or a part of civil society, and on terms that satisfy the needs of member states rather than indigenous peoples. For example, one of the most pressing issues for indigenous peoples over the past decade has been advocating for the protection of their human rights under the draft declaration on the rights of indigenous peoples. To many indigenous people this declaration represents a vital affirmation and acknowledgement of indigenous rights, rights that are intrinsically linked to the land, their environment and ultimately their full and meaningful participation in global environmental policy-making. Member states, however, continue to refuse to accept the draft declaration, leaving some indigenous people questioning the fundamental potential of the UN system for accomplishing anything with regards to indigenous peoples and their agendas.[2] As a result, some indigenous people refuse to participate in the UN system at all, seeing it as a colonising force comprised of countries engaged in the oppression of the world's indigenous population. For these people, participation in the United Nations legitimises this system, a system they find untrustworthy and ineffective in dealing with justice for the world's indigenous peoples.

Those indigenous people who choose to work within the United Nations are aware of and respectful of these perspectives, because often the traditional leaders and knowledge holders of their communities and nations hold these beliefs. They participate in global environmental policy-making initiatives with the purpose of changing and expanding existing institutional pathways for indigenous participation, viewing it as one potential avenue to promote justice and liberation for the world's indigenous peoples. They have used UN forums as opportunities to expose and bring attention to human rights abuses, continuing genocide, colonialism and environmental destruction. Indigenous organisations have also used these international meetings as opportunities for groups and individual nations to build political alliances and join in solidarity with other indigenous groups who refuse to compromise their rights and sovereignty in the face of extreme state pressures to do so.[3] Still other indigenous people choose to work from the margins of the UN system, often using non-institutional pathways for change, pushing for new decolonised relationships between indigenous nations and member states, in part based on the principles in the draft declaration. Indigenous peoples have been most successful in influencing the global agenda on environmental policy when these strategies are combined in a multifaceted approach. Yet given the barriers indigenous peoples face, these successes have been few and far between.

For indigenous peoples, the denial of national sovereignty, the lack of formal recourse for indigenous peoples to remedy human rights violations and the lack of political recognition of indigenous nations within the UN system provide the context for interactions with the United Nations. The destruction of indigenous lands has accompanied the oppression of indigenous peoples, with occupying governments facilitating large-scale industrial development on indigenous lands without the permission of their governments. This disrupts the sustainable relationships indigenous peoples have with their lands. For indigenous peoples, colonialism remains the major barrier to sustainability, as sustainability and the restoration of indigenous self-determination are intrinsically linked. A former Grand Chief of the Assembly of First Nations, Matthew Coon Come, makes this point in discussing the impact of the Rio Earth Summit on indigenous peoples colonised by Canada:

First Nations are concerned about environmental degradation and the impact this has on all our relations. The primary concern is our duty to the Creator to care for the land. However, First Nations are denied the inherent right to govern and manage our own lands in a sustainable way and are often denied access to the land. This lack of jurisdiction to manage our own lands has had many consequences, including the extinction of species, deforestation, water pollution, the decline in quality and quantity of wild foods, climate change and ozone depletion.[4]

Based on this perspective, the denial of indigenous nationhood is directly linked to the exploitation of the environment, and until these injustices are properly addressed both the environment and indigenous peoples will continue to suffer. Aroha Te Pareake Mead of the Maori nation clearly states that Maori will not achieve full and meaningful participation in international forums until their treaty is restored:

> Maori, however, will continue to be "third party stakeholders", rather than drivers of environmental decision-making, as long as treaty grievances remain unsettled and until the land, cash and other resources taken from them are returned.[5]

Indigenous representatives participating in UN forums relating to environmental policy-making have repeatedly raised these issues. Enfranchisement within the global arena requires that the global community address its colonial past, and the contemporary ways it continues to colonise and oppress indigenous peoples. Without addressing the systemic and root causes of indigenous disenfranchisement, solutions aimed at increasing indigenous participation and influence will serve only as "Band-aid solutions", falling short of affording the rightful place of indigenous peoples in global policy-making processes.

Decolonisation: Full enfranchisement

The full enfranchisement of indigenous peoples within the UN system requires extensive decolonisation of indigenous-state relations at the national level, in addition to the decolonisation of the relationship between indigenous nations and the UN system itself. Decolonisation is a political, social, physical and spiritual process which must take place both within indigenous nations and in the external political relationships formed with other indigenous and non-indigenous nations. It is a large and complex project that will span several generations and take on diverse forms and pathways, as individual indigenous nations revitalise their traditional forms of knowledge, governance and political relationships. They will have to address collectively and critically the impacts of colonialism and occupation on indigenous lands and peoples. Indigenous peoples are not a homogeneous entity, and colonialism has impacted on the indigenous peoples of the world in different ways. Decolonising pathways will be reflective of individual indigenous traditions, indigenous conceptualisations and diagnosis and indigenous visioning. The core of decolonisation relies upon strengthening indigenous political traditions, governance, worldviews, knowledge systems and education and health care systems. Still, in contemporary times, most indigenous peoples have not entered a post-colonial era, and they continue to fight for their lives, their way of life and their lands, making thinking about a decolonised future all the more difficult.

Although indigenous peoples have been discussing decolonisation for generations, academics have only begun to talk about decolonisation in the last few years.[6] Therefore, questions about *how* decolonisation will take place and *what* decolonised political relationships will look like remain unanswered in the academic literature. In fact, there will be no single answer to these questions, as indigenous peoples continue to envision for themselves a decolonised future. If any generalisations can be made on this topic, it is that decolonisation represents a process of rediscovery and recovery, of mourning and critically addressing current injustices and the injustices of the past, of envisioning future possibilities and of commitment and action.[7] State and global governing structures must also be willing to decolonise their relationships with indigenous nations. Discussions about decolonising global governance mean critically evaluating the current relationship and creating space for envisioning a better future.

The purpose of this chapter is to examine critically the ways in which indigenous peoples currently participate in global governance for sustainable development. It will begin by discussing the international community's interest in traditional knowledge as a motivation for enhancing indigenous participation. It will then examine measures attempting to enhance indigenous participation in global environmental policy-making, focusing on both institutional and non-institutional pathways. Finally, the chapter will conclude with a discussion of various "successful" attempts to enfranchise indigenous peoples, including a discussion of Inuit influence in the Stockholm Convention on Persistent Organic Pollutants, indigenous declarations and the Call of the Earth *Llamado de la Tierra* Initiative.

Global governance and indigenous peoples: The current situation

Over the past few decades the UN system has taken some measures to enhance and promote indigenous participation in sustainable development and environmental policy-making. In the early 1980s the world's scientists, policy-makers, political leaders, academics and civil society activists recognised the importance of indigenous knowledge for the promotion of sustainable development.[8] From an indigenous perspective, these legal measures were initiated not out of a sense of righting past wrongs or concerns over the rights of indigenous peoples, but because member states were interested in the traditional knowledge of indigenous peoples as a potential remedy for global environmental crises.[9] This interest has motivated member states to invite indigenous peoples to participate in a variety of working groups and forums regarding biodiversity and sustainability in order to learn how this knowledge might be applied to environmental crises.

Indigenous peoples have viewed this newfound interest in their knowledge and concern for their enfranchisement with scepticism. Indigenous academics Marie Battiste and Sakej Youngblood Henderson write:

> As the twenty-first century dawns, industrialised societies are demanding that indigenous peoples share our knowledge, our hearts, bodies and souls so that Eurocentric society can solve the various problems that its world-view has created. In view of the history of relations between the colonisers and the colonised, this is an extraordinarily bold request. The colonising peoples have done nothing to create trust or to build relationships with our ecologies or our knowledge. They have contaminated the land, and they have refused to have respectful relations with the forces of the ecologies. Indeed, they have competed with these forces.[10]

Unfortunately the interest of industrialised societies in indigenous *knowledge* was not coupled with an interest in indigenous *peoples*. This has forced indigenous peoples to engage in discussions in order to protect knowledge from exploitation without any resolution of human rights violations and continuing genocide against indigenous peoples worldwide. It is difficult to accept that states currently engaged in and benefiting from the occupation of indigenous national territories, the denial of the indigenous right to self-determination and the promotion of national policies aimed at destroying the foundations of indigenous knowledge could possibly be interested in their traditional knowledge in a manner that is not based on exploitation and oppression. Battiste and Youngblood Henderson continue:

> This interest [in indigenous knowledge] has reinstalled the predatory mentality of Eurocentric thought, raising questions about the ethics of the new global enterprise and about indigenous peoples' ability to survive it. The parallel between the dispossession of indigenous land and the dispossession of our intellectual knowledge is riveting. Without effective protection of the special interests that indigenous peoples have in our ways of knowing and heritage, indigenous cultures are threatened and endangered. Our heritage and teachings are open to pillage in the same way and by the same peoples who have been taking our lands and resources for more than five hundred years.[11]

Although indigenous, or traditional, knowledge systems have been sustaining indigenous nations for countless generations, informing their governance, health care, education and political systems, it is only in the past two decades that non-indigenous peoples have become interested in certain aspects of those knowledge systems. In 1987 *Our Common Future*, the report of the World Commission on Environment and Development, recognised the role of indigenous peoples in sustainable development. Five years after this report was released, the Rio Declaration reaffirmed this position, stating that indigenous peoples have a vital role in environmental management and development. Principle 22 of the Rio Declaration recognises the critical role of indigenous peoples in sustainable development, and calls for states "to recognise and duly support our identity, culture and interests". Principle 26 also discussed this role, stating the following as its three main objectives:

a) the empowerment of indigenous people and communities;
b) strengthening of the active participation of indigenous people and communities in national policies, laws and programmes from resource management;
c) the involvement of those people and communities in resource management and conservation strategies.

The rhetorical nature of Agenda 21 does not require that indigenous peoples *influence* national policies, laws, resource management or conservation strategies, merely that they *participate* and be involved in those strategies. This results in many cases where states have adopted the Agenda, but indigenous peoples' participation has remained superficial. Thus the *status quo* has persisted, and indigenous participation has not influenced national policy in any meaningful way. From an indigenous perspective, effective and meaningful participation means that different decisions will be made and that indigenous participation will be reflected in the overall decision-making of the organisation.

The Convention on Biological Diversity (CBD) opened for signature during the Rio Earth Summit. Article 8(j) of the convention deals specifically with indigenous peoples and traditional knowledge:

Each contracting Party shall, as far as possible and as appropriate: Subject to national legislation, respect, preserve and maintain knowledge, innovations and practices of indigenous and local communities embodying traditional lifestyles relevant for the conservation and sustainable use of biological diversity and promote our wider application with the approval and involvement of the holders of such knowledge, innovations and practices and encourage the equitable sharing of the benefits arising from the utilisation of such knowledge, innovations and practices.[12]

While international recognition of the importance of traditional knowledge is a major accomplishment for indigenous peoples, many indigenous peoples feel that CBD working groups on article 8(j) and on access and benefits-sharing have focused more on enabling state governments and industry *access* to traditional knowledge than assisting indigenous peoples in the *protection* of that knowledge from outside exploitation. These bodies have been slow to acknowledge that many indigenous groups are advocating *sui generis* mechanisms for the protection of knowledge to be recognised rather than working within existing Western intellectual property regimes, a position that has been virtually ignored by member states.

Despite the recognition of the role of traditional knowledge and indigenous peoples in sustainable development, they still face major barriers to full participation in the decision-making of these UN bodies. At the international level, these goals remain difficult to achieve given that settler governments continue to deny indigenous sovereignty, governance and land rights, thereby undermining indigenous identity, culture, knowledge and interests. The role of indigenous peoples in international governance remains shackled by the colonial and neo-colonial policies of state governments, aimed at continuing to undermine indigenous self-determination, nationhood and traditional systems of knowledge. The contradictions do not go unnoticed by those indigenous peoples participating in UN bodies, particularly around the issue of traditional knowledge and intellectual property rights (IPRs), and they represent a major structural barrier to indigenous peoples in the multilateral arena.

Institutional pathways

Although problematic for the reasons discussed above, principle 22 and article 8(j) have enhanced indigenous participation in global policy-making and have been a first step in enabling indigenous peoples to influence national positions and global agendas. Over the past decade they have expanded opportunities for indigenous peoples to participate in global environmental policy-making through institutionalised pathways. Indigenous peoples have participated on state delegations; represented indigenous groups, nations and communities at different meetings under observer status; participated on expert panels; and submitted case studies under the CBD. The following sections outline the nature of this enhanced participation.

State delegations

Canada and New Zealand are two state governments that have regularly included indigenous representatives on their delegations when negotiating international environmental policy agreements. The international community has applauded them for doing so. The effectiveness of these measures, however, is mixed from an indigenous perspective. The presence of an indigenous person on a state delegation gives legitimacy to the state's negotiating positions, positions that are often crafted without any indigenous input and are often detrimental to indigenous interests.

> **Box 5.1:** In my own experience, I have sat as part of the Canadian delegation negotiating the Biosafety Protocol under the CBD and as part of the delegation to the *ad hoc* open-ended working group on Article 8(j). I was the only indigenous delegate present at the negotiations for the Biosafety Protocol (several NGOs and indigenous groups were present in the corridors, but did not have access to the plenary). Despite the fact that the issues captured in these negotiations were of enough interest to the Assembly of First Nations to send me to the table on their behalf, the Canadian government categorically ignored all of my input into the process. I had absolutely no influence over their negotiating position and, although on paper I was a full member of the delegation, I was not allowed the same access to information as other governmental delegation members. For all intents and purposes, I might as well have not been there; my presence only gave legitimacy to the Canadian delegation, which regularly put forward negotiating positions that had the potential to endanger indigenous peoples. In some cases, I worried that I was actually assisting them in developing their positions; they knew how developing countries with opposing views would criticise them ahead of time. This was a particularly frustrating experience: although I was able to gain access to information and to negotiations, my presence was used by coloniser governments to legitimise Canada's negotiating position. This has been the experience of many other indigenous peoples in Canada to the point where many, including myself, refuse to sit on any government-sanctioned delegations.

Since the author has had extensive personal experience with this problem, it is both appropriate and helpful to share these experiences of the role of indigenous representation on national delegations (Box 5.1).

Aroha Mead describes her experience on New Zealand state delegations:

> It isn't uncommon in such situations for states to prevent indigenous delegates from participating in the smaller more technical working groups and committees as the states feel more exposed when discussions become detailed and specific. It is in this way that they tend to develop quite simplistic responses to what are complex matters. Indigenous peoples continue to be the "objects" of negotiation, but they themselves are most often not directly included in the policy development stages.[13]

Despite these problems, in meetings where indigenous organisations are not afforded observer status membership of a state delegation may be the only institutional pathway open for indigenous peoples to participate. In this case, membership on state delegations will afford indigenous peoples access to corridor discussions, side events and opportunities to meet with other member states that might be supportive of their concerns. Combined with a multi-pronged approach supported by other indigenous organisations, this may be one part of an effective strategy to influence global environmental policy-making. However, it requires substantial resources for it to be fully effective.

Indigenous organisations and observer status

Indigenous people representing organisations, nations or communities not willing or able to participate in state delegations can also participate in some global environmental policy negotiations as observers. Observer status affords some level of participation in these meetings, though considerably less than the level which delegates enjoy. Indigenous peoples have been able to use observer status to their advantage in several cases, using it as an opportunity to monitor countries' negotiating positions, to develop relationships with other delegates who may be supportive of indigenous causes, to educate delegates about issues that are important to indigenous peoples, to strategise with others through the Indigenous Caucus, to liaise with NGOs and other members of civil society who might have common interests and goals and to garner media attention for indigenous issues. To be fully effective, observer status must be combined with other non-institutional strategies to increase influence. For instance, the Maori nation has been able to use the observer status of some Maori groups, in addition to Maori membership on state delegations, to advance their political goals. Aroha Mead explains:

There have been times here in New Zealand, when the Maori activist movement, together with well placed Maori senior government officials, together with Maori politicians, have joined forces and been highly effective in pushing for change or for something to be squashed (i.e. the NZ position on the OECD Multilateral Agreement on Investment).[14]

This kind of effective strategising requires indigenous peoples to be actively involved in high-level state government and political affairs, something that for some is a compromise of indigenous sovereignty and for others, often in majority world countries, is simply impossible.

Participation in expert groups: The Ad-Hoc Open-Ended Working Group on Article 8(j)

One of the most successful of institutional pathways designed to enhance indigenous participation has been the Ad-Hoc Open-Ended Working Group on Article 8(j). Indigenous peoples have substantial and unprecedented participation in this working group and have participated as co-chairs, formally addressed the forum through interventions and have had some influence over setting the agenda for the group's work. Several indigenous nations have addressed the floor directly, as indigenous nations, although their interventions do not often hold the same weight as interventions by state governments. Some indigenous organisations, however, have advocated for this model of participation to be used in the Framework Convention on Climate Change, the Kyoto Protocol and the Ad-Hoc Open Ended Working Group on Access and Benefit Sharing of Genetic Resources (ABS) within the CBD.

Indigenous peoples do not agree on whether the Working Group on 8(j) is successful or not. While it represents an important first step, many people are concerned that it "ghettoises" indigenous issues in the CBD into one working group. By compartmentalising all indigenous issues within the CBD into one meeting, indigenous peoples have less access to other working groups. For instance, indigenous peoples are very concerned about access and benefit sharing with respect to traditional knowledge, yet they do not have the same level of participation in the ABS Working Group meetings because "indigenous issues" are dealt with in the Working Group on 8(j).

Some participants also question the ability of the Working Group to influence decision-making at the Conference of the Parties (COP). Indigenous participation at the COP, the supreme decision-making body of the CBD, is extremely marginalised. The COP meets every two years and its main functions are to monitor progress and to agree on a programme of work to implement the convention. The participation of observers is encouraged, but with over 100 indigenous peoples in attendance at COP7, they were only allowed to address the forum in one presentation for each agenda item. Participation in workshop groups was at the discretion of the chair.[15] Indigenous peoples also question the influence of article 8(j) within the larger system of global governance. The World Intellectual Property Organization (WIPO) is of particular interest to indigenous peoples because of its work on traditional knowledge and intellectual property. WIPO, however, will not consider the decisions of the Working Group; it will only consider the decision of the COP. This barrier makes it more difficult for the Working Group on 8(j) to influence WIPO on this very important issue.

The Indigenous Caucus

At most international meetings with indigenous peoples participating as observers, the Indigenous Caucus (open to all indigenous peoples and organisations) meets and operates in an attempt to provide a united position designed to influence both the procedures and content of meetings.

Indigenous participants have very little time and financial resources for setting agendas and strategies for participating in the Working Group ahead of time, especially in comparison to many member states; therefore, the Indigenous Caucus is not nearly as effective as it might be in presenting a united front to the Working Group. Language barriers further confound the effectiveness of this group. There are few resources available for translation at these meetings, making it difficult to include all indigenous delegates. There are also substantial differences in perspective, strategy and purpose for the indigenous peoples of the world and it can become exceedingly difficult to build any kind of consensus under these conditions. Nevertheless, the Indigenous Caucus has continued to meet, present interventions when possible and monitor the procedures of the Working Group meetings.

Case studies

Indigenous groups are often invited to submit case studies to help monitor and assess the effectiveness of national programmes of work. Under the CBD, case studies are submitted to the Secretariat and are considered "vital to the preparation of documents and the development of recommendations to be considered at Conference of the Parties meetings and meetings of the Convention's subsidiary bodies".[16] There are two issues with case studies. Many indigenous groups do not have the financial capacity or human resources to construct and submit case studies. Secondly, the issues that the case studies address more often reflect the agenda of member states than of indigenous peoples.

Side events

Indigenous peoples have been successful in organising various side events on the margins of important international meetings. Although these events are not formally part of the programme of work, they give indigenous peoples time and space to discuss issues, positions and concerns in a more detailed and complex manner. Side events can be an effective tool for influencing international policy-making, but they are dependent upon the attendance of individual delegates and the capacity of indigenous organisations to arrange them.

Barriers to effective participation in institutional pathways

The preceding section outlines the various ways indigenous peoples participate in international sustainable development policy-making through institutional pathways. There are, however, several barriers that limit the effectiveness of such participation.

Indigenous groups which participate, like NGOs, are self-selected and largely unaccountable to grassroots indigenous people. Larger, well-established groups tend to have the personnel and resources to participate. The Canadian Assembly of First Nations (AFN) is an example of an aboriginal political organisation that has participated in international environmental policy-making. Its funding comes from the Canadian government, and its membership is composed of First Nation chiefs elected under the Indian Act, a colonial system of government controlled by the Canadian government and imposed on First Nations communities. The funding the AFN receives from the Canadian government is dependent upon how well the two are getting along: the more critical the AFN is of Canada, the less funding it receives. The organisation is always short on funding and personnel, often with only one person looking at environmental issues in the 633 First Nation communities it represents. Clearly, this limits the AFN's capacity to participate effectively in international policy-making. The AFN has no funds to consult with the people in the communities it represents or to strategise and build networks with other indigenous peoples regarding policy issues.

At the same time, the AFN is the indigenous group in Canada with the *greatest* capacity to participate in international policy-making for sustainable development. Groups representing indigenous knowledge holders, traditional governments, clan mothers and elders have virtually no access to these forums and are completely disenfranchised. Individual indigenous nations, which sometimes are considered more legitimate in the eyes of local indigenous peoples than organisations like the AFN, often have virtually no resources to participate because their existence is ignored by the Canadian government. This is further complicated by international funding organisations which deny funding to indigenous groups from developed countries. Indigenous peoples from countries like Canada, the United States, New Zealand and Australia cannot access these funds because their national governments provide support to indigenous peoples to attend international meetings. Unfortunately, this state-sponsored support only goes to indigenous people and groups who are supportive of state governments' negotiating positions – positions that often have detrimental impacts on indigenous peoples.

Indigenous participants in the activities of Agenda 21 were also wary of the lack of resources to support their effective participation. Little if any funding is allocated nationally so that indigenous representatives can consult at the community level; as a result communities remain largely ignorant of UN processes. Despite the very best efforts of indigenous representatives, non-indigenous UN participants are mostly unaware of community issues. This is a problem that has been identified by indigenous delegates participating in the CBD:

It will not be enough to draft Convention language with the participation of a few delegates; indigenous communities will have to participate in the process by discussing the issues, and developing and implementing positions ... Effective participation must include participation at the international level as well as the national level, communication to and discussion among communities at home.[17]

Many indigenous peoples have expressed the reality that the Rio Earth Summit and Agenda 21 have little impact in indigenous communities. Matthew Coon Come, former Chief of the AFN, the largest political organisation of indigenous peoples in Canada, writes: "While some individuals from the Assembly of First Nations participated in the Rio Summit and others followed it closely, the percentage of First Nations individuals who even knew it was taking place was quite small."[18] Lucy Mulenkei of the African Indigenous Women's Organization echoes Coon Come's comments: "Rio had little impact for indigenous peoples in Kenya ... The process [in preparation for Rio+5] advanced slowly at the regional and national levels and participation was non-existent for indigenous peoples at the community level."[19]

Traditional indigenous processes of governance and decision-making require broad-based consultation and discussion with people at the community level. This requires a commitment of time and resources for sure, but these necessities do not guarantee that indigenous peoples will be willing to participate, particularly if they do not see the international community as an effective arena for the advancement of rights. The non-participation of indigenous peoples is often assumed to relate solely to capacity issues, when in many indigenous cultures it is a political signal of discontent and resistance.

A special note on the participation of indigenous women

Indigenous women face even more barriers to participating in global policy-making. It is especially difficult for indigenous women to participate in international processes and attend international meetings. Children are an integral part of indigenous communities and indigenous women often bring children with them when they attend meetings. Indigenous cultures are highly child-friendly environments. The UN system is not. This represents a substantial barrier towards participation for women with children. Both governmental and non-governmental donors will not provide monies for women to bring along young children or to bring family members to look after the children while the women attend meetings. This prohibits young women from travelling internationally because many of them nurse babies and toddlers long term, and their cultural parenting practices involve a high level of attachment, making separation from children impossible. As a nursing mother, the author has been forced to withdraw from all previous UN work including participation in the Article 8(j) Working Group because of an inability to find any organisation (with the exception of the Call of the Earth/*Llamado de la Tierra*) that will fund the travel costs of a child and a caregiver. Judging by the absence of women and children at international meetings, this appears to be true for many other young indigenous women.

Recommendations for improving institutional pathways for indigenous participation

- In order to build trust and demonstrate their commitment to indigenous issues, member states should sign on to the draft declaration on indigenous rights.
- Indigenous peoples should be invited to participate as observers in any global policy initiative that influences indigenous peoples or in which they have an interest.
- The influence of the Working Group on Article 8(j) should be expanded and should have greater impact on other bodies such as WIPO.
- Increased financial resources should be available to support the work of the Indigenous Caucus, to increase the participation of indigenous women and to allow broader indigenous participation on international policy issues.
- Increased measures should be taken to assist indigenous peoples in protecting indigenous knowledge using the mechanisms they choose.
- The participation of indigenous organisations at COPs must be expanded.

Non-institutional pathways

Deskaheh and Ratana began the tradition of using non-institutional pathways to influence global policy nearly nine decades ago. Although they were not permitted access to the League of Nations, they took every opportunity available to them to influence member states and educate them about their cause. Although this did not translate into influence, by using the media and meeting with member countries they were at the very least able to educate member states and the general public in Europe about indigenous issues.

In contemporary times, one of the most important examples of indigenous peoples exerting influence on global environmental policy comes from the Inuit and their fight to eliminate persistent organic pollutants

(POPs) from their territories. By employing both institutional and non-institutional strategies, the Inuit were able to influence the global agenda on POPs and the Stockholm Convention on Persistent Organic Pollutants far beyond their numbers. Several strategies contributed to their success. First, five aboriginal peoples' organisations concerned with contaminants in the North joined forces to create a coalition, called the Northern Aboriginal Peoples' Coordinating Committee on POPs – later known as the Canadian Arctic Indigenous Peoples Against POPS (CAIPAP) – with the purpose of monitoring and influencing the POPs negotiations under the Convention on Long Range Transboundary Air Pollutions (CLRTAP). By obtaining a small amount of funding, they were able to acquire technical expertise and travel monies to attend negotiating sessions. Using the observer status of one of their members, the Inuit Circumpolar Conference, the coalition monitored Canada's negotiating position, lobbied other states for support, sponsored side events, met with NGOs and used displays in the corridors to educate delegates about their plight. The role of the chair was also critical to the Inuit's success, as was the technical and political ability of their spokesperson.[20] The peaceful protests of the NGOs outside of the negotiating session helped garner media attention to the issue. When they were not attending negotiations as observers, the coalition met with members of parliament in Canada, wrote letters to the Canadian delegation based on the observations they made during the negotiations and used the media whenever they could to draw attention to the issue. In the end, the Inuit were successful in influencing the national negotiation position of Canada and the final text of the treaty.[21]

Indigenous declarations

Indigenous peoples have also organised themselves at international meetings related to sustainable development through declarations of individual nations and of the collective Indigenous Caucus. Unfortunately, as mostly rhetorical, political and legally non-binding, these documents are largely ignored by states.[22] Despite this, these declarations represent a united and clear international policy direction put forth by indigenous peoples. One such declaration is the Mataatua Declaration on Cultural and Intellectual Property Rights. In June 1993 the Nine Tribes of Mataatua in the Bay of Plenty region of Aotearoa, New Zealand, convened the First International Conference on the Cultural and Intellectual Property Rights of Indigenous Peoples. Over 150 delegates from 14 countries attended, including indigenous representatives from Ainu (Japan), Australia, the Cook Islands, Fiji, India, Panama, Peru, the Philippines, Surinam, the United States and Aotearoa. The conference met over six days to consider a range of significant issues, including the value of indigenous knowledge, biodiversity and biotechnology, customary environmental management, arts, music, language and other physical and spiritual cultural forms. On the final day a declaration on the cultural and intellectual property rights of indigenous peoples was passed by the plenary. Although the declaration is over a decade old, its content remains as relevant today as it did then, clearly outlining the link between the right to self-determination and the recognition of indigenous peoples as the exclusive owners of their knowledge.

Over the past 10 years this declaration has not influenced international policy-making around intellectual property issues to any measurable degree. Organisations like WIPO continue to advocate for intellectual property rights to protect indigenous knowledge, despite the fact that many indigenous people have voiced concern over their ability to protect cultural knowledge valued for its intrinsic worth. Some indigenous peoples are advocating the recognition in national law of the customary practices and laws of indigenous peoples, and for policy responses to emanate from indigenous perspectives rather than Western legal traditions.[23] One group actively articulating this position within global environmental policy-making initiatives is the Call of the Earth/ *Llamado de la Tierra*.

The Call of the Earth/*Llamado de la Tierra* Initiative

The Call of the Earth/*Llamado de la Tierra*: Indigenous Wisdom for Sustaining Livelihoods, Cultures and Environments was formally launched at the fourth session of the WIPO Intergovernmental Committee on Traditional Knowledge and Folklore in December 2002. The Call of the Earth/*Llamado de la Tierra*[24] Initiative is an independent, international indigenous peoples' initiative on cultural and intellectual property policy sponsored by the Rockefeller Foundation. It brings together leading indigenous experts in cultural and intellectual property from around the world, with the objectives of:
- providing indigenous peoples with an ongoing space for dialogue on intellectual property (IP) policy;
- supporting indigenous peoples' efforts to participate more substantively and meaningfully in the international IP policy arena;
- helping reconceptualise and reframe the policy discussion on IP and indigenous knowledge to focus on the rights of indigenous peoples, the collective and spiritual dimensions of indigenous knowledge and the ar-

ray of existing customary law approaches to the protection and management of indigenous knowledge;
- helping ensure that indigenous communities are able both to protect intellectual creations and benefit from them.

Many indigenous peoples have raised concerns that emerging international IP policies and discussions of traditional knowledge do not adequately reflect or respond to the experience, needs and priorities of indigenous peoples. The Call of the Earth/*Llamado de la Tierra* initiative will help to help ensure that indigenous perspectives are more effectively articulated and considered. The initiative involves four core activities.
- *Dialogues*. In partnership with local and international indigenous organisations, the initiative hosts dialogues on IP policy at the regional and thematic levels to promote the sharing of experiences and the gathering of perspectives that can be shared in regional, national and international policy forums.
- *Knowledge base of indigenous research, analysis and experiences*. The initiative documents and publishes indigenous research, analysis and experiences (by indigenous peoples) on customary approaches to the management of knowledge and innovation; local experiences related to indigenous knowledge and IP policy; and indigenous perspectives on ongoing policy debates related to indigenous knowledge at the national and/or global level.
- *Collaboration*. The initiative offers support and advice, where requested and where resources permit, to related local and global initiatives, particularly efforts to build capacity of upcoming indigenous experts on issues of knowledge and IP policy and giving the legal support to indigenous communities.
- *International strategy*. The initiative facilitates efforts among indigenous peoples to engage strategically in regional and international policy debates on IP policy matters.

The years since 2003 have not been easy for the initiative. Operating on a fraction of its proposed funding needs, the proposed activities have necessarily been cut back, and unfortunately, as with many other inadequately funded indigenous and environmental organisations, much time is spent on fund-raising activities. Despite these challenges, the COE Steering Committee has begun work on a variety of activities and continues to have a strong presence at international meetings concerning indigenous peoples, the environment and IP. The COE has been an active participant since 2003 in the WIPO Intergovernmental Committee (IGC) on Intellectual Property and Genetic Resources, Traditional Knowledge and Folklore. One of the primary ways indigenous peoples interact with the international community concerned with sustainable development is through traditional knowledge, and WIPO is a forum for international debate regarding the interactions of IP, traditional knowledge, genetic resources and traditional cultural expressions.[25] Of primary concern to the COE and many other indigenous peoples is the potentially negative impact of IPRs on the capacity of indigenous peoples to control, preserve and transmit their knowledge.[26] The agenda of the 173 member states that make up WIPO is focused solely on IPR solutions to the protection of traditional knowledge, and the pace of the debate has not allowed indigenous peoples to form policy responses to ensure that protection and respect for knowledge and innovation emanate from indigenous cultural perspectives.[27]

Of further concern is the lack of meaningful indigenous participation in the IGC, established by the WIPO General Assembly in October 2000. Indigenous participation in the IGC has been minimal, with member states driving the agenda and indigenous peoples participating as observers with the status of accredited or accredited 'ad hoc' organisations. During the Sixth Session of the IGC held in 2004, only four indigenous groups – COE, the Third World Network, Folklorica Departmental de la Paz, and Nara Instituto Indigena Brasileiro – were present. This is alarming since much discussion has taken place regarding increasing indigenous participation in the IGC, yet the *status quo* remains in place.

The COE also presented at the third meeting of the Permanent Forum on Indigenous Issues. The Permanent Forum is plagued by the same neo-colonial policies as other UN bodies. It has been criticised by indigenous peoples from its inception, when the member states refused to recognise indigenous peoples' right to self-determination. Fearing that the use of the word 'peoples' would imply recognition of this right, they instead chose to use the word "issues" in the naming of the forum. There remains no formal recourse for indigenous peoples to remedy human rights violations occurring in their territories, as the forum functions solely as an internal report-writing and data-gathering agency for state policy-making.[28] However, the Permanent Forum is the only permanent organ within the UN system for indigenous issues. As such, the COE has recommended greater participation of the Permanent Forum in WIPO as one means of increasing indigenous systematic participation in the IGC. The COE proposed several other concrete options for increasing this participation, yet little action has been taken on the part of the IGC. The COE is the only international organisation dedicated to advancing indigenous perspectives on IPRs and traditional knowledge in the international arena. Although the organisation is actively working to increase indigenous peoples participation in these processes and also increasing their capacity to do so, real change requires the commitment of state governments.

Recommendations

- Create opportunities for indigenous peoples to learn, from indigenous organisations that have been successful, how to build effective international strategies to influence global environmental policy.
- International funding organisations must increase their support of indigenous organisations to sustain campaigns to influence policy at both the national and international levels.

Decolonising international environmental policy-making

Addressing the disenfranchisement of indigenous peoples from global governance concerned with sustainable governance is a complex issue. The denial of indigenous nationhood and the right of indigenous nations to be self-determining represents a major barrier to effective participation, one where little progress has been made since the inception of the UN system. These rights are simply not respected when indigenous peoples are reduced from nations to stakeholders, and asked to be observers of proceedings that greatly impact on the lives of their peoples. When indigenous peoples are invited to participate in global environmental policy-making, they often lack the capacity to do so effectively. The lack of influence indigenous peoples have in this system then feeds into their reticence to participate in further policy-making activities. Indigenous peoples have been attempting to gain the recognition of indigenous national sovereignty by the international community since the days of Deskaheh, to no avail. This leaves some of them asking whether the UN system has the potential for accomplishing anything with regards to the aims of protecting indigenous peoples' interests and goals. Taiaiake Alfred and Jeff Corntassel suggest that indigenous peoples may need to spend less time participating in the UN system and shift towards engagement and activism within other global forums.[29] They point to the Unrepresented Nations and Peoples Organization (UNPO) as one possible avenue. This organisation comprises 52 nations, as opposed to state governments, working together to promote the common goals of self-determination.

UNPO is a democratic, international membership organisation. Its members are indigenous peoples, occupied nations, minorities and independent states or territories which have joined together to protect human and cultural rights, preserve the environment and find non-violent solutions to conflicts which affect them. UNPO provides a legitimate and established international forum for member aspirations and assists its members in effective participation at an international level. Although UNPO members have different goals and aspirations, they share one condition – they are not represented in major international forums, such as the United Nations. As a result, their ability to participate in the international community and have their concerns addressed by the global bodies mandated to protect human rights and address conflict is limited.[30]

Alfred and Corntassel's suggestion is worthy of lengthy reflection and discussion amongst indigenous peoples. By actively participating in the UN system in the limited capacity state governments allow, indigenous peoples bring legitimacy to that system, whether or not they support those outcomes. Furthermore, indigenous people devote their time, energy and limited resources responding to the agenda of state governments, rather than setting their own goals and working towards these. Alfred and Corntassel also suggest that indigenous peoples need to reinvigorate their traditions around global governance.[31] Instead of just engaging in alliance and solidarity work at the international level, they suggest that indigenous governments behave and act like legitimate governments, entering into the process of treaty-making with other indigenous nations.

Decolonising the UN system of global governance will not be an easy task, but it is a necessary process to engage into ensure the effective and meaningful participation of the world's indigenous peoples in global governance and international discussions regarding sustainability. Adopting the draft declaration on indigenous rights is a first step in this direction. Indigenous peoples have tremendous knowledge to offer the world in terms of sustainable development, and it is in the best interests of all parties to develop a new, decolonised and just relationship with indigenous peoples in global governance structures. These changes are necessary for the survival of all of the earth's peoples, both indigenous and non-indigenous.

State governments have tremendous power over the indigenous lands they are occupying and the indigenous peoples they are colonising. They have a vested interest in continuing to occupy and oppress indigenous peoples. State governments and indigenous peoples do not have the same perspectives, goals or agendas, yet member countries control UN processes. This power imbalance and the opposing agendas of state governments and indigenous peoples plague the effective participation of indigenous peoples in international environmental policy-making.

There have been so many efforts by indigenous peoples to participate in these international discussions, to voice opposition to continued exploitation of land, people and knowledge. Indigenous peoples continue to work within the UN system, despite the lack of motivation of state governments to remedy basic human rights issues, in order to ensure that knowledge and knowledge holders are protected from the potential yet blatant threat of exploitation. In the long term, effective, meaningful and just participation by indigenous peoples in the UN system can only be achieved through a new relationship between the UN system and indigenous peoples, a relationship that Deskaheh and Ratana began to forge over 80 years ago.[32]

Notes

1. Akwesasne, Notes (1995) *Basic Call to Consciousness*, Summertown, TN: Book Publishing Company, pp. 18–36; Washinawatok, Ingrid (1997) "International Emergence: Twenty Years at the United Nations", *Native Americas* XIV(2): 13–21.
2. Alfred, Taiaiake and Corntassel, Jeff (2004) *A Decade of Rhetoric for Indigenous Peoples*, available from www.Taiaiake.com.
3. Ibid.
4. Coon Come, Matthew (2002) "Let Us Govern", *Biodiversity: Journal of Life on Earth* 3(3): 31.
5. Mead, Aroha Te Pareake (2002) "Strengthen Our Participation (New Zealand)", *Biodiversity: Journal of Life on Earth* 3(3): 35.
6. Battiste, Marie, ed. (2000) *Reclaiming Indigenous Voice and Vision*, Vancouver: UBC Press; Smith, Linda (1999) *Decolonizing Methodologies: Research and Indigenous Peoples*, London: Zed Books.
7. Laneui, Poka (2000) "Processes of Decolonization", in Marie Battiste, ed., *Reclaiming Indigenous Voice and Vision*, Vancouver: UBC Press, pp. 150–161.
8. Simpson, Leanne (1999) "Traditional Ecological Knowledge: Issues, Insights and Implications", PhD dissertation, University of Manitoba, Canada, unpublished.
9. Ibid.
10. Battiste, Marie and Youngblood Henderson, James Sakej (2000) *Protecting Indigenous Knowledge and Heritage*, Saskatoon: Purich Publishing, p. 11.
11. Ibid., p. 12.
12. Convention on Biological Diversity, Secretariat of the CBD, UN Environment Programme.
13. Mead, Aroha Te Pareake (2004) personal communication, 7 January.
14. Ibid.
15. Mead, Aroha Te Pareake (2004) personal communication, 23 April.
16. UNHCHR (2001) *Leaflet No. 10: Indigenous Peoples and the Environment*, available from www.unhchr.ch/html/racism/indileaflet10.doc.
17. Fortier, Fred (2002) "International Perspectives on Biodiversity", *Biodiversity: Journal of Life on Earth* 3(3): 45.
18. Coon Come, note 4 above.
19. Mulenkei, Lucy (2002) "Increase Our Representation (Kenya)", *Biodiversity: Journal of Life on Earth* 3(3): 30.
20. Fenge, Terry (2003) "POPs and Inuit: Influencing the Global Agenda", in David L. Downie and Terry Fenge, eds, *Northern Lights Against POPs: Combating Toxic Threats in the Arctic*, Montreal: McGill-Queens Press, pp. 192–241; Watt-Cloutier, Sheila (2003) "Inuit Journey Towards a POPs Free World", in David L. Downie and Terry Fenge, eds, *Northern Lights Against POPs: Combating Toxic Threats in the Arctic*, Montreal: McGill-Queens Press, pp. 256–269.

21. For a complete and detailed discussion of this process and the strategy of the Inuit, see Downie, David and Terry Fenge, eds (2003) *Northern Lights Against POPs: Combating Toxic Threats in the Arctic*, Montreal: McGill-Queens Press.
22. Alfred and Corntassel, note 2 above.
23. *Call of the Earth Bulletin*, July 2002, available from www.earthcall.org.
24. Members of the COE Steering Committee include Aroha Te Pareake Mead (co-chair), Alejandro Argumedo (co-chair), Leanne Simpson, Debra Harry, Clark Peteru, Marco Terena, Parshuram Tamang, Robrigo de la Cruz and Jannie Lasimbang.
25. See www.wipo.int/tk/en/index.html.
26. Call of the Earth, Statement at the Fifth Session of the WIPO Intergovernmental Committee on Intellectual Property and Genetic Resources, Traditional Knowledge and Folklore, 8 July 2003.
27. *Call of the Earth Llamado de la Tierra Bulletin*, July 2002.
28. Alfred and Corntassel, note 2 above.
29. Ibid.
30. See www.unpo.org.
31. Alfred and Corntassel, note 2 above.
32. Many of the authors cited in the endnotes would like their nationalities to be known. These authors and their nationalities are detailed below.

Alfred, Taiaiake	Haudenosaunee
Battiste, Marie	Mi'kmaq
Coon Come, Matthew	Cree
Corntassel, Jeff	Cherokee
Fortier, Fred	Shuswap
Laneui, Poka	Hawaiian
Mead, Aroha Te Pareake	Maori
Simpson, Leanne	Anishinaabekwe
Smith, Linda	Tuhiwai
Youngblood Henderson, James Sakej	Chickasaw

Part II
Models

6
Civil society and the World Trade Organization

Kevin R. Gray

Introduction

The World Trade Organization is made up of 148 member states.[1] It is the prototype of an inter-state institution with each member state having one vote. Although there are obvious inequities in such a democratic system, where economic power renders disproportionate influence, decisions are still required to be made by consensus. As such, even the smallest developing country can play a significant role in negotiating new trading rules, if only as an obstructionist state. Perhaps due to this power, it is the last bastion of sovereignty for certain states.[2] Since decision-making is totally within the realm of the member states, the secretariat has little autonomy to alter working procedures substantively, limiting how far it can engage civil society.[3]

The ethos of the international trade system is to liberalise the trade in goods and services. Ironically, the sovereignty of the state is diminished in favour of opening up market access and breaking down trade barriers. The rules of international trade aim to open up such barriers, therefore increasing the availability and quality of goods in the marketplace. Moreover, these rules impact on the ability of states to regulate in the public interest where such governance leads to a violation of trade rules.[4] Such encroachment provides evidence for citizens that the international trading system has directly tangible effects at the level of individuals. Thus, the global trade regime could be seen as the agent, if not the progenitor, of globalisation, which has mobilised citizens to focus their disenchantment on an international institution such as the WTO.

The evolution of the WTO from the General Agreement on Tariffs and Trade (GATT) system has fostered this perception of the WTO's leading role in globalisation. Under GATT, only a few organisations were invited to GATT meetings, such as the International Chamber of Commerce (ICC); the primary route to channel civil society concerns about trade liberalisation was through national mechanisms.[5] Some non-governmental organisations did participate in the conference that drafted the ITO Charter. In fact, the ICC had been working with international bodies of the League of Nations for several years before the ITO Charter.[6] Some specific agreements in the GATT system also allowed for the establishment of councils that provided for cooperation and consultation between governments and NGOs.[7]

The advent of the Uruguay Negotiating Round broadened the international trade mandate and thereby provoked wider NGO interest in areas such as agriculture, development and food safety.[8] Academics joined civil society in calling for a greater democratisation of the GATT decision-making process.[9] In addition, GATT panel decisions came under increasing scrutiny. The Tuna-Dolphin rulings holding that trade bans pursuant to US conservation laws aimed at preventing dolphin by-catches in tuna fishing nets could not be justified under GATT rules. This decision drew strong criticism by environmentalists.[10]

The number of agreements under the WTO umbrella now touches upon several areas of domestic regulation. GATT was essentially a system of consensual reduction of tariffs. Now the WTO Agreements cover areas such as intellectual property, agricultural reform, government procurement and environmental regulation. Moreover, the rules-based system enforced by a strong dispute settlement body has placed the concerns of individuals under a mechanism distant from democratic systems within each member state. As the WTO broadens its mandate, it concurrently becomes more vulnerable to attacks.

The civil society international trade community

Awareness in civil society about the WTO can be traced in part to how trade rules began to encroach upon non-trade areas. Lessons can be drawn from civil society engagement in other areas of international affairs. NGO participation in international policy is entrenched in areas such as human rights[11] and the environment.[12] Many international organisations have included NGOs into their decision-making process, even allowing for NGOs to become "part of their international legal personality".[13] In relation to the environment, this is affirmed in international declarations such as the Johannesburg Declaration and the Rio Declaration.[14] Many Secretariats of multilateral environmental agreements have accredited a large number of NGOs to participate in Conference of the Parties proceedings. The privileges of accreditation provide for open access to all formal sessions and sometimes informal meetings, even being allowed to intervene in discussions upon the invitation of the chair.[15] Civil society has come together to thwart the dominance of some states which aim to confound, if not undermine, the negotiations altogether.[16]

Parallel to these developments, environmental NGOs (ENGOs) serve as an example of civil society actors that have been at the forefront of non-trade movements challenging the international trading system.[17] Trade and environment is one of the various "trade and ..." concerns that have undermined the legitimacy of the WTO in the eyes of civil society. A common perception is that the WTO deprives state legislatures of the necessary policy space in areas such as environmental or health regulation.[18] The Tuna-Dolphin dispute certainly motivated the environmental community into action, seeing the linkages between trade and environment as a realistic problem rather than rooted in abstract predilections. Developments in other areas such as labour rights, intellectual property and investment also generated momentum for civil society to find practical cause in their opposition, thereby stimulating new groups into action that had not previously registered their opposition to trade liberalisation.[19]

In some instances, civil society appears united in questioning the direction of the WTO or the positions of its member states. However, its occasional agreement disguises the wider plurality in the civil society community. Some organisations are supportive of the WTO and even engage in dialogue in order to advance their agenda. Others choose tactics including civil disobedience to show an oppositional front to the WTO. The distinction has been categorised by John Foster in chapter two of this volume as being "insider" or "outsider" groups. In addition, civil society views may differ across issues or across regions – for example, there is often a division between Northern and Southern NGOs.[20] The historical origins of NGOs are essentially Western in orientation, revealing a "missionary character".[21] Having such origins, Northern NGOs may be advocating for greater regulatory space, which can be pitted against the concerns of market access to developed countries, increasingly voiced by numerous civil society organisations (CSOs) from all parts of the globe. Such polarity also exists within some issue- or sector-specific civil society groups.[22]

Thus, civil society represents a wide plurality of interests, or what has been referred to as WTO "cosmopolitanicism".[23] Such interests can shape strategies and advocacy, establishing different roles for engaging with the WTO, from providing information, monitoring state activity and consulting on various committees to lobbying public opinion and street protests. Civil society input has been seen by some to be critical to advancing trade negotiations and therefore lending these greater legitimacy.[24] Civil society has also formed coalitions with other actors, despite having conflicting agendas. For instance, it was common in the United States for environmental groups and industry associations to join together in "green and greedy" coalitions in order to seek protectionist measures from their governments.[25] One does not have to search hard to see the irony of the Korean farmer, Lee Kyung-Hae, who unfortunately took his own life on the streets of Cancun. Many civil society representatives lamented the tragedy and championed his cause despite understanding that he was protesting the potential withdrawal of protectionist government support by the Korean government in the face of further agricultural liberalisation.

External versus internal tensions

Some WTO members symbolically view the institution as a pantheon for sovereign decision-making; this view fuels resistance to open the body to outside interests. The one-vote system serves to empower certain members that may not have such weight in other international venues. For those countries hoping to preserve their influence, civil society participation should be limited, so that it cannot erode state sovereignty.[26] However, WTO members' obstinacy to such participation places strain on the WTO that is attempting to build institutional links with civil society in order to quell criticism about its exclusivity. By making such inroads, the WTO gains legitimacy. In attempting to open up the institution in order to develop better public relations with world citizenry, it is risking estranging itself from the member states.

A commonly held view is that the proper arena for NGO consultation is at the national level, where the implementation of the WTO obligations, a product of national law-making, directly affects the citizenry. There is certainly an important role for opening up dialogue with civil society at the state level, precisely for this reason. However, diverting all civil society participation to the national level discounts the varying levels of acceptance for such participation inside the WTO member states' polities. Moreover, confining civil society participation to the national level is premised on the transparency of the international institution, which in turn informs positions advanced at the national level. However, most WTO negotiations are conducted *in camera*, with public exposure coming well after the meetings have taken place. A focus on national-level participation also leaves little room for transnational NGOs, whose platform is comprised of the international and non-state-specific concerns of the international population.[27] Moreover, it also overlooks the fact that although national decision-making on trade originates in the national capitals, these positions are often modified in the course of negotiations, where trade-offs on national positions are common. This bartering can go unchecked without involvement at the international level. The large number of parties to the WTO intensify the trade-offs made during the process, potentially increasing the number of decisions made without civil society involvement.[28] The democratic deficit emerges at this point in the process, since the reliance upon states to ensure that all goals reflected in the preamble of the WTO Agreement will be guaranteed in a negotiated outcome is misplaced.[29]

There is also a sequential argument against opening up the WTO processes to civil society. Some member states maintain that internal mechanisms for participation should be improved before civil society is granted greater participation privileges. Many WTO members highlight the problems inherent in the WTO itself regarding a lack of transparency and the equality of members. A "club" atmosphere still remains where only a small number of influential governments play any significant role.[30] Since the internal mechanisms are in need of improvement, the time may not be appropriate to allow civil society to have greater access to documents and deeper participation in WTO affairs when WTO members do not have such benefits. This external-internal tension is evident in the arena of dispute settlement. In 2000 the secretariat issued some rules of procedure[31] facilitating the receipt of *amicus curae* briefs, in advance of the consideration by the Appellate Body of the Asbestos panel decision.[32] As party submissions were being prepared and exchanged, the Appellate Body established a procedure for considering briefs by private individuals or groups.[33] This procedure required applicants to respond to a series of questions and to establish how the brief would make a contribution to the dispute not raised by the government parties themselves.

Although this did not prejudge the merit of the submissions, or whether they would be deemed relevant in the dispute by the Appellate Body, it was seen by many members as being outside the authority of the secretariat. The acceptance of *amicus* briefs was viewed as a political decision that could only be made by the member states. An emergency meeting of the General Council was called where several member states expressed their concern. Although the procedures were not annulled, the Appellate Body did not accept any of the *amicus* briefs and gave no reasons for this decision.

The general view was that civil society should not be given greater rights than the member states. Many developing countries are unable, unwilling or simply lack the capacity to bring disputes to the WTO. Considering that the NGOs having the resources and capacity to submit *amicus* briefs would be predominately from the North, opponents argued that the rule would only tip the balance further against developing countries which perceptively suffer from a institutionalised bias in dispute settlement. However, procedural rules in the Dispute Settlement Understanding make it difficult for third party states to participate. In fact, Morocco successfully submitted an *amicus* brief in the EC-Sardines dispute instead of submitting a third-party submission.[34]

WTO institutional mechanisms – Modalities of participation

In its early days the WTO promoted the use of domestic mechanisms to channel the concerns of civil society. It viewed the domestic level as the more appropriate forum, since effective avenues for this form of communication were available in all member states. Slowly, the WTO has begun to augment this view with mechanisms at the international level. It has begun to open up its processes and procedures to civil society. For example, many documents are now available to the public, enhancing the institution's transparency. Overall, the WTO has shown a slow "cautious but steady movement toward more consultation with civil society".[35] This has even had a knock-off effect, opening up decision-making at the national level to processes such as impact assessments[36] and public consultation. Civil society engagement is also formalised in NAFTA under the Commission on Environmental Cooperation,[37] as well as in MERCOSUR through the Economic and Social Advisory Council. CARICOM also has a Civil Society Charter that allows for public participation, including a CARICOM Forum. Several bilateral trade agreements allow for public participation in the development of national environmental laws and policies.[38] Newly forming trade regimes are also providing for civil society engagement in the formation of such regimes. For instance, the Free Trade Agreement of the Americas (FTAA) negotiations included a Committee of Government Representatives for the Participation of Civil Society. The FTAA draft texts were made available and opened up for public comment.[39]

The WTO is not subject to any prescribed rules regarding its relationship with civil society. The Marrakech Agreement did call for "suitable arrangements for consultation and cooperation with NGOs concerned with matters within the scope of the WTO", although no details were added. This provision was based on a similar one from the Charter of the International Trade Organization.[40] Further formalisation of such rules may have a minimal contribution to effective participation.[41] However, the rules would impose specific parameters to confine participation within narrowly construed limits.

Article V(2) of the Marrakech Agreement states that "the General Council may make appropriate arrangements for consultation and cooperation with NGOs concerned with matters related to those of the WTO". In 1996 the General Council approved the Guidelines for Arrangements on Relations with Non-Governmental Organizations.[42] This provided limited authority to establish more direct contact with NGOs through various means such as symposia and briefings.[43] Chairpersons of WTO councils and committees were permitted to meet with NGOs, although they would have to meet in their "personal capacity unless the council or committee decided otherwise".[44] However, the same guidelines noted that NGOs cannot be directly involved in negotiations and that the national level is where the "primary responsibility is for taking into account the different elements of public interest which are brought to bear on trade policy-making".[45]

In 1996 the General Council allowed NGOs to attend the WTO Ministerial Conference. Approximately 108 NGOs were accredited to attend.[46] Attendance was limited to "attending" rather than "observing". Civil society groups were not permitted to make a statement at the Ministerial although there were educational seminars set up outside of the Ministerial. Accreditation is normally given only for ministerial conferences that take place every two to three years rather than councils, committees and other bodies that serve as the ongoing inter-governmental negotiating forums.[47]

Accreditation processes imply some selectivity about who is accredited based on the level of expertise of the organisation or the legitimate interest in the substantive issues.[48] The three minimum criteria applied generally to international institutions for the purpose of accreditation are the accredited organisation must be distinguished from organisations established by inter-governmental agreement; the accredited organisation must be able to establish an expertise or other interest in the subject matter of the institution; and it must demonstrate that it is not part of any government and is free to express independent views.[49] Once accredited, such organisations may soften their criticism of the WTO since the process has opened up channels of communication to the benefit of their advocated positions.[50] Having a demonstrated interest in international trade issues also favours the better-resourced organisations that can afford to send representatives to international meetings and/or produce information material. This could even distort the trade agenda, where certain special interests dominate the decision processes.[51] The presence of civil society at ministerial meetings appears to be increasing, despite the secretariat not providing any funding to assist NGOs in attending meetings.[52]

Another mode of interaction with civil society is the use of public symposia. These were introduced in 1998, with one focusing on trade facilitation and the other on trade, environment and sustainable development. A high-level symposium on environment and development was hosted by the WTO the following year. At that event, a Joint Civil Society Statement called on the WTO to be accountable to parliaments and civil society.[53] Since then, public symposia have been organised by the WTO secretariat, although civil society is given some input into the agenda. There is relatively little participation by the WTO member states. It is unclear if or how the symposia actually impact on negotiated outcomes.

There are several additional ways in which civil society can engage in the development of the WTO system. These modalities of participation can range from participation in negotiations, observership at WTO committee and council meetings, transparency of WTO documents that may allow for opportunities to comment and dispute settlement. Civil society groups can also provide expertise to the WTO, and help inform member states of the issues and possible strategies prior to and during the negotiations. However, documents in the WTO that are under negotiation or discussion are not publicly accessible.[54]

The most effective way for the WTO to maintain its transparency is through its website. Here viewers can see WTO documents, dispute settlement rulings, calendars of meetings and other pertinent information about current activities at the WTO. There is also a specific website devoted to NGO issues. However, despite greater openness by the WTO through such ways as derestricting documents, there has been little direct impact on changes to individual members' positions.[55]

Another conduit for civil society engagement is participation in delegations at WTO ministerial meetings. In some cases this can even include NGOs serving as the sole representative of a state at a WTO meeting.[56] Some states are uncomfortable with the presence of non-state actors in a negotiating setting, disrupting the "sociology" of the discussions.[57] This can facilitate a possible transformation of non-state views into government positions, although it is more likely that the civil society members chosen will not deviate too much from the government positions. Failing to toe the party line can result in marginalisation from the rest of the delegation. However, the breakdown of talks in Cancun in 2003 can be traced to stronger developing country engagement, possibly associated with the provision of advice by NGOs to national delegations.

However, there has been an emergence of coalition-building of developing countries in the WTO, catalysed by civil society initiatives. For instance, organisations like the World Wildlife Fund have been pivotal in getting the fisheries subsidies issue on the negotiating agenda, recruiting numerous countries representing a variety of levels of economic development to push the issues. Similarly, the efforts of Oxfam International can be seen as providing the necessary stimulus for West African countries to call for a sector-specific solution to the problems arising from agricultural subsidies that their cotton farmers face in the international marketplace. Finally, the successful campaigns of securing greater access to medicines under the compulsory licensing provisions of the TRIPs Agreement is primarily the product of a partnership between Northern NGOs and developing countries.

There are very few provisions allowing for direct civil society participation in WTO operations, including monitoring implementation. One of these is provided in the Agreement on Preshipment Inspection:[58] its Independent Entity oversees binding arbitration between exporters and inspection entities. The Independent Entity was established through an agreement with the ICC and the International Federation of Inspection Agencies. Both of these organisations have assisted the WTO in its operational work on pre-shipment inspection. Despite the limited formal role, civil society advocacy performs an unofficial check on implementation.

In the future there may be a larger role for civil society in monitoring implementation. Considering the depth of civil society expertise and its increasing legitimacy as well as the WTO, as an institution, having an interest in being more inclusive, there may be some role in assisting in compliance review. Canada has proposed that the trade policy review mechanisms be opened to accredited observers.[59] In addition to implementation, NGOs can also assist in facilitating the ratification processes in various member states and highlight situations where a county may not be acting consistently with its obligations.

NGOs may also have some impact through standard-setting bodies that contribute to WTO rule-making. NGOs are mentioned in the WTO Agreements with relation to standard-setting under the TBT Agreement. States are obligated to ensure that local government and NGO standardising bodies within their territories accept and comply with the Code of Good Practice.[60] Members are also to take measures that have the effect of directly or indirectly requiring or encouraging such standardising bodies to act in a manner inconsistent with the code. This establishes an indirect obligation for such bodies, although the state is exclusively responsible for its enforcement. NGOs may also sit on ISO standard-setting bodies. For the Codex Alimentarius Commission, country delegations often include representatives of industry, consumers' organisations and academic institutions, in addition to government representatives. A number of international non-governmental organisations also attend as observers.

Overall, there appears to be a divergence between the official mechanisms available to civil society and those activities that have been more effective in practice in allowing civil society to get its messages across. The existing modalities of such participation present limitations to effecting any concrete changes in member state positions. Symposia do not engage WTO members in a substantive fashion. Greater transparency may contribute to a more informed civil society, but the timing of the release of official documents perhaps comes too late to change previously made, and now entrenched, decisions. Although these institutional pathways to the WTO are widening, it is more challenging to discern any real impacts where decision-making is influenced by civil society.

Despite the limited role of formal participation of civil society, there are less tangible (or non-institutional) but equally effective influences that civil society can generate in the WTO. Overall, civil society has heightened the awareness of the concerns by highlighting the wider application of trade rules and their impact on states' ability to regulate. Through political activity, states have responded. In fact, many states are using the data and expertise from civil society to inform their negotiating positions. Readily apparent in Cancun, civil society input and experts have filled in the gaps for some member states which lack the capacity and knowledge to match the prowess of the more developed economies in negotiations. The overall results of the Doha Round are perhaps the best time to reflect on civil society's contribution to the outcome. In the interim, dispute settlement provides a high-profile arena to reveal civil society concerns, offering a venue to critique particular aspects of the international trading system.

Dispute settlement

Dispute settlement is singled out as a particular modality of interest in light of its rapid evolution in the WTO system. The adjudication of disputes at the WTO forms one of the three functions of the WTO: the others are its executive and legislative powers.[61] In contrast to the closed nature of WTO legislative proceedings, dispute settlement provides an avenue for openness and transparency, arguably rendering it, and perhaps the WTO as a whole, more legitimate and acceptable in the eyes of civil society.[62] In turn, some WTO members have agreed to post their submissions on a publicly accessible website.[63]

Civil society has used *amicus* briefs to channel its advocacy efforts, innovatively borrowed largely from public interest litigation tools employed in domestic jurisdictions.[64] These efforts have been duplicated in international legal proceedings.[65] Although the use of *amicus* briefs is not explicitly permitted under the rules of the Dispute Settlement Understanding, therefore constituting a non-institutionalised pathway for civil society, its acceptance by dispute settlement panels and the Appellate Body has transformed the conduit to the WTO, giving it a more institutionalised nature.

Attempting to participate in dispute settlement proceedings mirrors the lobbying efforts of civil society approaching international institutions to launch litigation proceedings.[66] In fact, several claimants in WTO cases can be traced back to efforts by affected groups urging governments to bring cases to the WTO. The use of *amicus* briefs may be effective where the WTO member state is not adequately reflecting the interests of civil society in its submissions.[67] These views may even have direct relevance to the legal questions before the panel, such as consumer tastes and preferences when interpreting the Technical Barriers to Trade Agreement.[68] The civil society groups that engage in the dispute settlement process through instruments such as *amicus* briefs are seen to reflect a broad array of interests, dispelling myths that this practice is predominated by Northern-based NGOs.[69] Moreover, NGOs may strategically see *amicus* briefs as a way to influence institutional changes in the WTO through the adjudicative process, especially where the negotiating outcomes may fall short of civil society aspirations.[70]

There is no prescribed role for civil society under the Dispute Settlement Understanding.[71] Cases are heard in closed proceedings with the availability of submissions resting solely at the discretion of the parties to the dispute. Despite the formal state-to-state model of dispute settlement, panels and the Appellate Body have broadened the role of public participation by recognising their discretion to "seek information and technical advice from any body which it deems appropriate".[72] This includes the admittance of unsolicited *amicus* briefs,[73] as well as correspondence.[74] NGOs have even submitted *amicus* briefs with content relating to their eligibility to submit them.[75] Although the panels and the Appellate Body have the authority to consider the NGO briefs, they are not obliged to accept such submissions. In practice, such briefs are assumed to be reviewed by the Appellate Body judges. In the Shrimp-Turtle dispute the Appellate Body even raised such points in its comments to the parties to the dispute.[76]

As demonstrated in several WTO disputes, *amicus* briefs have been appended to WTO member submissions.[77] Information in such briefs can complement the country claims by providing additional technical, scientific or even policy analysis. Although such opportunities will be limited to civil society organisations that carry a significant amount of influence and corresponding resources, as well as advocating a position similar to the WTO member, this does open up an avenue of participation that could be pursued more often in the future. Even where no *ami-*

cus briefs are submitted, civil society can still be instrumental in the preparation of country positions, elevating their chances for success in WTO litigation.[78]

Many WTO members have concerns regarding the judicial interpretation of the Appellate Body's authority to receive *amicus* briefs. Primarily, many WTO members, mainly developing countries, feel that the WTO as an institution still has inherent barriers concerning its internal transparency, which need to be resolved before questions regarding external transparency can be considered. Giving civil society rights to submit information in the dispute settlement process could result in members having lesser rights in the process. The recent EU-Sugar dispute aggravates this concern since dispute settlement rules regarding confidentiality were applied to an NGO that submitted an *amicus* brief, placing obligations on the NGO corresponding with its rights to participate in dispute settlement.[79] Moreover, many countries in the developing world feared an influx of Northern-driven NGO submissions that would bias the partiality of the adjudicators, guaranteed in a closed inter-state proceeding. As discussed above, the "disconnect" between member states' positions and the institutional need to have a more inclusive dispute settlement system reached a zenith in the Asbestos dispute. Since then, *amicus* briefs have been received, although the decision to admit them rests solely with the panels and the Appellate Body rather than being directed by the WTO secretariat.

Since dispute settlement plays a vital role in the development of the WTO regime, it is inevitable that civil society will further its causes through *amicus* briefs. In fact, the frustration associated with the slow pace of the Doha Round and the lack of success some groups have in attracting attention at the national level could result in a larger number of submissions. More members states should begin to embrace the benefits of having civil society, including business groups, contribute its expertise, buttressing their claims in some cases. This may help to stem the obstinate position of some members which would like to keep dispute settlement an exclusive inter-state affair.

The Cancun Ministerial

This discussion merits a brief review of the 2003 Cancun Ministerial, where negotiations broke down and where civil society was heavily involved. Many countries, both developed and developing, saw a valuable opportunity lost for further international trade talks in the direction of achieving a good result for its citizens. The popular support for a non-outcome at Cancun was not unanimous. However, the absence of any result was also seen as a template for some countries to assert their sovereign muscle, refusing to fall back from their negotiating positions in the face of pressure from other WTO members.

Parallel to the development of a stronger presence of developing countries in negotiations, NGO empowerment, measured by the impact that civil society had on developing country negotiators, was also evident.[80] Civil society certainly featured the highest in numbers at the Cancun Ministerial that were accredited (although many non-accredited NGO representatives were on the outside of the compound).[81] Many NGOs provided free advice to developing countries and opened up a dialogue with WTO members. Many WTO members, in turn, adopted positions that did not differ too much from the claims of civil society.

It is difficult, however, to link civil society participation directly with the lack of result or consensus at Cancun. Entrenched developing country positions were at least informed, if not strongly influenced, by voices of civil society. However, this may overstate civil society's contribution to the collapsed talks. The WTO system is already starting to expose its weaknesses in trying to cover a broad agenda, with many states continually calling for a minimisation of the Doha Round agenda. Two if not three of the Singapore issues (competition, investment and government procurement) were effectively taken off the table in the face of a mandate of the WTO members to agree to the modalities for negotiations in these areas.[82] Adopting a bad deal appeared to be a worse option to not agreeing to anything at Cancun – a sentiment shared by many civil society members. Although any causal relationship between civil society participation and the negotiating outcome is tentative at best, what transpired at the Fifth Ministerial is that both civil society and developing countries emerged as considerable constituencies that had to be accounted for by the stronger economies represented at the WTO.

Conclusions

In order to gain a better understanding of how civil society has in fact transformed the international trading system, and the underlying sovereign-based system, it is important to look at this dichotomy in the overall shifting paradigm in international law and relations. The role of non-state actors has flourished in many areas of multilateral decision-making, each having unique roles in relation to the international system that affords their participation. In turn, this has altered the role of states not so much in their normative significance but in terms of their function and the extent of the power they render.[83] This is consistent with the general "federalisation" in the international order with a wider plurality of participants.[84]

However, the rooted inter-state system in the WTO imposes an artificial barrier to any real and effective role for civil society. Although some progress has been made in making the WTO more transparent and inclusive in terms of process, the question remains whether such cosmetic changes can ultimately overcome the "disenfranchisement" of civil society.[85] If states remain as the dominant actors in the system, it will be hard pressed to remedy the "democracy deficit".[86] The institutional mechanisms within the WTO that are available to civil society may secure piecemeal gains. This complements the mainstream techniques of civil society activities aimed to publicise issues, name and shame governments and generally raise the public profile of issues that normally reside behind closed doors. Efforts at the national level can parallel the use of such techniques in Geneva, bringing forth changes in members' negotiating positions.[87]

As the institutional response by international organisations to civil society participation loosely tracks the transformation of international relations, including the horizontal and vertical growth in the number of actors engaged in its development, civil society will continue to play an essential role. Incidentally, the institutions themselves become more transparent.[88] The concerns of civil society are already addressed by member states through consultations at the national level. *Amicus* briefs will be seen as a viable way to influence the judicial development of WTO law and therefore more civil society actors will take advantage of the opportunity.

Ultimately, such evolution can be viewed as an agent for eroding the sovereignty-based WTO system. However, sovereignty is already under threat by international trading rules that have tangible effects on the ability to govern in the public interest. Policy space is never more important than in the current contemporary climate. Where civil society can be co-opted to assist in defence of this, this may strengthen state efforts in this regard. Reflexively, civil society can have legitimacy justifying its presence at the negotiating table.

Acknowledgements

The author would like to thank Jessica Green, Richard Tarasofsky and Steve Charnovitz for their comments. The views expressed in the chapter, including any errors or omissions, are entirely those of the author.

Notes

1. As of October 13, 2004; see www.wto.org/english/thewto_e/whatis_e/tif_e/org6_e.htm.
2. Some critics in the academic world have questioned the idea of sovereignty as being an outdated concept in the contemporary reality of international relations. See Jackson, John H. (2003) "Sovereignty Modern – A New Approach to an Outdated Concept", *American Journal of International Law* 97(4): 782–802.
3. For the purpose of this chapter, the term civil society is intended to refer to the conglomerate of diverse interests and organisations that are not states. This can include NGOs, business groups, religious institutions and industry associations. However, a majority of the literature on the topic does examine the civil society – WTO relationship from the perspective of NGOs which arguably, due to lesser financial resources and access to decision-makers, have less influence over WTO member state positions than their business and industry counterparts. This could be offset, however, by the powers civil society wields over public opinion. See Shaffer, G. C. (2001) "The World Trade Organization under Challenge: Democracy and the Law and Politics of the WTO's Treatment of Trade and Environment Matters", *Harvard Environmental Law Review* 25: 1–93.
4. This not only applies to direct violations but also measures that nullify or impair the benefits of the international trading rules. See article XXIII of the General Agreement on Tariffs and Trade (hereinafter GATT).
5. Jackson, John (1969) "Private Citizen and GATT Obligations", in J. Jackson, ed., *World Trade and the Law of the GATT*, Indianapolis: Bobbs-Merrill Company. For a general historical account of NGO participation in the GATT system, see Charnovitz, S. and Wickham, J. (1995) "Non-Governmental Organizations and the Original International Trade Regime", *Journal of World Trade* 29(5): 111–122.
6. See Ridgeway, G. L. (1938) *Merchants of Peace: Twenty Years of Business Diplomacy through the International Chamber of Commerce, 1919–1938*, New York: ICC.
7. See *Arrangement Regarding Bovine Meat* (1979), GATT B.I.S.D. (26th Supp.) at 84 and *International Dairy Arrangement* (1979) GATT B.I.S.D. (26th supp.) at 96.
8. Charnovitz, Steve (2000) "Opening the WTO to Non-Governmental Interests", *Fordham International Law Journal* 24: 173–216.
9. See Roth-Arriaza, N. (1992) "Precaution, Participation, and the 'Greening' of International Trade Law", *Journal of Environmental Law & Litigation* 7(57): 92–98; Housman, R. F. (1994) "Democratizing International Trade Decision-Making", *Cornell International Law Journal* 27(3): 699–749. Such calls were also echoed after the advent of the WTO. See Shell, G. R. (1995) "Trade Legalism and International Relations Theory: An Analysis of the World Trade Organization", *Duke Law Journal* 44: 829–907; Charnovitz, Steve (1996) "Participation of Non-governmental Organizations in the World Trade Organization", *University of Pennsylvania Journal of Economic Law* 7: 331–357. For an opposing view, see Nichols, P. M. (1996) "Realism, Liberalism, Values, and the World Trade Organization", *University of Pennsylvania Journal of Economic Law* 17: 295; Nichols, P. M. (1996) "Extension of Standing in World Trade Organization Disputes to Non-government Parties", *University of Pennsylvania Journal of Economic Law* 17: 295–330.
10. *United States – Restrictions on Imports of Tuna*, GATT B.I.S.D. 39S/155 (3 September 1991). See Jackson, John H. (1992) "World Trade Rules and Environmental Policies: Congruence or Conflict?", *Washington & Lee Law Review* 49: 1227–1278.
11. NGOs are given an opportunity to consult with the UN Economic and Social Council pursuant to article 71 of the UN Charter. See resolution 1996/31 (49th plenary meeting 27 July 1996). For general information regarding civil society participation in the human

rights sphere, see Otto, D. (1996) "Non-Governmental Organizations in the United Nations System: The Emerging Role of International Civil Society", *Human Rights Quarterly* 18: 107–141.
12. See Oberthür, Sebastian (2003) "Participation of Non-Governmental Organisations in International Environmental Governance", in R. A. Kraemer and S. Müller-Kraenner, eds, *Ecologic Briefs on International Relations and Sustainable Development*, Berlin: Ecologic; Raustiala, Kal (1997) "The Participatory Revolution in International Environmental Law", *Harvard Environmental Law Review* 21: 537–586; Sands, Philippe (1992) "The Role of Environmental NGOs in International Environmental Law", *Journal of the Society for International Development* 2: 28–32.
13. See Charnovitz, Steve (1997) "Two Centuries of Participation: NGOs and International Governance", *University of Michigan Journal of International Law* 18(2): 183–286.
14. See points 26 and 31 of the Johannesburg Declaration, chapter XI of the WSSD Plan of Implementation, principle 10 of the Rio Declaration and chapter 27 of Agenda 21. See also Organization of American States (2001) *Inter-American Strategy for the Promotion of Public Participation in Decision-making for Sustainable Development*, Washington: OAS, available from www.ispnet.org.ISPpubl/EngPolicyFramew.pdf.
15. See Oberthür, note 12 above. For instance, article 15 of the Basel Convention grants direct access with observer status to negotiating sessions and Conferences of the Parties for any national or international organisation, governmental or non-governmental, with competence in the field of hazardous wastes. The Convention on Biological Diversity (1992) has created the clearing-house that facilitates public access to information.
16. See Foster, this volume, discussing the role of civil society organisations that showed great effort to unite other states and disseminate information in the face of mounting opposition by the United States during the negotiations to the Cartagena Protocol on Biosafety. See also Egziabher, T. (2000) "Civil Society and the Cartagena Protocol on Biosafety", in P. Brown and A. Simard, eds, *Promoting Human Security: Civil Society Influence*, Montreal: FIM.
17. This certainly does not negate the importance of other issues the civil society organisations rally around. As the Doha Development Round has moved on to the agricultural and developmental agenda, newer organisations are emerging that focus primarily, and quite effectively, on these concerns.
18. Shaffer, note 3 above.
19. Esty, Dan (1994) *Greening the GATT: Trade, Environment and the Future*, Washington, DC: Institute for International Economics.
20. Although North-South interests will not be so easily divisible, there are certain key trade issues that will be more likely to drive geo-political divisions such as trade and environment or even NGO participation in dispute settlement. See Shaffer, note 3 above.
21. Thürer, Daniel (1998) "The Emergence of Non-Governmental Organizations and Transnational Enterprises in International Law and the Changing Role of the State", in R. Hoffman, ed., *Non-State Actors as New Subjects of International Law: International Law – From the Traditional State Order Towards the Law of the Global Community*, Proceedings of an International Symposium of the Kiel Wlather-Schücking-Institute of International Law, 25–28 March, Kiel: Duncker and Humblot, p. 41.
22. For instance, business interests can include advocates for greater liberalisation or stronger protectionism.
23. Charnovitz, Steve (2001) "WTO Cosmopolitics", *NYU Journal of International Law and Politics* 34: 299–354.
24. See Esty, Dan (1998) "Non-governmental Organizations at the World Trade Organization: Cooperation, Competition or Exclusion", *Journal of International Economic Law* 1: 123–148.

25. See DeSombre, Elizabeth (1995) "Baptists and Bootleggers for the Environment: The Origins of United States Unilateral Sanctions", *Journal of Environment and Development* 4: 53–75.
26. For a conflicting view see Slaughter, Anne Marie (2004) *A New World Order*, Princeton: Princeton University Press.
27. See Esty, note 24 above, and Charnovitz, note 23 above.
28. Professor Kal Raustiala notes that rules and processes should be adjusted to allow for interest groups to get involved in decision-making as the locus of such decision-making is increasingly shifting upwards. See Raustiala, K. (2000) "Sovereignty and Multilateralism", *Chicago Journal of International Law* 1: 416.
29. See Charnovitz, note 8 above.
30. See Keohane R. and Nye J. S. Jr (2001) "Between Centralization and Fragmentation: The Club Model of Multilateral Cooperation and Problems of Democratic Legitimacy", John F. Kennedy School of Government Faculty Research Working Paper Series, Kennedy School of Government Working Paper No. -1-004, available from http://papers.ssrn.com/paper.taf?abstract_id=262175.
31. The procedure allowed for "any person, whether natural or legal, other than a party or a third party to the dispute, wishing to file a written brief" being invited to apply.
32. Civil society has also been given the opportunity to submit *amicus curae* briefs in other judicial forums such as in the areas of investment disputes pursuant to chapter 11 of NAFTA. See *Methanex Corporation* v. *United States of America*, Decision of the Tribunal on Petitions from Third Persons to Intervene as "Amicus Curiae", 15 January 2001.
33. See *European Communities – Measures Affecting Asbestos and Asbestos – Containing Products*, Communication from the Appellate Body, WT/DS135/9 (20 November 2000).
34. Some commentators have claimed that the Appellate Body was required to accept the submission from Morocco since by not doing so, it would be accrediting private parties who had submitted *amicus* briefs greater participatory rights. See Shaffer, G. and Mosoti, V. (2002) "Ec Sardines: A New Model for Collaboration in Dispute Settlement?", *BRIDGES* 6(7): 15–16, 22.
35. Segger, M. C. and Caberra, J. (2004) "Sustainability Smoke Signals? Strengthening Public Participation, Access to Information and Access to Justice in Americas Regimes", unpublished paper on file with the author.
36. See Government of Canada (2004) *Canada's Environmental Assessment Framework for Trade Negotiations*, available from www.dfait-maeci.gc.ca/tna-nac/backgrounder-en.asp.
37. The North American Agreement on Environmental Cooperation provides for an access to information process including specific reports about the state of the environment that have to be made public. The Council must also hold public meetings in all of its ordinary sessions and consult with NGOs in decision-making processes. See arts. 2, 9. In addition, the Commission may compile a fact-finding record that can be requested by civil society groups.
38. See Canada-Costa Rica Environmental Cooperation Agreement, art. 1(d). The bilateral trade agreement between Chile and the United States establishes an Environmental Affairs Council pursuant to chapter 19 on the environment.
39. The FTAA Committee of Government Representatives on Civil Society has created an open and permanent invitation to civil society to provide written submissions on issues of relevance to the FTAA. Ironically, the current text does not allow for NGO participation in the dispute settlement system. For a good analysis of civil society in the FTAA negotiations process, see Segger and Caberra, note 35 above.
40. See Havana Charter for the International Trade Organization.
41. Oberthür, note 12 above.
42. Decision adopted by the General Council on 18 July 1996, WT/L/.162 (23 July 1996).

43. Ibid., para. 4.
44. Ibid., para. 5.
45. Ibid., para. 6.
46. These groups comprised (in descending order of overall numbers) businesses, development, environment, labour and other assorted interest groups. See (1996) *Final Statistics of the First WTO Ministerial Conference in Singapore: Non-Governmental Organizations (NGOs)*, available from www.wto.org/english/forums_e/ngo_e/statsi_.htm.
47. See ICTSD (1999) *Accreditation Schemes and Other Arrangements for Public Participation in International Fora: A Contribution to the Debate on WTO and Transparency*, Geneva: ICTSD.
48. See ibid. The controversial nature of the accreditation system is seen in other international institutions such as the UN ECOSOC. See Alston, J. D. (2001) "The United Nations Committee on Non-Governmental Organizations: Guarding the Entrance to a Politically Divided House", *European Journal of International Law* 12(5): 943–962.
49. See Oberthür, note 12 above.
50. See Keohane, R. O. and Nye, J. S. Jr (2000) "The Club Model of Multilateral Cooperation and the WTO: Problems of Democratic Legitimacy", available from www.ksg.harvard.edu/cbg/trade/papers.
51. See Esty, Dan (1999) *Why the World Trade Organization Needs Environmental NGOs*, Geneva: ICTSD.
52. By contrast, the secretariat of the UN Convention to Combat Desertification (CCD) and the Global Environmental Facility has granted money for participation in the CCD negotiations. See Oberthür, note 12 above, p. 12.
53. *Joint Civil Society Statement on the WTO High-Level* Symposia, March 1999, available at www.globalpolicy.org/cosecon/bwi-wto/wto99-2.htm.
54. By contrast, the FTAA trade ministers devoted six paragraphs to the topic of transparency and civil society participation. The Committee on Government Representatives on the Participation of Civil Society is to make recommendation to the Trade Negotiations Committee "on the means to broaden the mechanism for disseminating information on the discussions, drawing upon the experiences of countries for distributing information to their civil societies".
55. Shaffer, note 3 above.
56. A representative of the Foundation of International Environmental Law and Development, a London-based NGO, represented the government of Sierra Leone at a meeting of the Committee on Trade and Environment. For an account of the experiences of FIELD lawyer Beatrice Chaytor, see Chaytor, B. (2000) "Cooperation between Governments and NGOs: The Case of Sierra Leone in the CTE", in P. Konz, ed., *Trade, Environment and Sustainable Development: Views from Sub-Saharan Africa and Latin America: A Reader*, Tokyo: UNU/IAS.
57. See Foster, this volume.
58. WTO Agreement on Preshipment Inspection, annex 1A, art. 4, 1994.
59. See *External Transparency*, informal paper by Canada, WT/GC/W/415 (17 October 2000).
60. Article 4.1, Technical Barriers to Trade Agreement.
61. Charnovitz, note 8 above.
62. Cottier, T. (1998) "The WTO and Environmental Law: Three Points for Discussion", in A. Fijalkowski and J. Cameron, eds, *Trade and Environment: Bridging the Gap*, London: Cameron May.
63. For instance, the United States regularly posts its submissions on the USTR website.
64. See Charnovitz, note 8 above. See also Shaffer, note 3 above; Shelton, D. (2000) "The

Participation of Non-governmental Organizations in International Judicial Proceedings", *American Journal of International Law* 88: 611–642.
65. In the ICJ nuclear test case (ICJ Reports 288, 1995), NGOs prepared draft pleadings for New Zealand. Found in Sands, Philippe (2003) *Principles of International Environmental Law*, Cambridge: Cambridge University Press, p. 199.
66. For instance, civil society strongly lobbied for the World Health Organization's request for an advisory opinion on the legality of the use of nuclear weapons before the International Court of Justice.
67. One of the *amicus* briefs in the present GMO dispute at the WTO was partly motivated by dissatisfaction with the defence raised by the European Union.
68. See the appended letter from UK Consumers' Association to the Peruvian complaint in the EU-Sardines dispute. In that dispute, the panel explicitly noted that they considered the letter in determining what European consumers associate with the term "sardines". At the Appellate Body, the letter was affirmed as an appropriate piece of evidence for the panel to consider.
69. For instance, one of the *amicus* briefs submitted in the GMO dispute was made by a consortium of both Northern- and Southern-based NGOs. In the EU-Sardines dispute a Northern NGO (UK Consumers' Association) submitted a brief that was attached to the developing country complainant's pleadings, arguing that the EU narrow classification of what are sardines acted against the economic and information interests of Europe's consumers. See Shaffer and Mosoti, note 34 above.
70. See Robertson, D. (2000) "Civil Society and the WTO", *World Economy* 23: 1127.
71. See WTO Agreement, Understanding on Rules and Procedures Governing the Settlement of Disputes, annex 3, 1994.
72. Article 13.1, Dispute Settlement Understanding.
73. Whereas in the Shrimp-Turtle dispute, the *amicus* briefs were attached to the US briefs qualifying them as being within the Appellate Body's ambit of consideration, in *United States – Imposition of Countervailing Duties on Certain Hot-Rolled Lead and Bismuth Carbon Steel Products Originating in the United Kingdom (Carbon Steel)*, Report of the Appellate Body, WT/DS138/AB/R (10 May 2000), the Appellate Body held that it had the authority to accept the NGOs briefs directly from the petitioner NGO when the information is "pertinent and useful". However, in that case, the Appellate Body concluded that it was not necessary to take the two briefs into account.
74. In *Australia – Measures Affecting Importation of Salmon, Recourse to Article 21.5*, Report of the Panel, WT/DS18/RW, para. 7.8 (18 February 2000), the compliance review panel accepted a letter from the concerned Fishermen and processors in South Australia.
75. See the Shrimp-Turtle Appellate Body proceedings, which included an American appeal of the panel decision regarding their lack of authority to consider NGO briefs. *United States – Import Prohibitions of Certain Shrimp and Shrimp Products*, Report of the Appellate Body, WT/DS58/AB/R (12 October 1998).
76. See Charnovitz, note 8 above. Some of those arguments even appeared in the rulings themselves.
77. For example, see the Shrimp-Turtle and EU-Sardines disputes.
78. See Shaffer, G. (2003) *Defending Interests: Public-Private Partnerships in WTO Litigation*, Washington, DC: Brookings Institute Press.
79. See EU-Sugar (2004). In turn, the application of dispute settlement rules to non-state actors creates a horizontal relationship between states and civil society in terms of the dispute settlement process.
80. Primack, D. and Bilal, S. (2004) "The Journey from Cotonou to Cancun, and Beyond:

The Changing Dynamics of WTO and EPA Negotiations", *Trade Negotiations Insights* 3(1): 1–5.
81. The number of accredited NGOs in Doha was limited, due to spatial concerns as well as concerns with security in the post-11 September environment. The Seattle Ministerial accredited 686 NGOs.
82. This has been confirmed by the WTO members in the July Package agreed to in July 2004. Despite this result, the contributions of civil society towards that outcome are difficult to gauge, especially in light of the strict party-to-party discussions leading up to the July Package. See Public Citizen (2004) "Public Citizen Condemns Process, Outcome of Geneva WTO Framework Talks", available at www.citizen.org/pressroom/release.cfm?ID=1759.
83. Thürer, note 21 above.
84. Schreuer, C. (1993) "The Waning of the Sovereign State: Towards a New Paradigm for International Law", *European Journal of International Law* 4: 447.
85. Disenfranchisement is defined by J. F. Green as "being deprived of the capability to participate and to influence agenda-setting and decision-making in international regimes for sustainable development". See Green, J. F. (2004) *Engaging the Disenfranchised: Developing Countries and Civil Society in International Governance for Sustainable Development – An Agenda for Research*, UNU-IAS Report, Tokyo: United Nations University.
86. Keohane, and Nye, note 50 above. Some argue that moving the WTO from an "intergovernmental model" to a "civil society/stakeholder model" is fraught with similar power imbalances between the diverse members of civil society. See Shaffer, note 3 above.
87. See Shaffer, note 3 above. *Review* 25: 1–93.
88. This has certainly been the case with multilateral environmental agreements such as CITES. See Sands, P. and Bedecarré, A. (1990) "Convention on International Trade in Endangered Species: The Role of Public Interest Non-Governmental Organizations in Ensuring the Enforcement of the Ivory Trade Ban", *Boston College Environmental Affairs Law Review* 17: 799.

7
The politics of inclusion in the Monterrey Process

Barry Herman

"It happened in Monterrey ... in old Mexico".[1]

The UN International Conference on Financing for Development (FfD) in Monterrey, Mexico in March 2002 was unprecedented. It brought together key economic and political decision-makers, including more than 50 heads of state and over 200 ministers of finance, foreign affairs, development and trade. They were joined by the heads of the United Nations, the International Monetary Fund (IMF), the World Bank and the World Trade Organization (WTO), and by the chairs of the major inter-governmental committees that deal with international financial issues, including the Financial Stability Forum (whose chair was also president of the Bank for International Settlements), the Group of 10 (the major developed countries in monetary and financial affairs), the Group of 20 (major developed and "systemically important" developing countries) and the Group of 24 (the caucus of developing countries at the Bretton Woods institutions).

The heads of the major regional development banks and other development finance organisations or their representatives also participated, as did all the relevant UN specialised agencies, funds and programmes. They were joined by prominent individuals from the world of business and finance and by a range of civil society leaders, including Jimmy Carter, a former president of the United States. In short, this was the largest and most diverse gathering of officials and other stakeholders ever to have met at such a senior level on international financial matters. Also unique, for the most part, they actually talked to each other.[2]

Throughout the period since the end of the Second World War, international decisions on monetary, financial, trade and development matters have been made in multilateral forums, albeit ones limited to a few countries or a restricted range of issues, and usually behind closed doors. The Monterrey Process invited all countries to come and consider the issues together, in public and with non-governmental stakeholders watching and speaking. It turned out to be the right mechanism at the right moment.

As will be described here, however, it took five years to build sufficient confidence among the relevant decision-makers for them to agree to participate in the Monterrey Process. Even with that, real-world events helped propel them beyond their standard forums and processes. When the 9/11 tragedy raised the urgency of making a sincere global political gesture for development, the gathering momentum and interest in the Monterrey Process of governments, international institutions, private sector and civil society organisations provided a compelling opportunity.

Diplomats at the United Nations had successfully paved the way by developing a new modality of informal international discussions for consensus-building and by getting it accepted as the approach to use in preparing the Monterrey Process. The United Nations can be the most rigid and stale inter-governmental forum, routinely discouraging initiative and good will. But it can also be a flexible tool for international convergence when the situation warrants it and enough actors recognise it, as happened in FfD.

This chapter will seek to demonstrate that Monterrey was a departure from the norm in several ways. First, the conference was the initiative of developing countries whose main message to the developed countries was something like "this time it's serious and we can reach a deal to do better". Over time, they convinced sceptical governments of developed countries, not to mention the leadership of the World Bank and other institutions, to take a chance on the United Nations. This was central.

The FfD preparatory process was also unusual in that the standard UN negotiating practices on economic and social affairs, under which so little is usually accomplished, were held in abeyance through most of the Monterrey preparations. Moreover, while civil society organisations that advocate on financial issues usually avoid the United Nations as irrelevant for their issues, several of them decided to engage in New York and, in doing so, enriched the process. So too did a number of Wall Street emerging market professionals and some private sector organisations that saw something special happening at the United Nations. In both sets of non-governmental stakeholders, forms of engagement with governmental representatives were tried out that were simply not available in any other international financial and trade forum.

More than four years have passed since Monterrey and, as the chapter will also argue, the future of the process has become uncertain. The Monterrey Consensus adopted at the conference – if not every paragraph – remains an effective point of reference in the Bretton Woods institutions and in donor government forums, where finance and development assistance ministries meet and make policy. However, in the UN bodies responsible for the follow-up to Monterrey, the sense of mission and political innovation that characterised the FfD process has weakened, allowing the standard maggoty politics of the United Nations to feed on its body. Yet FfD can have a future as the unique process that it was. It requires a new concurrence of the factors that were responsible for its initial success.

What Monterrey delivered in policy reform

The central feature of the Monterrey Process was that it dared to reach for agreement with political commitment – not just a paper text – on a new North-South understanding on what UN delegates referred to as the "hard" issues of international trade and monetary, financial and development policy. All through the 1990s the United Nations had been a forum for agreement on the "soft" issues such as the rights of children, social development, gender equality, population policy and environmental sustainability, albeit too often only at the level of principles and broad intentions rather than concrete actions. In 2000 some of these intentions were brought together and codified into specific targets to be achieved by 2015 in the Millennium Declaration of the General Assembly (adopted as Resolution 55/2), following an unprecedented gathering of heads of state in New York as the Millennium Summit. However, even this kind of political event was a far cry from what FfD had proposed, i.e. turning the United Nations into a serious political forum on financial matters.

Some argue that the Monterrey Consensus never delivered the concrete advances promised on financing for development. However, certain real political commitments were made at Monterrey, if not necessarily as many or as deep as some observers might have wished. Also, not all of these commitments are leading to significant real changes in policy. After all, Monterrey did not and could not overturn actual power relations. However, it did forge political alliances that increased opportunities for some important reforms.

The reform that has received most attention is the reversing of the decade-long decline in official development assistance (ODA). The Millennium Declaration had been a grand commitment, but there was little money behind it. One of the contentious points in the negotiations of the Monterrey Consensus was what to say about increasing aid. In the end, a fairly non-committal text was adopted: "We recognise that a substantial increase in ODA and other resources will be required." A separate paragraph referred to the UN target for donor governments to give ODA equivalent to 0.7 per cent of their gross national product,[3] which was more than three times the actual figure in 2001 (0.22 per cent). In fact, no stronger consensus text was possible and Japan has continued to cut back its aid effort in the years since Monterrey. Nevertheless, overall ODA measured in constant prices and exchange rates has risen 11 per cent in the two years since the conference and is projected to rise a further 25 per cent by 2006, based on existing commitments.[4]

Several individual commitments to raise ODA were made in 2002 in the context of the Monterrey conference.[5] In the case of the United States and the European Union, there seemed to be a "bidding war" in early 2002, as the first announcement by US President George Bush was followed later by an explanation that in effect raised the pledged amount when it seemed small next to the EU commitment at its Barcelona meeting. It should be noted that in both Europe and the United States, civil society advocates had been pressing for the aid increases and should receive a significant amount of the credit for realising them. On the other hand, translating the commitments into cash in each case requires continued pressure on national governments, and far more resources are needed than have been pledged thus far.[6]

In this context, the agreement in the Consensus on "staying engaged" for an effective follow-up contained an interesting feature, in that it explicitly recognised the need for a "global information campaign" to continue to press countries to help reach for the Millennium Development Goals.[7] This effort is being implemented through the MDG Campaign Unit of the UN Development Programme. "Staying engaged" also gave a fresh impetus to reform of the UN inter-governmental machinery, in particular as it concerned the General Assembly's Economic and Financial Committee ("Second Committee") and the Economic and Social Council (ECOSOC). Governments had decided in Monterrey that the follow-up should be undertaken using the existing inter-governmental machinery, which could mean duplicating some of the existing work in these bodies or consolidating different efforts under FfD. Thus far, however, there has been no consolidation of secretariat reporting or of inter-governmental discussion and the effort may end up stillborn.[8]

The Monterrey Process also sought to reform inter-governmental processes outside the United Nations, with the aim of making them more democratic. Here, as in the case of aid noted above, the text adopted in the Monterrey Consensus looks weak. The relevant paragraph pertaining to the major institutions and forums began, "A first priority is to find pragmatic and innovative ways to further enhance the effective participation of developing countries and countries with economies in transition in international dialogues and decision-making processes." Subsequent sentences then addressed specific institutions and bodies, more or less following the model of the one addressed to the IMF and the World Bank, namely "to continue to enhance participation of all developing countries and countries with economies in transition in their decision-making".[9]

The commitment to address the issue embodied consensus recognition that there was a problem in institutional governance. However, the consensus did not extend to how to fix it. On the plus side, the governance issue entered the agenda of the Development Committee the September following the Monterrey meeting. The committee is a joint forum of ministerial-level governors of the IMF and the World Bank, and it set both institutions into active motion on the issue. So far, as might have been expected, only marginal improvements have been agreed. These reflect an obvious need that is also easy to satisfy to strengthen the overwhelmed offices of the executive directors for sub-Saharan Africa through "capacity-building" assistance.[10]

Moreover, a higher-level ministerial grouping, the International Monetary and Financial Committee (IMFC) of the IMF, has acknowledged the deep political importance of the issue, as in its 24 April 2004 communiqué it says, "The IMF's effectiveness and enhanced credibility as a cooperative institution also depends on all members having appropriate voice and representation. Efforts should continue to be made to enhance the capacity of developing and transition countries to participate more effectively in IMF decision-making."[11]

The central obstacle to addressing the problem is that a few small developed countries have to move aside to let certain large developing countries take their seats on the executive boards of the institutions so as to reflect international economic realities better. In addition, as became clear during the selection of the new managing director of the IMF in March and April 2004, it is impossible to continue to justify the informal arrangements by which a European is always elected managing director of the IMF and a US national always heads the World Bank. Monterrey, as an inter-governmental initiative led by developing countries, raised the visibility of the governance issues of representation and transparency, and while that did not solve the problems, it did help put them into play politically.

Monterrey also provided an opportunity to give further political impetus to international cooperation on some of the donor-advocated domestic policies, such as better confronting corruption. In this case, the genuine interest expressed by civil society, business and governmental representatives in Monterrey helped speed the successful conclusion of negotiations that had already started on a treaty to combat corruption. The UN Convention against Corruption was agreed on schedule and opened for signature in December 2003. When it enters into force it will criminalise a number of corrupt practices, add protections for "whistle-blowers", establish rules for freezing illicit assets and otherwise strengthen cooperation between states. It will also make it more difficult to hide illicit gains and help developing countries recover their stolen assets.[12] The proof will, of course, be in the implementation, but the quick launch and the broad support at high levels are encouraging.

Again, what Monterrey provided was an opportunity for policy reform that may or may not be captured. In some cases, however, it appears that the critics are correct that there were no significant new commitments to even consider reform underneath the words that had recognised the need to do so. For example, the Consensus called on the WTO "to ensure that any consultation is representative of its full membership".[13] One of the difficulties that emerged at the WTO Cancun Ministerial Meeting in September 2003 was that developing countries were seriously disappointed in how few of their views were reflected in post-consultation negotiation texts. This frustration seems to have been an impetus to the "galvanising of developing countries into issue-based coalitions [which] has led to conclusions about their latent empowerment, and also to concerns about North-South polarisation".[14] Nevertheless, recent developments suggest that developed countries in the WTO are hearing more clearly the concerns and voices of developing countries in the give and take of negotiations. This is not to say that the final negotiated outcome will make the "Doha Agenda" into a "Development Round", but there is today more serious engagement by developed country trade policy negotiators on developing country concerns.

In short, Monterrey gave political credibility to some of the global governance demands of developing countries, while also providing a forum in which governments of developed countries could respond to public pressure at home by collectively committing to enhance development cooperation. Developed countries also extracted pledges from developing country governments to handle their own development requirements more effectively. These pledges were relatively easy for the latter to make, as the substantive points had already been agreed, for example, in the New Partnership for Africa's Development (NEPAD) for the Africans. However, the commitments by all developing countries in coming to Monterrey and embracing the Consensus provided a handle that the multilateral institutions could use to press the donor governments for additional aid funds and that the donor governments, in turn, could take to their legislatures.

How the Monterrey Process evolved

If in March 2002 the Monterrey conference became an important political forum on international financial issues, few would have believed it possible when the process began in 1997.[15] Unlike some other UN conferences that began with the intention of holding a global summit, governments did not have any agreed vision of what they were inventing. Certainly, few delegates expected that it would become a summit meeting and several expected it would collapse, as had a number of failed initiatives to launch a round of "global negotiations" on development at the United Nations. Indeed, FfD succeeded because it began as a vague notion and opportunistically evolved over time into an increasingly precise project.

The starting point for understanding the history of FfD is seeing it in the context of the general impotence of the UN General Assembly as a global policy-making institution. As there is no global government, there is no obligation on the powerful countries to share decision-making with the weak except on those occasions when the cooperation of the weak is essential for the decisions to have effect. In those cases, the powerful may offer to take up an issue through the United Nations and the *quid pro quo* is that the weak participate with the strong in making the decisions. Monterrey was a case in point.

In FfD an additional problem was that delegations to UN bodies are drawn from foreign ministries, which have no responsibility for international financial matters (except for development assistance in a number of donor countries). As foreign ministries were unlikely to be given responsibility over the content of FfD, they would have to build new working relationships at home in their capitals with their brethren in finance.[16] In many cases, this was no small undertaking. At one time foreign ministers may have had primacy in the cabinets of government leaders, but in the globalising 1990s finance ministers were usually the most senior ministers. More than that, diplomacy at the United Nations was generally not regarded as very important, except with respect to the Security Council, and FfD had no relationship to that portfolio.

The United Nations does undertake a number of development assistance activities and is a forum in which political commitments on aid can be made, such as the famous aid target of 0.7 per cent of gross national product. However, when the donor governments want to make a joint policy decision they do so in their own forum, the Development Assistance Committee of the Organization for Economic Cooperation and Development, or in the World Bank or the Development Committee, where the developed countries control a clear majority of votes (if votes ever need to be taken). By the same token, international financial policy decisions are reached in the IMF, where developed countries also control the decisions, or in developed country forums, such as the Paris Club for deciding on developing country relief from obligations to official government creditors, or in specialised financial institutions like the Bank for International Settlements or the regulatory oversight committees that it services. An even more limited forum largely guides coherence in all these financial areas, namely the finance ministers of the Group of 7 major industrialised countries (sometimes also the Group of 8 at summit level, when it includes the Russian Federation).

And yet the United Nations has always held an attraction to governments as the world's main political forum. The General Assembly is the place that most heads of state want to address, not the annual meetings of the IMF and the World Bank. Indeed, the heads of the IMF and the World Bank have addressed ECOSOC annually since its early years. This is a relatively safe venue in that ECOSOC is a coordinating body and not a potential instruction-giving body. The General Assembly is in theory the senior inter-governmental deliberative body and potentially could interfere in decisions of the Fund and Bank, except that agreements had been signed in the early years of the United Nations saying that the General Assembly would not interfere in the decision-making at either Bretton Woods institution (or the WTO and its predecessor, the General Agreement on Tariffs and Trade).

So the central challenge that UN delegates had to face in FfD was to bring the finance ministries and other relevant officials into a UN process and engage the institutions they oversee in a serious way. More than just serve as a place to make a speech, Monterrey did just that. The official sessions in Monterrey comprised typical opportunities for set speeches by leaders or ministers in plenary, while the President of Mexico also hosted a private leaders-only meeting. More interestingly, several days were devoted to informal roundtable discussions, first at ministerial level and then including heads of state. The roundtables focused on building bridges among institutions and stakeholders, including seriously listening to non-governmental points of view presented by business leaders and articulate NGO speakers.

The Monterrey conference was also notable in not having to go through contentious negotiations over formal texts that typically absorb much of the energy at large UN conferences. The negotiations had been completed in January in New York at the final preparatory meeting. Indeed, more than the summit conference itself, the real revolution was in the final meeting of the Preparatory Committee in January 2002, as many governments sent finance ministry officials from capitals and the offices of executive directors at the Bretton Woods institutions to work beside their UN mission staff in negotiating the final text of the Monterrey Consensus.

A different approach to UN diplomacy

From its beginnings and continuing until Monterrey itself, FfD has had enemies as well as friends among UN missions and in different parts of the secretariat. FfD held out a promise of creating a new form of North-South cooperation in development, although it was unclear that it could deliver anything at all. The pessimists saw it as selling out the unrealised ideals of an independent South to a dominating North.

In that view, confrontation was the better approach, steadily challenging the North and the institutions it dominated. Cooperation meant cooptation. Country by country, the South was fundamentally weak, but at least the concerns of the South could be kept before the world through disciplined negotiation on texts put forward by the Group of 77 (G-77), the developing countries' caucus at the United Nations on economic and social affairs. The proper role of the secretariat, in this view, was to give the South arguments to use in its collective confrontation with the North in their debates, whether in New York, Geneva or Washington. FfD with its emphasis on inclusion and cooperation was a major threat to this process. It would disrupt the way the G-77 worked without delivering anything in return.

Other UN missions saw it differently (although this was never for public discussion). They saw the standard approach to UN negotiations on economic issues as emphasising the weakness of the South. The only power of the G-77 was over words on texts that did not matter, and even that was highly limited. In the standard UN consideration of an economic policy issue, the G-77 first negotiates a text among its own members and then presents it to the developed countries. Their representatives find it unacceptable and then the North (usually led by the European Union) and the South (G-77) negotiate to a watered-down version of the G-77 proposal. Nothing in the real world changes as a result.[17] That is not how policy change happens. In this view, only solidarity among G-77 member countries and inertia keep the process going.

In fact, the seed of FfD had actually been sown in one of the most unpromising of these North-South negotiations, one that had dragged on for more than four years and was finally coming to a close in 1997, mainly so delegations could adopt it and allow it to die a well-deserved death.

This was the Agenda for Development, 287 paragraphs filling over 100 pages with platitudes and bland statements of principle on development policy, plus hortatory statements about reform of the UN bodies and the secretariat. However, one section contained an opportunity to establish a dialogue between the inter-governmental processes of the Bretton Woods institutions and ECOSOC, and the prescient final paragraph of the "Agenda" said that "Due consideration should be given to modalities for conducting an intergovernmental dialogue on the financing of development."[18]

Venezuela's deputy permanent representative at the time, Ambassador Oscar de Rojas, had introduced that last sentence into the negotiations at virtually the last minute. Apparently, it was accepted because it was only an agreement to think about doing something, not actually to do it. A few months later, in the fall of 1997, he interested first a number of Latin American and then Asian and African countries in pursuing the idea further. It thus became a proposal of the G-77. It seemed headed for defeat, as had similar proposals over the past 20 years, until in November the United States announced its support for the initiative. That gave it the momentum to bring in the other countries, including the somewhat reluctant European Union.

Agreement was possible, in part, because the resolution embodying the proposal was intentionally non-committal. As adopted by the General Assembly on 18 December 1997, it called for a "high-level international intergovernmental consideration of financing for development".[19] That could mean anything from a summit conference to a seminar of senior officials. The resolution also asked the Assembly to reconvene its Second Committee in March 1998 to consider what information needed to be collected to decide what type of event to organise, and called for an *ad hoc* working group of the Assembly (a committee of the whole) to be formed in 1999 to draw up a specific proposal. This gave the proponents of FfD two years to build consensus around the "form, scope and agenda" of the proposed event. The initial resolution thus reflected both that there was no consensus at the end of 1997 that any such meeting at senior level was warranted, and also that no one was insisting on permanently ruling it out.

Meanwhile, the proposal for a joint meeting of senior government representatives from the Bretton Woods committees and ECOSOC was quietly percolating through inter-secretariat channels, and although nothing had been decided before the end of 1997, it was becoming increasingly clear that some meeting would take place, and it did in April 1998. The prospects for that meeting might have been helped by the very positive tone at the special Second Committee meeting in March that the Assembly convoked to follow up on the FfD proposal. US Ambassador to the United Nations, Bill Richardson, gave his government's statement; it was probably the first time the US permanent representative ever addressed this committee.[20] Many other governments also sent their permanent representatives to give their statements, together signalling that something unusual and important was happening.

Ambassador Richardson indicated strong interest on the part of the US government in the new FfD process, but cautioned that it would not countenance a new Bretton Woods conference to restructure the IMF and World Bank. In other words, and as others echoed, there were things to discuss in an FfD event but on condition that the initiative would be practical and that the developing countries would not push for unrealisable commitments. There would be some interesting negotiations over the next few years on what constitutes "unrealisable", but the essential point is that the process immediately took on a positive momentum.

Furthermore, the genius in drafting the initial FfD resolution was maintained as the governing prescription all the way to Monterrey: commit to formal negotiation the fewest words possible and do not press to include text on which there is no real agreement. In other words, a strategy evolved in the FfD process to hold off any negotiations on texts as long as possible, and then negotiations should be about nuance and appropriate phrasing of essentially agreed points. Moreover, instead of the standard G-77 initiation of negotiations, all texts were tabled either by co-chairs of committees or by "facilitators" who they appointed, the latter being trusted diplomats with thick skins whose job was to take into account different views, produce their own "compromise" text and then absorb the criticism of their text from all sides as they iterated towards a consensus.

The idea was that the substantive points should be argued out not in text negotiations but in informal dialogues and, indeed, in open discussion involving "all relevant stakeholders", a term that would become an essential aspect of the FfD process. These stakeholders included, in particular, relevant government representatives and international institutions, business and civil society. Agreements, when they could be reached, would be among government representatives – the United Nations is an inter-governmental forum, after all – but non-voting participants were welcomed to seek to influence the consensus-building process through dialogue.

The open and informal approach allowed participants to hear and weigh a broad range of views, as the restrictions on permitted speakers in a formal meeting of a General Assembly committee could be waived in an informal session. The informal structure also allowed a frank give and take, as no official records were kept of what each speaker said. Instead, the co-chairs, typically one ambassador from the North and one from the South, would produce balanced summaries of the discussion, assisted by the secretariat. In this way, a sense of participation among the different stakeholders grew. Broad participation would be followed, if slowly, by a measure of ownership, which would make it easier to pass through the difficult moments, of which there would be many.

In the end, the process worked. The developing countries did not press for rhetorical victories but sought practical actions from their "partners". Developed countries promised to deliver on some policies, like aid, and agreed to make Monterrey a North-South summit. All sides welcomed proposals from the private sector and civil society, as long as they held out realistic promise. The leading political themes of the FfD process quickly became and remain pragmatism and ownership. Pragmatism characterised the entire FfD process, sometimes to the frustration of non-governmental organisations (NGOs) and some government representatives, but it held together the relevant stakeholders and produced the Monterrey conference and the "Monterrey Process". As noted earlier, the texts so negotiated were typically bland, but in some cases contained political commitment behind them. In other cases the discussions had ended without a strong consensus and without a strong text. People understood that what mattered were not the words on the page but the actions that would follow.

Engaging stakeholders in the new UN process

The Ad Hoc General Assembly Working Group in 1999 did not manage to deliver the agenda as had been requested. It did, however, set the stage by instituting the FfD informal meetings strategy, arranging for business and civil society inputs in panel presentations to meetings of delegates, bringing senior officials from the Bretton Woods institutions into the meetings, preventing the tabling of any premature draft texts by the G-77 and otherwise keeping those who were doubtful about the process from undermining it. After the working group completed its task in June 1999 there was enough confidence – enthusiasm would be an exaggeration – for the Assembly to agree to go to the next step and convoke the Preparatory Committee for the FfD "event". It was not agreed at the time that the event would be a conference; nor was it agreed where or when it would be held or what the agenda would contain. However, there was a sense that something important could come out of the process based on how the discussions had been evolving.

Thus, in early 2000, the "Prep Com" began its work. It was another committee of the whole, but with an innovative 15-member bureau and again co-chairs at ambassadorial level from the North and South. The bureau would guide the work of the Prep Com and seek to engage the institutional and non-governmental stakeholders in the FfD meetings process. In June 2000 the Prep Com reached a crucial milestone when it adopted an agenda for the conference. The developed countries urged emphasis on domestic policy issues in developing countries and for the newly fashionable domestic "governance". Developing countries pressed for international policy commitments, including "global governance". Developed countries viewed this as dangerous, since their dominance of decision-making in the international financial and trading "architecture" could be challenged. The United States finally agreed to include "systemic issues" on the agenda when it was offered an escape clause by the facilitator, Minister Mauricio Escanero of Mexico, which was to allow for a reconsideration of including that agenda item if the United States saw its national interest being threatened. The Europeans then found themselves isolated and hard pressed not to accept a deal to which the Americans had agreed.

Besides, by then the World Bank and the IMF had been brought inside the secretariat team that was servicing the process, along with other parts of the UN system. That in itself should have been a confidence-building measure for the developed countries. The World Bank lent its support, perhaps initially in a defensive spirit, on the watch for a potential need for damage control. However, the Bank made a major commitment to support the FfD process, including seconding a staff member to the FfD coordinating secretariat in New York and assigning a senior official to participate in and draw other Bank staff into substantive preparations and inter-governmental discussions as the process developed. After a time, the IMF also assisted the FfD secretariat, albeit from Washington. The WTO came to be involved as well, but mostly offered moral support from the management and staff. In any event, Geneva was a lot further from New York than Washington and trade was less central (while still being essential) to FfD.

In fact, the agreement to allow "systemic" issues on to the FfD agenda could not have been otherwise if the process was to have any credibility after the severe financial crises of 1997–1998 in East Asia and the Russian Federation, and the near meltdown of the US Treasury market that followed soon after. It was widely believed that the IMF had made mistakes that had worsened the situation in certain cases, and in any event that the global financial system had become quite fragile. "Financial architecture reform" had entered the international vocabulary. But which reforms, drafted by whom and with whose mandate? FfD could not ignore these issues.

For the essential FfD outreach to the inter-governmental process in the Bretton Woods institutions, the bureau was able to build on the activities of ECOSOC, which had held its second meeting with senior government officials of the Bretton Woods ministerial committees in 1999 and a third meeting in 2000. ECOSOC ambassadors also held meetings with the boards of executive directors of both institutions in Washington and New York in 1998 and 1999, although the purpose of these meetings was unclear. The new FfD Prep Com then offered a focused reason for executive board meetings with UN delegates, which took place in the FfD context in 2000 and 2001. FfD also made it to the agenda of the Development Committee at its November 2001 meeting, which had been postponed from its scheduled time by the events of 9/11. Coming a few months before the Monterrey conference, this gave a boost to the importance of Monterrey, albeit on the back of a horrible tragedy.

The series of meetings with the Bretton Woods institutions from 1998 onwards turned out to be an important interface between foreign and finance ministry representatives and over time helped build confidence in the FfD process. However, in the beginning there was considerable coolness to overcome. Former UN Under-Secretary-General Nitin Desai, who helped organise these meetings, described them as being like new neighbours talking awkwardly over the back fence. Indeed, supporters of FfD welcomed the initiative of the Quaker UN Office to organise a retreat in the Catskill Mountains in the summer of 2001 where a number of UN and Bretton Woods representatives could become more familiar with each other.

In addition, country representatives to the New York and Washington institutions began to interact, the most sustained being the "Philadelphia Group" comprising about half a dozen developed country representatives to the World Bank and United Nations who in 2004 still met semi-annually in Philadelphia, about half-way between Washington and New York. In other cases it has remained very hard to bridge the ministerial divide, other than on an *ad hoc* and unsustained basis. Despite this, the FfD interactions with the inter-governmental machinery of the Bretton Woods institutions were far more successful that those with the WTO. Members of the FfD bureau travelled to Geneva in 2000 and met with members of the General Council, the senior WTO body, after which the Council appointed its Trade and Development Committee as interlocutor with the FfD process in New York. In 2001 the bureau visited the committee on what was thought to be a genuine invitation to dialogue. The committee and bureau members listened to a set of briefings by WTO staff on the state of various trade negotiations and then heard statements from the FfD bureau. It then rose, not allowing an interchange with the New York delegates. The stated reason was that the committee had not finished negotiating a text that it had wanted to submit to the FfD Prep Com giving the WTO view on a variety of trade-related matters. Whatever the reason, it sent a chilling message on the distance the intergovernmental process of the WTO wished to keep between itself and the United Nations in New York.[21]

Besides outreach to international institutions, the Prep Com bureau sought to engage the private sector in FfD. In this case, emerging market financial professionals from Wall Street began to show increasing interest in the United Nations, as they looked for venues where they could consider how to breathe new energy into international lending and investing in developing countries. Furthermore, as individuals they increasingly had time on their hands because much of their main business activities in emerging economies had disappeared in the financial crises.

The pragmatic nature of the FfD process was attractive to business interests. FfD was not about making woolly statements on the social role of business, but addressed its fundamental economic role. Governments in the FfD process wanted to hear from business about concrete ways to promote the financing of development, which perforce is mainly private financing. Developing countries explicitly sought to discuss how to bring more foreign business to their shores. Major business organisations, in particular the International Chamber of Commerce and the World Economic Forum, thus became involved, and the Business Council for the United Nations in New York organised informal discussion groups of private financial executives and specialists with UN diplomats on techniques for financing development. The engaged private sector people also became important advocates for FfD, especially with the US government. In Monterrey itself, business organisations held a pre-conference conference on the Monday of the week of the official conference. A number of prominent financial leaders from the South (primarily Latin America) and the North participated in the business conference and in "side events" during the conference. After Monterrey, some of the private sector proposals tabled at those meetings would be implemented independently or with support of certain donor governments and foundations.

Of course, the FfD bureau also reached out to civil society; indeed, it welcomed a large number of NGOs into FfD that did not already have standard consultative status with the United Nations through ECOSOC.[22] Civil society groups, as well as business organisations, thus became important participants in the FfD process and helped to shape the tone and content of the Consensus.[23] Admittedly, however, civil society advocacy groups first had to overcome their initial dismissal of FfD as just another UN process that would produce nothing but an empty declaration. Ultimately they came to argue effectively for important policy initiatives, such as how to handle the debt of poor countries in crisis. They also were important advocates in their national capitals for strong governmental participation in FfD and they advocated in Washington for serious engagement by the Bretton Woods institutions in the New York preparatory meetings.

Civil society groups were also an important presence in the UN meetings themselves. They produced generally well-attended, provocative and technically competent public presentations in "hearings" and "side events" at the United Nations and made concerted efforts to influence key delegations through direct lobbying campaigns. Indeed, being present in the Prep Com meetings, the NGOs could hear the views of different governments, day by day, and respond to them. NGOs divided themselves up into caucus groups by topic, which would meet each morning before the official meetings began in order to discuss negotiating positions and target individual delegates to lobby and how to approach them. Also NGOs, like the business representatives, could take the floor at the end of each morning and afternoon Prep Com meeting, providing an opportunity to add their views to the debate. They were also able to circulate their position papers in the meeting room.[24]

In Monterrey NGOs, like their business counterparts, organised a pre-conference conference running through the weekend before the official start, which was attended by several international organisation staff but few representatives of governments. However, NGOs more effectively reached deep into the Monterrey Process through important "side events" during the conference. Indeed, NGO-organised meetings during the January Prep Com in New York and in Monterrey were the first public discussions involving IMF staff and financial market professionals, let alone NGO debt campaigners, of the emerging IMF proposal for a sovereign debt restructuring facility. In this regard, NGOs created a number of meetings that governments just had to cover.

Overall, civil society also played a political role in support of FfD in Europe and North America, and global NGOs were effective advocates during the preparatory meetings and in Monterrey ("effective" means that some of their concerns influenced the negotiations and a few proposals were even taken up, but it does not mean that all their views were taken on board). Developing country individuals that were well plugged into the main international NGO networks participated in the FfD meetings in New York and Monterrey, as well as in "side events" during meetings of the Bretton Woods institutions in Washington on issues that were also part of FfD.

However, in developing economies themselves, civil society input on FfD – indeed, FfD itself – was less evident. There is little indication of significant activities in developing countries aimed to influence government participation or policy in the Monterrey Process. The one exception was in Mexico, which as host country for the conference provided an opportunity for local NGOs to put pressure on domestic politicians on a range of social and economic concerns under the gaze of the international press corps that would assemble for the conference.

Backsliding after the conference

It was inevitable that after the Monterrey conference ended there would be a redirection of attention to other issues and forums. Another big international meeting followed on its heels in Johannesburg, South Africa in September 2002, the World Summit on Sustainable Development, marking 10 years since the "Earth Summit" in Rio de Janeiro, the first of the big UN global conferences of the 1990s. Other events would also require attention. Meanwhile, the Monterrey Process spiralled down over the ensuing two years with increasing speed. The politics of inclusion was faltering.

The Monterrey Consensus had stipulated two bases on which a continuing important role for the FfD process could be predicated. One was recognition that the specialised international forums on trade and financial issues were somewhat like separate silos of activity and that the world could benefit from a "coherence forum" where their impacts on each other and on development could be discussed. The other was that the United Nations had demonstrated in the FfD process that it could be that forum, having successfully brought together in Monterrey "all the relevant stakeholders" on international monetary, financial, trade and development policy. Thus governments pledged in the Consensus to "stay engaged" through the Monterrey process, not only to follow up on the commitments they had made but also to bring the different international forums into regular contact with each other through the United Nations to strengthen international policy coherence.

The mechanism for the follow-up was unlike that in other UN conferences. Instead of establishing a special forum, like the Commission on Sustainable Development for the follow-up to the Earth Summit, FfD would make use of existing forums. First, the meetings of ECOSOC with the Bretton Woods institutions, that had by then become annual affairs, would be turned into FfD meetings to focus on "coherence, coordination and cooperation" on Monterrey issues. They would operate as in Monterrey, with a formal segment and with informal, multi-stakeholder dialogues. There would be no attempt to negotiate an agreed text on any of the discussions, but the president of ECOSOC would prepare a summary that could include recommendations under his or her own authority. The first president under the new structure, Ambassador Gert Rosenthal of Guatemala, took this initiative, which was especially germane in this case because his summary was also to be a document of the first FfD High-Level Dialogue in the General Assembly, described below.[25]

The WTO was invited to join the ECOSOC/FfD meeting at intergovernmental level, which it did in 2003 in the person of one of its committee chairs, but this was not continued in 2004. Also, ECOSOC invited the Trade and Development Board of the UN Conference on Trade and Development (UNCTAD) to join the discussions in 2004, which it did in the person of its chair. However much UNCTAD was welcomed, especially by the G-77, the WTO was the primary forum for international trade negotiations and its absence was significant. Unfortunately, as may be recalled from above, the WTO had been the one inter-governmental body to keep a significant distance from FfD during the preparatory phase, and thus this policy was apparently simply resumed in 2004. Indeed, the WTO General Council hosted a meeting on policy coherence in trade and financial matters in the spring of 2003 in which the IMF and World Bank heads participated, but at which the United Nations was no more than a silent witness.

In fact, there is a history to the distancing of the WTO from the United Nations that goes back to the Uruguay Round negotiations that led to the creation of the WTO in 1995. The negotiators addressed the coherence issue at that time, but solely in the context of WTO/Bretton Woods interactions. The WTO also had decided then not to affiliate formally with the United Nations as a "specialised agency", which is the status of the IMF and the World Bank. All of this underlined that ECOSOC was going to have a difficult time engaging WTO at inter-governmental level (although WTO senior management has attended all major post-Monterrey meetings).

The second part of the inter-governmental follow-up to Monterrey was agreement to hold a High-Level Dialogue on FfD in the General Assembly every two years. The first one was held in 2003 and it, like the ECOSOC meetings, brought a number of government representatives with ministerial rank to New York. Although a small number of development cooperation and finance ministers participated, the meeting was at a significantly lower level than Monterrey had been. This too was expected, as Monterrey had been exceptional and this dialogue would take place every two years. And yet, the dialogue was important. While it was structured somewhat like Monterrey and the ECOSOC meetings, in combining informal roundtables and a formal plenary, it had the potential for significant consequences. In this case, the Second Committee of the Assembly had pledged to consider adopting a resolution based on the dialogue after it ended.

The exercise, however, was a great disappointment. The original concept was for the president of the Assembly, Foreign Minister Julian Hunte of St Lucia, to serve as facilitator for a draft resolution. The great prestige of his position was expected to help guide the negotiations, but in reality he had little involvement. In fact, competing draft resolutions circulated and even the very skilled facilitator selected, Minister-Counsellor Félix Mbayu of Cameroon, had great difficulty holding the pieces together, especially as the negotiations turned out to be contentious, even bitter at times, and without involving any ambassadors or senior officials stepping in to resolve disputes, as sometimes happens when important negotiations bog down. In the end, the agreed resolution pertained primarily to planning subsequent FfD meetings and activities. It was the last resolution to be adopted by the Second Committee in 2003 and required delaying its closing. The Assembly plenary adopted it on 23 December. Quite a number of delegates left for their Christmas holiday break with a sour taste in their mouths.

Moreover, part of the agreement embodied in the FfD resolution was already dead by January 2004. In that part, the new president of ECOSOC, Ambassador Marjatta Rasi of Finland, "in consultation with all major institutional stakeholders" was expected to "focus the annual special [ECOSOC] high-level meeting on specific issues, within the holistic integrated approach of the Monterrey Consensus".[26] In other words, the president was supposed to work with partners to reach an agreed focus of the meeting, including through consultations with management and the inter-governmental processes of the IMF, the World Bank, the WTO and UNCTAD. As January turned into February and then March, it became clear that there was no agreement on a focus and that the difficulty was internal to New York and not with the institutional partners. The result was that the 2004 ECOSOC discussions "focused" on:

- the impact of private investment and trade-related issues on financing for development;
- the role of multilateral institutions in reaching the Millennium Development Goals;
- debt sustainability.

This was a very broad "focus" indeed, which almost guaranteed the discussion would be at the level of broad generalities instead of an in-depth discussion of coherence aspects of any one of the topics alone.

Post-Monterrey, but especially in 2004, the New York delegations have also challenged the continued enthusiasm of civil society and business partners in the FfD process. The coordinating groups for both sets of non-governmental partners planned with the UN secretariat to organise "hearings" with delegations on the theme of the April 2004 meeting. These "hearings" had been an important part of the inclusiveness of the Monterrey Process, although slackening attendance of delegates in the fall 2003 hearings was a sign that something was amiss. The fact that there was no agreed focus to the coming ECOSOC meeting that the hearings were suppose to enrich made it difficult to plan them, but both sets of partners in fact produced substantively rich meetings. Unfortunately virtually none of the delegates came to hear them. In the case of the NGO "hearings", an effort was made to encourage attendance by setting up what was expected to be an active debate between NGOs and selected government representatives to which delegates were expected to contribute from the floor. The overall theme was provocative enough: "coherence of the international financial and trading systems in support of development: national responsibilities and international obligations". The hearings were structured as a presentation by two NGO experts followed by a critique and questions from two UN representatives. The United States, supporting this process, sent a deputy assistant secretary of state as its commentator. The other commentators were the ambassadors of Jamaica, Pakistan and the European Commission (which speaks for the European Union on trade matters). Very few representatives of other countries came into the room during the three hours of the hearings (most who did were from other European countries and a small number of developing country representatives who had been active in the FfD process in earlier years).

The problem seemed to be that FfD was not on delegates' "radar screens". They had no engagement at this time with the substance of the hearings. That cogent and provocative analyses were being presented by NGO experts and challenged by senior diplomats in a collegial yet critical atmosphere was a lost opportunity for the country representatives who did not attend. It was a valuable use of time for the secretariat staff and NGOs who did attend.

Virtually the same reception was given to the business sector participants. If anything, there were even fewer government representatives in the room. The "business hearings" were structured differently, as the group of "business interlocutors" on FfD had organised a technical working group meeting the day before and wanted to report to government representatives at the United Nations on the results of their discussions. Some governments had participated in the technical meeting (United States, United Kingdom, India [State of Kerala] and Uganda), but from finance-related ministries or semi-independent official entities. A number of senior executives from the private sector and multilateral agencies drew from personal experience in discussing "critical information needs" and "risk-mitigation needs" of investors and in considering concrete mechanisms to help address them. The discussions were very rich. There was much to report to the UN representatives, but it fell on mainly empty chairs (again, secretariat staff and NGOs learned from the presentations).

Thus, the explicit efforts to institutionalise the strengths of FfD in the Monterrey follow-up have not taken hold. Perhaps, more than was realised, talented diplomats and top management of key institutions, plus momentum from business and civil society, and then a pressing political context accounted for the success of Monterrey. That combination would be hard to sustain. Many – but not all – of the diplomats who made up the core of interested parties in FfD have moved on to new postings, as have some of the key officials in the institutional partner organisations. Also, some of the issues from Monterrey have moved to the table for decision in Washington, as noted at the outset. Meanwhile, old methods of working on economic issues in the United Nations continued alongside the new FfD processes, and with the weakening of the momentum of Monterrey the old ways appear to have captured FfD as well.

Conclusion: Lessons for continued dialogue

The Monterrey Process can be reinvigorated. Whether or not that happens depends on whether the factors that accounted for its success come to operate adequately once again.

The first factor is leadership stepping forward from among the country representatives to the United Nations. Unlike the Bretton Woods institutions, General Assembly initiatives in the economic and social area are typically led by country missions and not by the secretariat. The Assembly processes allow capable and articulate leaders from even small countries to take initiatives and build coalitions around issues. FfD began as the initiative of a representative of a middle-sized middle-income country. It spread first to enough of the members of the group of developing countries to win the G-77 endorsement and then garnered support of certain important developed and other relatively advanced countries. Participants in the coalition may have been seeking disparate ends, but one aspect of effective leadership in a parliamentary context like the General Assembly is in helping them all see FfD as a promising path to their ends.

The second factor is that there is sufficient flexibility – even ambiguity – in the process and its goals so as to allow the leaders to hold the interested parties together. The explicit strategy in the FfD process to prevent the tabling of G-77 texts for negotiation used the confusion from not tabling national positions to prevent defections from the supporting coalition of governments from North and South. Positions of governments that are written down for consideration by other countries, *ipso facto*, become matters for change through negotiation. It is best to leave this to the last stages of the process, when the starting positions will have come closer together. In addition, beginning that final negotiation with a "facilitator's text" relieves governments of having to state explicitly and defend their national positions, except in so far as necessary in making comments on the facilitator's text. Moreover, participation of other multilateral institutions was contingent on not being trapped into negotiation over matters usually decided in their own inter-governmental forums. Premature specificity, especially through written texts, not only might have forced the institutions to withdraw, but it could have led their major shareholders to gut the entire prospect of potential positive results.[27]

The third factor is that a core group of officials needs to become committed to the project and fight for it, as it will have to overcome both active enemies and the studied indifference of needed partners. In the case of FfD, a major challenge was to involve finance ministries and in some cases central banks in a UN exercise. As noted earlier, foreign ministries are responsible for country representation at the United Nations, and while they have often engaged less powerful ministries in UN affairs (social, environmental, health, etc.), for FfD they had to engage the generally more powerful finance ministries. The core country representatives at the United Nations led in this effort in the FfD process. The core included, besides a number of government representatives, individuals in the staffs of the secretariat and the Bretton Woods institutions, and important individuals in senior management of those institutions. Each helped to bridge the ministerial divide, without which the project would have failed. Some of those links have atrophied and need to be strengthened for a successful FfD future.

The fourth factor is being able to maintain both the leadership and the core support group over time. While senior management of the United Nations and other institutions may turn over each decade and while staff members are usually on a long-run career path (albeit often with changing assignments), diplomats and governmental representatives in the United Nations and the financial and trade institutions usually change postings every three to five years. The core is thus bound to lose important individuals and it needs to be big enough and have enough overlapping tenures to survive the departure of key individuals.[28] In the case of FfD, core members from the UN missions were not necessarily elected into formal leadership positions in the inter-governmental structures. Indeed, the core was informal and mainly discussed what should happen in the formal structures.

The fifth factor is that non-official stakeholders are engaged in the process in a serious way. The FfD Prep Com facilitated this by establishing easy rules for engagement in official meetings by individual NGOs and business executives, and by offering many opportunities for interaction. The non-official actors have to believe that their views are being considered as part of the work programme of the process, i.e. that it is worth their time and effort. In the case of FfD, both business and NGO groups also advocated in relevant ministries for their governments to participate seriously and at senior level. Keeping this flame alive (or rekindling it) is a major challenge today in the FfD process.

The final factor is that real-world developments should bolster the political value of effective international cooperation. FfD was born in the midst of the Asian financial crisis and "Afro-pessimism", and then the Millennium Declaration announced a new international commitment to development cooperation for global peace and security, as well as human solidarity over development. On top of this, a new level of urgency suddenly emerged after 9/11 when the feeling spread that a world forever divided into rich and poor was no longer feasible politically, let alone desirable. But there also needed to be a sense that multilateral processes could address the root causes of the security threats, or that it was at least worth gambling that multilateralism held the answer. The final factor, then, pertains to leadership at the most senior levels of governments about the most fundamental aspects of international relations.

In sum, the main challenge facing those wishing to nurture the politics of inclusion in the Monterrey Process is how to continue to engage the large and small countries of the world, the main international institutions and the non-official stakeholders. It is not a matter of better "enfranchising" developing countries and civil society in international processes that are otherwise dominated by developed countries, which may be the political challenge in other international processes. FfD began as a developing country initiative among foreign affairs ministries represented at the United Nations. The challenge has all along been to engage first the Northern foreign ministries, then the finance ministries of North and South, the relevant multilateral institutions and the non-official actors. This remains the challenge today.

Acknowledgements

Views expressed are those of the author and not necessarily of the United Nations. The author wishes to thank Eva Hanfstaengl and Daniel Platz for comments on an earlier draft, along with the participants at the UNU-IAS/IIASA workshop at Laxenberg in June 2002.

Notes

1. Lyric by Billy Rose, 1930; recorded by Frank Sinatra in 1955.
2. For details on participants, see United Nations (2002) *Report of the International Conference on Financing for Development, Monterrey, Mexico, 18–22 March 2002*, New York: United Nations (Sales No. E.02.II.A.7), pp. 19–22. See United Nations (2002) *Fi-*

nancing for Development: Building on Monterrey, New York: United Nations (Sales No. E.02.II.A.5), for speeches, press conferences and relevant documentation.
3. United Nations E.02.II.A.7, ibid., p. 9.
4. Organization for Economic Cooperation and Development (2004) "Aid Ministers Note Rise in Aid Volume and Push for Aid Reform and New Approaches to Security-Development Linkages", press release, 16 April 2004.
5. For a country-by-country listing, see United Nations (2003) "Implementation of and Follow-up to Commitments and Agreements Made at the International Conference on Financing for Development", Report of the Secretary-General (A/58/216), table 3.
6. Following Monterrey, donor governments also agreed in Rome in 2003 and in subsequent meetings to strengthen the effectiveness of aid, including by reducing its transaction cost. Something as routine as reducing paperwork might not seem a development policy victory, but donor governments have heretofore jealously guarded their paperwork prerogatives. See IMF and World Bank, *Global Monitoring Report 2004*. Issued as background document for Development Committee meeting of 25 April 2004 (DC2004-0006/Add.1), pp. 11.7–11.14.
7. United Nations E.02.II.A.7, note 2 above, p. 17.
8. For many years the Assembly has annually adopted separate resolutions on North-South aspects of international trade, commodities, external debt and financial architecture reform, which typically have a considerable overlap. In 2002 delegations in the Second Committee negotiating the first substantive FfD follow-up resolution agreed to take selected texts from four other resolutions (57/235, 57/236, 57/240 and 57/241) into the FfD resolution (57/272) to ensure consistency, at least as far as specific wording was concerned on the selected paragraphs. In 2003 the FfD resolution dealt primarily with organisational issues (58/230) and the four other resolutions were negotiated as before (58/197, 58/202, 58/203, 58/304).
9. United Nations E.02.II.A.7, note 2 above, p. 14.
10. At each institution, two executive directors represent all of sub-Saharan Africa, around 45 countries in each case. Additional assistance will now be provided to their offices in Washington and in capitals.
11. IMF (2004) "Communiqué of the International Monetary and Financial Committee of the Board of Governors of the International Monetary Fund", Press Release 04/84, 24 April, para. 18.
12. United Nations (2003) "General Assembly Adopts UN Convention Against Corruption, Opens Treaty for Signature at High-Level Conference in Merida, Mexico, 9–11 December 2003", Press Release GA/10199.
13. United Nations E.02.II.A.7, note 2 above, p. 14.
14. United Nations (2003) "International Trade and Development", Report of the Secretary-General (A/58/414), p. 6.
15. The account in this section draws, *inter alia*, on Herman, Barry (2002) "Civil Society and the Financing for Development Initiative at the United Nations", in Jan Aart Scholte with Albrecht Schnabel, eds, *Civil Society and Global Finance*, London: Routledge, pp. 162–177; Herman, Barry (2003) "Financing for Development and the New North-South Dialogue", Centre for Banking Studies, Central Bank of Sri Lanka, Occasional Paper No. 47. A chronology of the FfD process from 1997 to 2003 may be found on the FfD web page at www.un.org/esa/ffd/chronologyffdprocess97-03.htm.
16. International trade policy was added after some years to the FfD agenda, which was initially mainly focused on financial issues *per se*. The same jurisdiction problem arose here, even though in many countries foreign ministries are responsible for trade negotiations and UN diplomats sometimes have had trade negotiation postings. That is, there

seems to have been as little interaction between United Nations and trade policy departments in the foreign ministries that were responsible for both as there was when the portfolios were held by separate ministries, thus fully echoing the mandate issue *vis-à-vis* finance ministries.
17. Negotiators are often junior-level diplomats without instructions from senior national officials that would have allowed a substantive give and take. Without authority to commit their governments, the negotiation is instead about finding words that will make it look like some policy change is advanced but which actually commits nobody to anything. Indeed, the exercise usually leads to reiteration of "agreed language" from another political process where policies are actually made or from a previous year's consideration of the item.
18. See United Nations (1997) *Agenda for Development* (General Assembly Resolution 51/240, annex), New York: United Nations (Sales No. E.98.1.3), p. 108. In fact, the General Assembly had proposed in May 1996 to invite the Bretton Woods institutions and members of their ministerial oversight committees (the Interim Committee, which would later become the IMFC, and the Development Committee) to meet with ECOSOC (Resolution 50/227, para. 88) and the Council responded to the Assembly proposal in July when, *inter alia*, it requested the Secretary-General to consult the institutions by early 1997 on the possibility of organising such a meeting (Resolution 1996/43, para. 5). The intention at that time was to strengthen collaboration of the institutions in light of the global UN conferences in the 1990s, including on environmental, social, gender, population, food and habitat issues, as well as on the needs of special groups of developing countries, rather than address the institutions' own "bread and butter" issues of financing for development, which came later.
19. See Resolution 52/179.
20. Usually the countries with large UN missions, like the United States, would send ambassadors with the rank of deputy permanent representative to meetings on economic and social issues when they warranted a higher level of participation.
21. This aside, relations have largely been cooperative and cordial during the FfD preparatory process, including WTO staff working with the FfD staff in the preparation of reports to the Prep Com. Indeed, the bureau began its disappointing day in Geneva with a useful dialogue about FfD with the director-general and the chair of the General Council.
22. From the beginning, the FfD secretariat reached out as well through its internet web page and list-serve broadsides, and by addressing various NGO audiences to inform them about the emerging process at the United Nations.
23. For more detail on NGO activities in FfD from 1998 to 2001, see Herman (2002), note 15 above, pp. 172–175.
24. See Tennessee, Paul N. (2004) "Lobbying International Institutions", *Guyana Journal* 9(1): 17–19. A detailed examination of NGO participation in the FfD process has been prepared as part of Schumacher, Lene (2003) "Invited to Dialogue: NGOs' Participation in the UN Preparatory Process for the Conference on Financing for Development in Mexico, March 2002", unpublished masters' thesis, Institute of Intercultural Communication and Management, Copenhagen Business School.
25. In addition to the president's summary of the ECOSOC meeting and his recommendations, summaries of the hearings and dialogue that were held a few weeks before with civil society and business were made documents of the Council and of the ensuing High-Level Dialogue. See United Nations (2003) "Summary by the President of the Economic and Social Council of the Special High-Level Meeting of the Council with the Bretton Woods Institutions and the World Trade Organization (New York, 14 April

2003)" and Notes by Secretariat containing summaries of the hearings and dialogues of the Council with members of civil society and business interlocutors (A/58/77-E/2003/62 and Add. 1 and Add. 2).
26. See Resolution 58/230, para. 11(c).
27. A range from ambiguity to specificity can be relevant at any level of an international discussion process, but does not solve all problems. For example, the inability to agree before March 2004 on substantive areas of focus for the April 2004 ECOSOC meeting, as discussed above, did not reflect a premature move to specificity. Whatever topics would be selected, they could be expressed with more or less precision, which the wording in the topics actually chosen as cited above showed. The delay seemed rather to be about a lack of willingness on the part of some countries to enter into any discussion beyond the most inconsequential at that time in the FfD process.
28. An anecdote may give the flavour of the passion of the core team in the case of FfD: a newly arrived diplomat from a major country whose predecessor had been part of the core group of supporters reported that this predecessor promised to geld him personally if the FfD project failed.

8

The Åarhus Convention: Engaging the disenfranchised through the institutionalisation of procedural rights?

Marc Pallemaerts

Introduction

The purpose of this chapter is to explore whether the forms of public participation institutionalised by the 1998 Åarhus Convention on Access to Information, Public Participation in Decision-Making and Access to Justice in Environmental Matters might serve as a model for broader international efforts to promote wider participation of civil society in governance processes in sustainable development at the national and international levels. Since the Åarhus Convention's system of procedural rights is essentially designed to ensure the enfranchisement of civil society actors in decision-making processes within states, and not to address the much broader issue of disenfranchisement within the international political and economic system, the focus of this contribution will be on the relevance of the convention as a model for the creation of institutionalised pathways for civil society participation in decision-making. While the institutional reforms provided for by the Åarhus Convention could contribute to a shift of norms towards a more inclusive model of international policy-making at the global level, as far as civil society participation is concerned, they would not necessarily at the same time contribute to achieving better parity of participation between North and South. Ways and means of addressing the latter issue are comprehensively addressed by other authors in this volume.

It is important to stress that the object and purpose of the Åarhus Convention is not to establish an international regime for sustainable development. Its scope is considerably more limited. It is also fundamentally different from that of most other multilateral environmental treaties. The convention does not primarily aim at establishing a legal and institutional framework for *international* governance in a specific substantive issue area of sustainable development, but at laying down a set of obligations to be applied by states in their *internal* decision-making procedures. It does not as much focus on defining the obligations of state parties *vis-à-vis* each other as on defining their obligations towards members of civil society subject to their jurisdiction. It is an international legal instrument specifically aimed at empowering civil society actors at the national and subnational levels, within a particular, rather limited field of decision-making related to sustainable development, namely environmental governance. But, as we shall see, it may have implications for sustainable development governance at the international level, and influence the further development of norms for the enfranchisement of civil society actors in international forums and even non-party states.

Before proceeding with an analysis of the Åarhus model of participation, the background, negotiating history, purpose and scope of the convention will first be explained. After describing the system of procedural environmental rights established by the convention, the chapter will conclude by examining its significance for and potential influence on sustainable development governance in a global context.

Background and history

The history of the Åarhus Convention goes back to the Ministerial Conference on Sustainable Development held by the UN Economic Commission for Europe (ECE), a regional preparatory meeting for the UN Conference on Environment and Development held in Bergen, Norway, in May 1990, where the ECE member states agreed "to contribute to the preparation of a document on environmental rights and obligations for possible adoption at the 1992 Conference on Environment and Development".[1] A preliminary draft of an "ECE Charter on Environmental Rights and Obligations", which explicitly recognised the individual right to a healthy environment and further contained provisions on access to information, public participation in decision-making and legal protection, was elaborated by an informal meeting of experts on environmental law convened jointly by the Dutch and Norwegian Ministries of Environment in October 1990.[2] Though it was subsequently considered by an *ad hoc* meeting open to participation by all member governments of the ECE, this draft charter was never formally endorsed by the ECE nor submitted to UNCED on its behalf, due to a lack of consensus within the region on the desirability of such an instrument.

When the ECE resumed its work on environmental rights after the Rio Conference, it chose to focus on the implementation of the procedural rights set out in Principle 10 of the Rio Declaration. Accordingly, a set of non-binding "Guidelines on Access to Environmental Information and Public Participation in Environmental Decision-Making" were developed by an ECE expert group and adopted by the "Environment for Europe" Ministerial Conference held in Sofia in October 1995.[3] The Sofia Conference also instructed the ECE Committee on Environmental Policy to prepare a draft convention on access to environmental information and public participation in environmental decision-making, based on the Sofia guidelines. Negotiations started in a new working group of experts in early 1996, with a view to finalising the proposed convention for adoption and opening for signature at the next "Environment for Europe" Ministerial Conference, scheduled to be held in Åarhus, Denmark, in June 1998.

The Convention on Access to Information, Public Participation in Decision-Making and Access to Justice in Environmental Matters was completed in time for its formal adoption by this conference and signed by 35 member states of the ECE and by the European Community in Åarhus on 25 June 1998. It entered into force on 30 October 2001, following ratification by 16 states. The convention now has 39 contracting parties: about half of them are member states of the European Union, and the other half are countries in transition from Central and Eastern Europe and Central Asia and the Caucasus region.

Although the convention was negotiated in a pan-European forum, within the framework of a political process for environmental cooperation in Europe which includes all former Soviet republics in Europe and Asia, as well as the United States and Canada, it was not conceived as an exclusively European instrument, since it is open for accession by any member state of the United Nations "upon approval by the Meeting of the Parties". Thus far, however, no non-European state has officially expressed interest in becoming a party to the Åarhus Convention, though the convention has been rather widely discussed in various international forums, including, *inter alia*, the UNEP Governing Council and the 2002 World Summit on Sustainable Development (WSSD). The United States and Canada, though full members of the ECE, elected not to participate in the negotiations and have stayed outside the Åarhus regime since its inception.[4] Ironically, the European Union and its member states, which like to position themselves as champions of environmental democracy in global forums such as the WSSD, constituted a small minority of the contracting parties to the Åarhus Convention until the latest enlargement of the European Union on 1 May 2004. It is only due to its new member states, most of which had already ratified the convention prior to their accession to the European Union, that a majority of the EU member states are now contracting parties. The European Community itself became a contracting party in early 2005.

Purpose and scope

The Åarhus Convention is the first multilateral treaty on the environment that primarily aims to impose obligations on states in respect of their own citizens. As a result, this new convention bears close similarities to international legal provisions on the protection of human rights. By undertaking to guarantee a series of "citizens' rights in relation to the environment",[5] of a procedural nature, the European states signatory to the convention wished to encourage what they described in their Ministerial Declaration as "responsible environmental citizenship", acknowledging that "an engaged, critically aware public is essential to a healthy democracy".[6] As the preamble to the instrument states, "citizens must have access to information, be entitled to participate in decision-making and have access to justice in environmental matters" in order to "be able to assert" their right to live in a healthy environment and to "observe" the associated duty "to protect and improve the environment for the benefit of present and future generations". The purpose of the procedural rights of access to information, public participation in the decision-making process and access to justice guaranteed by the provisions of the convention is clearly set out in article 1, which states that the aim of this unusual instrument is "to contribute to the protection of the right of every person of present and future generations to live in an environment adequate to his or her health and well-being". As mentioned above, the drafting of the Åarhus Convention was prompted by Principle 10 of the Rio Declaration, which enunciates the same procedural rights at the global level, albeit in much vaguer terms that are not legally binding.

The full engagement of civil society in the environmental policy-making process with a view to increasing its democratic nature and legitimacy is clearly perceived as the main purpose of the convention. In its preamble, the contracting parties state their belief "that the implementation of this Convention will contribute to strengthening democracy in the region of the United Nations Economic Commission for Europe". The Ministerial Declaration of the Åarhus Conference, by which the convention was adopted, praised it as "a significant step forward both for the environment and for democracy".[7] The aim is therefore to increase the transparency and democratic legitimacy of government policies on environmental protection, and to develop a sense of responsibility among citizens by giving them the means to obtain information, to assert their interests by participating in the decision-making process, to monitor the decisions of public bodies and to take legal action to protect their environment. The "engaged, critically aware public" is seen as both an essential player and a partner in the formulation and implementation of environmental public policies.

The Åarhus Convention articulates a detailed system of individual environmental rights, the implementation of which is already having a considerable impact on national systems of environmental law and administrative practices in many countries, including some countries which have not yet become parties to the convention.[8] In assessing the impact of the Åarhus regime, it is important to look at the dynamic interplay between international law, EU law and national law in the ECE region. Soon after the European Community had signed the convention, the EU institutions initiated a process aimed at transposing many of its provisions into binding provisions of EU law. The existing EC directives on access to environmental information,[9] environmental impact assessment[10] and integrated pollution prevention and control,[11] which already guaranteed some but not all of the rights provided for by the Åarhus Convention, were reviewed and legislative proposals formulated to bring them into conformity with Åarhus standards. As a result, new directives on public access to environmental information[12] and public participation in environmental permitting, impact assessment and planning procedures[13] were adopted by the European Parliament and the Council in 2003 and had to be fully implemented by EU member states in their national legislation by February and June 2005 respectively, regardless of whether they had individually ratified the Åarhus Convention or not. Since the expiry of these periods for transposition into national law, provisions of these EC directives also have direct effect in the national legal systems of the member states which may have failed to transpose them fully or correctly. National courts in these states are bound to apply them notwithstanding any conflicting provisions of national law and are able to refer issues concerning their interpretation to the Court of Justice of the European Union for a preliminary ruling if necessary. A separate, more recent and controversial Commission proposal for an additional directive on access to justice,[14] designed to implement the provisions of Article 9 of the Åarhus Convention, is still pending in the Council. The latest Åarhus-related legislative initiative of the European Commission is a proposal for a regulation on pollutant release and transfer registers, which provides information on inventories of pollution. It is designed to implement the provisions of the convention's Kiev Protocol, which was submitted to Parliament and Council in October 2004.[15]

In practical terms, the Åarhus Convention requires the states parties, in response to requests from any member of the public, and without the latter having to state any particular interest, to make available information on the environment held by public authorities, subject to a limited number of exemptions that may be invoked on grounds of public interest.[16] The parties must also take steps to collect and disseminate a whole range of information on the condition of the environment and activities and measures likely to affect it.[17] The provisions on public participation in decision-making processes require the parties to implement procedures enabling members of the public to obtain information and to assert their interests where public authorities are considering whether to permit specific activities that may have a significant impact on the environment.[18] Measures must also be taken to enable the public to participate in the preparation of plans and programmes relating to the environment,[19] and in the preparation by public authorities of regulations and other generally applicable, legally binding rules that may have a significant impact on the environment.[20] Last but not least, the convention guarantees access to review procedures in the event that public authorities fail to comply with their obligations in respect of access to information and participation in the decision-making process.[21] The public must also have access to administrative and judicial procedures to be able to challenge acts and omissions by private individuals or public authorities that contravene national legal provisions on the environment.[22]

It could be argued that the procedural environmental rights guaranteed by the Åarhus Convention simply give practical form, in the specific context of environmental policy, to the general principles of democracy and the rule of law already enshrined in other international instruments on the protection of human rights. On the other hand, the very emergence of specific rules of international environmental law concerning public participation in decision-making processes reflects broader concerns relating to developments in democracy and citizenship in a changing world.[23] As a popular target for citizen activism, environmental policy has, in a way, become a testing ground for efforts to transcend traditional models of representative democracy.

The convention provides evidence that, in Europe at any rate, NGOs continue to be seen as the primary agents of civil society in environmental policy-making, though its provisions are, by and large, designed to grant equal procedural rights to all members of "the public", a notion which it defines as referring to "one or more natural or legal persons, and, in accordance with national legislation or practice, their associations, organisations or groups".[24] For the purpose of establishing the right of public participation in decision-making on specific activities, the convention defines a more circumscribed notion: "the public *concerned*", which refers to "the public affected or likely to be affected by, or having an interest in, the environmental decision-making".[25] In this particular context, a special status is granted to "non-governmental organisations promoting environmental protection", which "shall be deemed to have an interest" in the decision-making, provided they meet any requirements which may have been established under national law. Moreover, the convention contains a general provision which requires its parties to "provide for appropriate recognition of and support to associations, organisations or groups promoting environmental protection".[26] Thus the special role of environmental NGOs is duly recognised, though without disregarding other actors within civil society. Informal grassroots organisations, social movements and individual citizens can equally avail themselves of the rights of access to information, public participation and access to justice laid down in the Åarhus Convention, since all of them are covered by the convention's broad definition of "the public".

The very purpose of the Åarhus Convention is to institutionalise pathways to enable civil society actors to influence environmental policy-making at the national and subnational levels and to grant international legal recognition and protection to procedural environmental rights. The capability of the beneficiaries of those rights to make use of them to participate effectively in the policy-making process is somehow presumed, though the convention contains a number of preambular and operative provisions which recognise that formal legal recognition of rights is not sufficient to achieve its objectives, but that this also requires additional, proactive efforts on the part of public authorities to assist citizens and their organisations in exercising these rights.

In the preamble, for instance, the contracting parties acknowledge "that citizens may need assistance in order to exercise their rights".[27] They also recognise that "the public needs to be aware of the procedures for participation in environmental decision-making ... and know how to use them".[28] Consequently, the importance of environmental education "to encourage widespread public awareness of, and participation in, decisions affecting the environment and sustainable development"[29] is stressed in yet another recital. A number of corresponding operative provisions, generally couched in rather exhortatory terms, require efforts by states parties with a view to the promotion of environmental education and awareness;[30] the provision of "assistance" and "guidance" to the public by public officials and authorities;[31] the provision of transparent information to the public about the type and scope of environmental information held by public authorities to ensure that such information is "effectively accessible";[32] and the provision of information to the public about access to administrative and judicial review procedures and the consideration of mechanisms to "remove or reduce financial and other barriers to access to justice".[33]

It is outside the scope of this chapter to evaluate to what extent such provisions are effectively enhancing the capability of civil society actors, for whose benefit the Åarhus Convention's system of procedural environmental rights has been created, to make use of those rights and actually influence environmental decision-making in the countries which have subscribed to the convention. The question of the actual capacity and influence of civil society actors is considered by other contributors to this volume.

The significance of the Åarhus Convention for sustainable development governance

The Åarhus Convention does not cover the whole field of sustainable development governance, but by affirming, in the convention's preamble, the need "to ensure sustainable and environmentally sound development" as well as the desire "to encourage widespread public awareness of, and participation in, decisions affecting the environment and sustainable development", the parties intended that the scheme relate to the broader objectives of sustainable development. However, the specific obligations which the convention imposes on its parties with respect to their internal decision-making procedures relate to decisions on whether to permit certain proposed activities which may have a significant effect on the environment, to the preparation of plans, programmes and policies relating to the environment and to the preparation of legislation and regulations that may have a significant effect on the environment. So, in all cases, the criterion to determine whether particular policy-making processes are subject to the provisions of the convention is their environmental impact or relevance, without any direct reference to their effect on or relationship with the other two so-called "pillars" of sustainable development.

Nevertheless, it seems obvious that the Åarhus Convention is highly relevant to sustainable development decision-making as more broadly defined. Indeed, the activities to which its public participation provisions apply are important economic development projects in such sectors as energy, transport infrastructure, mining, metallurgy, the mineral and chemical industry, waste management, management of water resources, intensive animal husbandry and industrial food processing, etc. These projects obviously have social and economic as well as environmental effects and are likely to come under public scrutiny from a variety of civil society actors concerned with various aspects of sustainable development other than environmental protection only. Similarly, policies, plans and programmes "relating to the environment" are bound also to have wider economic and social implications, as does legislation "which may have a significant effect on the environment", a notion which is considerably broader than environmental law *sensu stricto*. Likewise, while the convention's provisions on access to information relate to a particular category of information held by public authorities, defined as "environmental information", and the definition of this concept is also rather broad. It includes, for example, "cost-benefit and other economic analyses and assumptions used in environmental decision-making", as well as "the state of human health and safety" and "conditions of human life" to the extent that these may be affected by environmental factors.[34]

Though its provisions primarily address *internal* decision-making processes within states, the Åarhus Convention is also likely to have "spillover" effects on certain aspects of international sustainable development governance. These result from the interesting provisions of article 3, paragraph 7, which require convention parties to "promote the application of the principles" laid down in the convention in international environmental forums. The "principles" referred to in this article are not explicitly defined, but can be presumed to cover the general principles of transparency and accountability, public access to information, public participation in decision-making and public access to review procedures. To the extent that the parties to the convention comply with this obligation, one may expect that this will contribute to the ongoing debate at the international level on the transparency, public accountability and legitimacy of inter-governmental policy-making processes and bolster the increasing calls from civil society actors from around the world for measures to overcome barriers to participation in such processes. Exactly how this may occur will be further analysed in the following section.

The potential impact of the Åarhus Convention on supranational and inter-governmental governance processes

Even if the Åarhus Convention primarily focuses on decision-making processes within its parties at the national or subnational level, it may also indirectly serve as a catalyst for the democratisation of supranational and international decision-making processes, which are playing an increasingly significant role as a result of regional economic integration and globalisation. In the European Union, for instance, supranational institutions are responsible for much of the legislative process in respect of the environment, and even for some administrative and judicial decisions.

By signing the Åarhus Convention, the European Community declared its willingness to apply the provisions of that convention to its own institutions, thereby fuelling the ongoing debate over the latter's openness and democratic legitimacy. In this context, it is worth noting that "The principle of participatory democracy" is enshrined in article I-47 of the Treaty establishing a Constitution for Europe, which provides, *inter alia*, that "Union Institutions shall maintain an open, transparent and regular dialogue with representative associations and civil society" and that "the Commission shall carry out broad consultations with parties concerned in order to ensure that the Union's actions are coherent and transparent". In October 2003 the European Commission submitted to the Council of the European Union and the European Parliament a proposal for implementing the Åarhus Convention in its own institutional framework,[35] as well as a draft decision on its ratification by the European Community.[36] While the latter proposal was adopted by Council on 6 July 2005,[37] the former is still under consideration by Council and Parliament. The adoption of the draft regulation on the application of the Åarhus Convention provisions to EC institutions would have far-reaching legal and institutional consequences, by granting more extensive participation rights to civil society in the area of EC environmental policy than it enjoys for other policy areas within the general institutional framework of the European Union.

Moreover, the implications of the Åarhus Convention may go beyond the European institutional framework, since the contracting parties also undertook to "promote the application of the principles of [the] Convention in international environmental decision-making processes and within the framework of international organisations in matters relating to the environment".[38] In the Lucca Declaration adopted at the first meeting of the parties to the Åarhus Convention, ministers "recognise[d] the need for guidance to the Parties on promoting the application of the principles of the Convention in international environmental decision-making processes and within the framework of international organisations in matters relating to the environment and ... therefore recommend[ed] that consideration be given to the possibility of developing guidelines on this topic".[39] Acting on this ministerial mandate, the Working Group of the Parties to the Convention, at its first meeting in November 2003, decided to establish an *ad hoc* expert group "to consider the scope, format and content of possible guidelines and the appropriate process for their development".[40] This group succeeded in elaborating draft guidelines, which were submitted to the Working Group of the Parties. After further negotiations in that forum, during which the experts' draft was substantially watered down, a revised draft was eventually submitted for adoption to the second meeting of the parties in Almaty, Kazakhstan, in May 2005. The meeting adopted the "Almaty Guidelines on Promoting the Application of the Principles of the Åarhus Convention in International Forums" and recommended their application by all parties, while at the same time inviting the international forums concerned "to take into account the principles of the Convention as reflected in [the] Guidelines and to consider how their own processes might further [their] application".[41] Of course, the adoption of the Almaty guidelines, as such, has no immediate effect on the institutional practices of the forums they are intended to influence. Ultimately, their impact will depend on the extent to which Åarhus parties are willing to take seriously their commitment to promote the application of the guidelines in the forums in which they participate, and the other members of these forums are receptive to such efforts. The success of the Almaty guidelines in ensuring wider civil society participation in international environmental decision-making processes will depend in no small measure on the cooperation of states which are not parties to the Åarhus Convention.

At any rate, the convention bodies themselves have already established an important precedent by granting NGOs an unprecedented role in their activities and proceedings. When it adopted its rules of procedure, which also apply to its subsidiary bodies, the meeting of the parties to the convention specifically "acknowledge[d] the unique role that the Convention has in promoting the participation of civil society in international environmental decision-making processes" and "recognise[d] that this leads to a special role for non-governmental organisations established for the purpose of and actively engaged in promoting environmental protection and sustainable development".[42] Accordingly, the rules of procedure contain a number of remarkable provisions allowing for extensive public access to convention meetings and documents. Thus, for example, it is provided, as a general rule, that meetings "shall be open to members of the public, unless the Meeting of the Parties, in exceptional circumstances, decides otherwise".[43] Representatives of NGOs which are "qualified or have an interest in the fields to which the Convention relates" shall automatically "be entitled to participate in the proceedings of any meeting [of a convention body], unless one third of the Parties present at that meeting objects".[44] Although such representatives formally have the status of observers without the right to vote, they nevertheless have the right to speak. Normally, representatives of parties and observers shall be called upon to speak in the order in which they have requested the floor, without precedence, although the chair "may at his or her discretion decide to call upon representatives of Parties before observers".[45] All official meeting documentation is to be published on the ECE website at the same time as it is sent to the parties and "shall be provided to members of the public on request".[46] Perhaps the most far-reaching example of an institutionalised role for civil society organisations in the framework of the convention bodies is the provision of the rules of procedure which require an NGO representative to be invited to attend all meetings of the convention's bureau, which is composed of government representatives elected by the meeting of the parties, albeit in an observer capacity.[47]

Similarities between the convention and international human rights law have been noted above. The convention's provisions on compliance review have opened up the possibility of a review mechanism accessible not only to states but also to individuals through some form of individual recourse procedure for the first time in international environmental law. The mechanism seems partly inspired by procedures already in force under some UN human rights treaties. Article 15 provides for the establishment of "arrangements" for reviewing compliance by parties which "shall allow for appropriate public involvement and *may include the option of consideration of communications from members of the public on matters related to this Convention*". Based on this provision, the first meeting of the parties to the Åarhus Convention, in October 2002, adopted detailed provisions on a procedure for the review of compliance by a compliance committee composed of independent experts.[48] This procedure provides for the examination, by this committee, of communications brought before it "by one or more members of the public concerning [a] Party's compliance with the Convention". In addition, the committee may also consider submissions by parties as well as referrals by the convention's secretariat. Furthermore, under the same rules, "the member of the public making a communication shall be entitled to participate in the discussions of the Committee with respect to that ... communication". Such provisions, granting individual citizens and NGOs the right actually to participate in the monitoring, by an international body, of state compliance with legal obligations is unprecedented in international environmental law. The Åarhus Convention's compliance mechanism has entered the stage of practical application, as 15 communications from the public have already been submitted to the Compliance Committee.[49] The committee completed its consideration of the first five cases prior to the second meeting of the parties in 2005. Its findings and recommendations to the parties concerned were endorsed by the meeting of the parties, which thereby demonstrated its confidence in this unique compliance system.

The global relevance and influence of the Åarhus Convention as a model for enhancing civil society participation

In many respects, the Åarhus Convention is an innovative instrument, whose potential significance for environmental protection, sustainable development, democratisation and even the promotion and protection of human rights extends well beyond the limits of the ECE region. To quote UN Secretary-General Kofi Annan, the convention constitutes "the most ambitious venture in the area of 'environmental democracy' so far undertaken under the auspices of the United Nations".[50] While states outside the ECE region are reluctant to subscribe to its provisions wholesale – by making use of the possibility of acceding to it – the growing interest in strengthening procedural environmental rights in all regions of the world[51] unmistakably reflects the influence of this bold European venture in international environmental law-making, though, in some regions, this interest actually predates the adoption of the Åarhus Convention and even that of the Rio Declaration and Agenda 21.

In the pre-Rio period it is worth recalling in particular the provisions of the World Charter for Nature. Adopted by the UN General Assembly in Resolution 37/7 of 28 October 1982, the charter already reflected a recognition of certain rights of the public in the specific context of the management and conservation of living natural resources. According to the text, "strategies for the conservation of nature ... and assessments of the effects on nature of proposed policies and activities ... shall be disclosed to the public by appropriate means in time to permit effective consultation and participation".[52] The charter also provides that "all persons, in accordance with their national legislation, shall have the opportunity to participate, individually or with others, in the formulation of decisions of direct concern to their environment, and shall have access to means of redress when their environment has suffered damage or degradation".[53] An implicit link between environmental protection and the fundamental rights of political participation and freedom of association is even established in the final clause of the World Charter, which states that "acting individually, in association with others or through participation in the political process, each person shall strive to ensure that the objectives and requirements of the present Charter are met".[54]

The provisions of the World Charter for Nature manifestly inspired the member states of the Association of South-East Asian Nations (ASEAN) when they decided to include, in their 1985 ASEAN Agreement on the Conservation of Nature and Natural Resources, a specific article on education, information and participation of the public, laying down an obligation for parties, *inter alia*, to "circulate as widely as possible information on the significance of conservation measures and their relationship with sustainable development objectives", and "as far as possible, [to] organise participation of the public in the planning and implementation of conservation measures".[55] This far-sighted regional environmental treaty, unfortunately, never entered into force.

During the UNCED preparatory process in the late 1980s and early

1990s, political declarations supporting wider recognition of procedural environmental rights were adopted in several regional forums. The role of the 1990 preparatory ministerial conference for the ECE region in initiating the process that eventually led to the Århus Convention has already been mentioned. But similar meetings in other regions also addressed the rights of individuals and NGOs. Thus, for example, the Ministerial Declaration on Environmentally Sound and Sustainable Development in Asia and the Pacific, adopted by a regional preparatory meeting in Bangkok in October 1990, affirms "the right of individuals and non-governmental organisations to be informed of environmental problems relevant to them, to have the necessary access to information, and to participate in the formulation and implementation of decisions likely to affect their environment".[56] The Arab Ministerial Conference on Environment and Development, held in Cairo in September 1991, stressing the importance of "popular participation", affirmed procedural environmental rights in very similar terms.[57] These various regional declarations in effect established the consensual basis for universal recognition of these rights in Principle 10 of the Rio Declaration. But after Rio the debate on their further elaboration and implementation moved back to the regional level, in Europe and elsewhere.

Following the adoption of the Århus Convention, an inter-regional effort to promote public participation in environmental decision-making was launched within the framework of the broader political dialogue between the European Union and a number of Asian countries[58] known as the Asia-Europe Meeting (ASEM). One of the areas covered by this dialogue is environmental policy, and cooperation has materialised in the form of regular meetings of environment ministers of the ASEM partners, the first of which was held in Beijing in January 2002, and the establishment, in 1999, of the Asia-Europe Environmental Technology Centre (AEETC) in Bangkok. In June 2000 a project on public participation in environmental governance in ASEM countries was initiated under the auspices of the AEETC, with funding from the government of Finland, which held the presidency of the European Union during the second half of 1999.[59] This project resulted in a number of expert reports,[60] a recommendatory policy document entitled "Towards Good Practices for Public Involvement in Environmental Policies" and two international conferences on public participation held in Asian ASEM partner countries with financial support from the European Commission and the AEETC. High-level political support for these activities was expressed by ASEM environment ministers at their Beijing meeting, where "the Ministers agreed that exchange of experiences concerning good practices for public involvement should be promoted",[61] and subsequently even by the participating countries' foreign ministers when they met in Madrid a few months before the WSSD. According to the chair's statement of the Madrid meeting, "Ministers gave special recognition to the valuable work carried out by the AEETC in promoting public participation in environmental affairs".[62] The second ASEM Environment Ministers Meeting, which took place in Lecce, Italy, in October 2003, again devoted political attention to the issue of public participation. The chairman's summary of the meeting states:

Ministers also recalled that business, mass media, major groups and all the people of civil society are important forces in promoting sustainable development. They stressed the importance of promoting access to information, public participation in decision-making and access to judicial and administrative proceedings according to Principle 10 of the Rio Declaration on Environment and Development and agreed that exchanges of experience, dissemination of good practice and development of guidelines for public participation should be promoted.[63]

However, ministers did not formally endorse the "Good Practice Document" developed by the AEETC experts. The chairman's summary merely notes that this document "provides a good basis for further work on public participation, for example within the UN regional framework".[64] Thus, while no further work on the issue is planned within the ASEM framework,[65] the partners apparently hope that the results of the project will inspire further initiatives at the regional level, e.g. within the forum of the UN Economic and Social Commission for Asia and the Pacific (ESCAP). At an international conference on public participation organised by the AEETC in Bangkok in June 2002, representatives of ESCAP and the ECE reportedly agreed to initiate cooperation to this end.[66]

Another inter-regional forum in which procedural environmental rights have gained a foothold is the Barcelona Convention for the Protection of the Marine Environment and the Coastal Region of the Mediterranean, which was negotiated within the framework of UNEP in 1976 and subsequently revised in 1995. One of the features of the amendments adopted by the meeting of the parties in 1995 is a new article on "public participation and information", which requires contracting parties to "ensure that their competent authorities shall give to the public appropriate access to information on the environmental state ... on activities or measures adversely affecting or likely to affect it and on activities carried out or measures taken in accordance with the Convention", as well as to "ensure that the opportunity is given to the public to *participate in decision-making processes* relevant to the field of application of the Convention and the Protocols, as appropriate".[67] These new provisions, which were manifestly inspired by Rio Principle 10, are particularly significant not so much because of their specific content, which remains relatively vague, but because they are included in a multilateral environmental treaty which includes not only the European riparian states of the Mediterranean but also developing countries of Northern Africa and the Middle East among its parties.[68]

From an African perspective, these subregional developments[69] could be viewed as somehow foreshadowing the broader legal recognition of environmental rights at the level of the continent as a whole, which was achieved later, following the entry into force of the Åarhus Convention. At their Maputo summit of July 2003, the heads of state and government of the member states of the African Union adopted a new African Convention on the Conservation of Nature and Natural Resources, which contains a specific article on "procedural rights". This clause is wider in scope than the above-mentioned provisions of the amended Barcelona Convention, as it also covers access to justice. It requires African countries to:

adopt legislative and regulatory measures necessary to ensure timely and appropriate
a) dissemination of environmental information;
b) access of the public to environmental information;
c) participation of the public in decision-making with a potentially significant environmental impact; and
d) access to justice in matters related to protection of environment and natural resources.[70]

These important provisions of the new African Convention should also be viewed against the background of the long-standing inter-regional partnership between the European Union and the African, Caribbean and Pacific (ACP) states, in which the important role of civil society and public participation in the development process has been formally recognised by all partners. According to the latest ACP-EU Partnership Agreement, signed in Cotonou in June 2000, whose scope is much broader than environmental cooperation and covers many other areas of sustainable development, "the contribution of civil society to development can be enhanced by strengthening community organisations and non-profit non-governmental organisations in all spheres of cooperation".[71] More specifically, EU and ACP states have undertaken to "establish arrangements for involving such organisations in the design, implementation and evaluation of development strategies and programmes",[72] and recognised the importance of access to justice and "greater involvement of an active and organised civil society" for "sustainable and equitable development".[73] Thus the procedural environmental rights recognised in the 2003 African Convention are fully consistent with the more general provisions on civil society participation subscribed to by African states in the ACP-EU framework.

The post-Rio developments in the Western hemisphere are equally noteworthy. In their North American Agreement on Environmental Cooperation, concluded in 1993 as a "side agreement" to the North American Free Trade Agreement (NAFTA), Canada, Mexico and the United States undertook, *inter alia*, to "promote transparency and public participation in the development of environmental laws, regulations and policies".[74] The trilateral Environmental Cooperation Agreement actually lays down a number of specific obligations with respect to procedural environmental rights of citizens and non-governmental organisations. In a wider regional context, the heads of state of the member countries of the Organization of American States (OAS), at their 1996 Santa Cruz Summit Conference on Sustainable Development, "recognising that the achievement of sustainable development requires a long-term commitment to strengthen participation by all citizens", decided to develop an "Inter-American Strategy for the Promotion of Public Participation in Decision-Making for Sustainable Development", which was formally adopted by the OAS Inter-American Council for Integral Development in April 2000.[75] This strategy, referring *inter alia* to the "commitments" contained in Principle 10 of the Rio Declaration, establishes a set of "basic principles of public participation", "general" and "specific" objectives and "policy recommendations" aimed at "direct[ing] the efforts of the member countries of the OAS, toward the formulation and implementation of policies that will ensure the participation of civil society in planning, environmental management and decision-making for sustainable development".[76]

Since the adoption of the Åarhus Convention, procedural environmental rights have also been on the agenda of the UN Environment Programme (UNEP). At its first meeting following the signing of the Åarhus Convention, the UNEP Governing Council adopted a decision "taking note of the various activities at the national and regional levels to promote enhanced participation by the public and major groups", including the Åarhus Convention, "affirming its commitment to promoting access to information and participation of all concerned citizens at the relevant levels" and requesting the executive director of UNEP to "seek appropriate ways of building capacity in and enhancing" access to procedural environmental rights.[77] While the cautious wording reflected hesitation on the part of many governments to recognise the universal validity of the Åarhus model, the decision did mandate further UNEP consideration of issues related to the enhancement of civil society participation in environmental policy-making worldwide. The same session of the Governing Council also adopted measures to ensure better public access to the environmental information collected and generated through UNEP's own INFOTERRA information exchange programme.[78]

Following the 1999 Governing Council decision, UNEP undertook a number of research and capacity-building activities, including the joint organisation with the ECE of an expert meeting on "promoting the application of Principle 10 of the Rio Declaration". At the first Global Ministerial Environment Forum convened by UNEP in Malmö in May 2000, ministers expressed high-level political support for strengthening "the role of civil society at all levels ... through freedom of access to environmental information to all, broad participation in environmental decision-making, as well as access to justice on environmental issues".[79] But, despite this high-level political attention, the further work of UNEP in this area has been progressing very slowly. In February 2001 the Governing Council elaborated on the Malmö Declaration by "urging" governments "to take steps to enhance access to environmental information held by public authorities and to encourage participation by all relevant sectors of society in the decision-making process in environmental matters, in accordance with relevant legislation or arrangements, bearing in mind the crucial role which it plays in institution-building for environmental protection and sustainable development", as well as "to take measures to establish, where appropriate, at the national and regional levels, judicial and/or administrative procedures for legal redress and remedy for actions affecting the environment that may be unlawful or infringe on rights under the law".[80] It is striking that the more specific the language of these recommendations becomes, the more it is qualified by references to national law. The same Governing Council decision also requested the UNEP executive director "to present a report on international legal instruments reflecting provisions contained in Principle 10 of the Rio Declaration on Environment and Development including an assessment and evaluation of their actual coverage vis-à-vis Principle 10".[81] Though such a report was duly presented to the next Global Ministerial Environment Forum in early 2002,[82] no consensus could be reached at that special session of the Governing Council on a draft decision on the subject proposed by the European Union, which was eventually withdrawn.[83]

The fate of this EU proposal as well as the subsequent debate at the WSSD in Johannesburg in the late summer of 2002 indicate that the elaboration of a global instrument on the subject remains controversial. No consensus could be reached in Johannesburg on a recommendation to develop "global multilateral guidelines" on public access to information, public participation in decision-making and access to justice, building on Rio Principle 10.[84] Consequently, the WSSD merely reiterated language from an earlier decision of the UN Commission on Sustainable Development (CSD) urging governments to "ensure" such access and participation "at the national level ... so as to further Principle 10 of the Rio Declaration on Environment and Development", and specifying that this is to be done "taking into full account Principles 5, 7 and 11 of the Declaration".[85] The only difference is that the reference to public participation in the WSSD Plan of Implementation can be interpreted as applying to *all decision-making with respect to sustainable development*,[86] whereas, in Principle 10 of the Rio Declaration as well as in the relevant CSD decision, it relates to environmental matters only. On the other hand, the explicit cross-references, in this context, to Principles 5, 7 and 11 of the Rio Declaration – qualifications that did not feature in the original wording of Rio Principle 10 – reflect the apprehensions of many developing countries about the political and resource implications of granting civil society extensive rights of access to their decision-making processes. Principle 5 refers to poverty eradication as "an indispensable requirement for sustainable development", while Principle 11 stresses the contextual nature of environmental standards and Principle 7 enshrines the well-known principle of the "common but differentiated responsibilities" of developed and developing countries in addressing global environmental problems. Together these references could be interpreted as implying that a lower standard of public participation should apply in developing countries, in view of resource constraints and the priority to be given to economic development. But, ironically, these apprehensions which manifested themselves at the global summit in Johannesburg seem to be at odds with the latest developments in regional forums, where developing countries increasingly express their commitment to participatory environmental rights for civil society.

After Johannesburg the debate within UNEP took a new turn, as the executive director, in a report to the 2003 session of the Governing Council, expressed the view that:

it is clear that [UNEP] must now press forward in developing further ways and means of enhancing the application of Principle 10 as a tool for improving and strengthening environmental governance.... [A] process might be initiated to investigate *the need for and the feasibility of a new international instrument on access to information, public participation in processes leading to decision-making and access to judicial and administrative proceedings relating to environmental matters*. The immediate results of such a process could be a set of *non-binding global guidelines* on access to information, public participation in decision-making and access to justice in environmental matters to further strengthen the institutional framework for environmental management.[87]

The Governing Council, however, was reluctant to give the executive director an unqualified mandate to initiate an inter-governmental process for the preparation of such global guidelines. Instead, it rather cautiously instructed him to *"assess the possibility* of promoting, at the national and international levels, the application of Principle 10 of the Rio Declaration ... and *determine, inter alia, if there is value in initiating an intergovernmental process* for the preparation of global guidelines on the application of Principle 10".[88] It remains to be seen what will be the eventual outcome of UNEP's ongoing work in this obviously controversial area of its activities on environmental governance and law. The executive director was unable to report significant progress, let alone submit further policy recommendations, to the meeting of the Governing Council in early 2005.[89]

Conclusions and recommendations

The Åarhus Convention on Access to Information, Public Participation in Decision-Making and Access to Justice in Environmental Matters represents a unique experiment in promoting the empowerment of civil society actors through international law. Though it originated in a particular regional context and therefore necessarily reflects the perspectives and values prevailing in that region, it might nevertheless serve as a model, or at least as a catalyst and source of inspiration, for international efforts in other regions and at the global level to promote wider participation of civil society in national and international governance processes in the field of sustainable development. As the Cardoso Panel on relations between the UN system and civil society noted in its report to the Secretary-General, the ECE's experience with the Åarhus Convention process is "an interesting example to learn from".[90]

Governments and civil society organisations committed to furthering the implementation of Principle 10 of the Rio Declaration and, more generally, the transparency, accountability and democratisation of governance processes at all levels may wish to consider the following recommendations.

- *The fastest and most decisive way of demonstrating this commitment and translating it into legally binding norms is for states outside the ECE region to accede to the Åarhus Convention.* Obviously, it will be for each government to judge whether the provisions of the convention are appropriate to and can be applied in its national context, and, if so, to take the necessary steps to implement the procedural environmental rights laid down in the convention in its internal law. Civil society groups will have a role to play in preparing the ground for such national policy decisions. The meeting of the parties to the Åarhus Convention, which formally must "approve" requests for accession by non-member states of the ECE, is likely to welcome such requests,[91] as they will increase the number of parties and bolster the convention's standing in the international legal order. If a significant number of non-European states eventually become contracting parties, they will be able, through their participation as full members in the meeting of the parties, to influence the further development of the Åarhus Convention regime, which, it should be recalled, already comprises a second legally binding instrument in addition to the convention itself, the PRTR Protocol, which is also open for accession by non-ECE states.

- *Åarhus Convention parties should fully implement their commitment under the Convention to promote its principles in international environmental organisations and forums, in order to contribute to the ongoing debate on civil society participation in global governance.* The adoption, by the meeting of the parties, of the Almaty Guidelines on Promoting the Application of the Principles of the Åarhus Convention in International Forums is an important first step in this direction. These guidelines establish international standards for access to information, public participation and, to a lesser extent, access to review procedures which may serve as a benchmark for the evolution of law and practice in other forums.

- *For those regions and states which feel unable to subscribe to the Åarhus model as it stands, regional standard-setting and law-making efforts based on Principle 10 of the Rio Declaration should be further encouraged and developed.* Regional forums such as, for example, the African Union, the Barcelona Convention, ESCAP, ASEAN and the OAS have already shown an interest in supporting the application of Principle 10 in their respective regions. The elaboration of legally binding regional instruments reflecting the specific interests and priorities of states and civil society in these regions could be a promising strategy.

- *UNEP should pursue and further develop its ongoing efforts in the field of capacity-building and, eventually, global standard-setting for the application of Principle 10 of the Rio Declaration.* While attempts to elaborate a global convention on the subject might be politically unfeasible and possibly even counter-productive, in view of the already more advanced normative efforts in many regional forums, non-binding global guidelines on access to information, public participation and access to justice in environmental matters, as proposed by the UNEP executive director, could play a useful role in support of regional and national efforts by establishing minimum standards of a universal nature.

Notes

1. *Bergen Ministerial Declaration on Sustainable Development in the ECE Region*, 16 May 1990, para. 16 (g).
2. UN Doc. ENVWA/R.38, 14 December 1990.
3. UN Doc. ECE/CEP/24, October 1995.
4. It should be noted, however, that both North American member states of the ECE did participate in the recent negotiations leading to the adoption of a Protocol on Pollutant Release and Transfer Registers, adopted and opened for signature at the Fifth Ministerial Conference on "Environment for Europe", in Kiev on 21 May 2004, although neither of them signed it. The text of the Kiev Protocol and the list of signatories can be found on the Åarhus Convention website at http://www.unece.org/env/pp/prtr.htm.
5. Declaration by the Environment Ministers of the Region of the United Nations Economic Commission for Europe, in "Environment for Europe" Fourth Ministerial Conference, Åarhus, 23–25 June 1998, Conference Proceedings, Copenhagen, Ministry of Environment and Energy/Danish Environmental Protection Agency, 1999, p. 16, para. 40 (hereafter referred to as Åarhus Ministerial Declaration).
6. Ibid., p. 17, para. 42.
7. Ibid., p. 16, para. 40.
8. For a discussion of the convention's impact on law and practice in East European and Central Asian countries, see Zaharchenko, Tatiana R. and Goldenman, Gretta (2004) "Accountability in Governance: The Challenge of Implementing the Åarhus Convention in Eastern Europe and Central Asia", *International Environmental Agreements* 4: 229–251. For a comprehensive assessment of national systems of access to environmental information, public participation and access to justice in nine countries both within and outside the ECE region, see Petkova, Elena, Maurer, Crescencia, Henninger, Norbert and Irwin, Frances (2002) *Closing the Gap: Information, Participation, and Justice in Decision-Making for the Environment*, Washington, DC: World Resources Institute.
9. Council Directive 90/313/EEC of 7 June 1990 on the freedom of access to information on the environment, OJ No. L 158, 23 June 1990, p. 56.
10. Council Directive 85/337/EEC of 27 June 1985 on the assessment of the effects of certain public and private projects on the environment, OJ No. L 175, 5 July 1985, p. 40.
11. Council Directive 96/61/EC of 24 September 1996 concerning integrated pollution prevention and control, OJ No. L 257, 10 October 1996, p. 26.
12. Directive 2003/4/EC of the European Parliament and of the Council of 28 January 2003 on public access to environmental information and repealing Council Directive 90/313/EEC, OJ No. L 41, 14 February 2003, p. 26.
13. Directive 2003/35/EC of the European Parliament and of the Council of 26 May 2003 providing for public participation in respect of the drawing up of certain plans and programmes relating to the environment and amending with regard to public participation and access to justice Council Directives 85/337/EEC and 96/61/EC, OJ No. L 156, 25 June 2003, p. 17.
14. Proposal for a Directive of the European Parliament and of the Council on access to justice in environmental matters, Doc. COM(2003) 624 final, 24 October 2003.
15. Proposal for a Regulation of the European Parliament and of the Council concerning the establishment of a European Pollutant Release and Transfer Register and amending Council Directives 91/689/EEC and 96/61/EC, Doc. COM(2004) 634 final, 7 October 2004.
16. Åarhus Convention, art. 4. For a more detailed analysis of this provision and its context, see Larssen, Christine (2003) "L'accès aux informations sur l'environnement en droit international: la Convention d'Åarhus", in Christine Larssen, ed., *Dix ans d'accès à l'in-*

formation en matière d'environnement en droit international, européen et interne: bilan et perspectives, Brussels: Bruylant, pp. 25–48.
17. Åarhus Convention, art. 5.
18. Ibid., art. 6.
19. Ibid., art. 7.
20. Ibid., art. 8.
21. Ibid., art. 9, paras 1 and 2.
22. Ibid., art. 9, para. 3.
23. See generally Ebbeson, Jonas (1997) "The Notion of Public Participation in International Environmental Law", *Yearbook of International Environmental Law*, 8: 51–97.
24. Åarhus Convention, art. 2, para. 4
25. Ibid., art. 2, para. 5.
26. Ibid., art. 3, para. 4.
27. Ibid., 8th preambular para., *in fine*.
28. Ibid., 12th preambular para.
29. Ibid., 14th preambular para., *in fine*.
30. Ibid., art. 3, para. 3.
31. Ibid., art. 3, para. 2.
32. Ibid., art. 5, para. 2.
33. Ibid., art. 9, para. 5.
34. Ibid., art. 2.
35. Proposal for a Regulation of the European Parliament and of the Council on the application of the provisions of the Åarhus Convention on Access to Information, Public Participation in Decision-making and Access to Justice in Environmental Matters to EC institutions and bodies, Doc. COM(2003) 622 final, 24 October 2003.
36. Proposal for a Council Decision on the conclusion, on behalf of the European Community, of the Convention on access to information, public participation in decision making and access to justice regarding environmental matters, Doc. COM(2003) 625 final, 24 October 2003.
37. Council Decision 2005/370/EC of 17 February 2005 on the conclusion, on behalf of the European Community, of the Convention on access to information, public participation in decision-making and access to justice in environmental matters, OJ No. L 124, 17 May 2005, p. 1.
38. Åarhus Convention, art. 3, para. 7.
39. Lucca Declaration, adopted by the First Meeting of the Parties to the Convention on Access to Information, Public Participation in Decision-making and Access to Justice in Environmental Matters, Lucca, Italy, 21–23 October 2002, UN Doc. MP.PP/2002/CRP.1, 20 October 2002, para. 31.
40. Report of the first meeting of the Working Group of the Parties, UN Doc. MP.PP/WG.1/2003/2, 26 November 2003, p. 9, para. 47.
41. Decision II/4, adopted at the second meeting of the parties held in Almaty, Kazakhstan, 25–27 May 2005, UN Doc. ECE/MP.PP/2005/2/Add.5, 20 June 2005, para. 3.
42. Rules of Procedure, Decision I/1, adopted at the first meeting of the parties held in Lucca, Italy, 21–23 October 2002, UN Doc. ECE/MP.PP/2/Add.2, 2 April 2004, preamble.
43. Ibid., rule 7, para. 1.
44. Ibid., rule 6, para. 2.
45. Ibid., rule 27, para. 1.
46. Ibid., rule 11.
47. Ibid., rule 22, para. 2.
48. Review of compliance, Decision I/7, adopted at the first meeting of the parties held in Lucca, Italy, 21–23 October 2002, UN Doc. ECE/MP.PP/2/Add.8, 2 April 2004.

49. For further information on the Åarhus compliance mechanism and these cases, see the convention's website at www.unece.org/env/pp/compliance.htm.
50. Foreword to the *Implementation Guide to the Åarhus Convention*, United Nations, Geneva, 2000, UN Doc. Sales No. E.00.II.E.3.
51. See generally Bruch, Carl E. and Czerbiniak, Roman (2002) "Globalizing Environmental Governance: Making the Leap from Regional Initiatives on Transparency, Participation and Accountability in Environmental Matters", *Environmental Law Reporter* 32(4): 10428–10453.
52. UNGA Res. 37/7, 28 October 1982, Annex, para. III.16.
53. Ibid., para. III.23.
54. Ibid., para. III.24.
55. ASEAN Agreement on the Conservation of Nature and Natural Resources, Kuala Lumpur, 9 July 1985, art. 16, para. 2.
56. UN Doc. A/CONF.151/PC/38, para. 27.
57. Arab Declaration on Environment and Development of Future Perspectives, issued by the Arab Ministerial Conference on Environment and Development, Cairo, 10–15 September 1991, UN Doc. A/46/632 (1991), Annex.
58. Brunei, China, Indonesia, Japan, South Korea, Malaysia, the Philippines, Singapore, Thailand and Viet Nam.
59. See generally Hildén, Mikael and Furman, Eeva (2002) "Towards Good Practices for Public Participation in the Asia-Europe Meeting Process", in Carl E. Bruch, ed., *The New "Public". The Globalization of Public Participation*, Washington, DC: Environmental Law Institute. For background see also Hofman, Peter S. (1998) "Participation in Southeast Asian Pollution Control Policies", in F. H. J. M. Coenen, D. Huitema and L. J. O'Toole, eds, *Participation and the Quality of Environmental Decision-Making*, Dordrecht: Kluwer Academic Publishers, pp. 287–305.
60. See in particular *Public Involvement in Environmental Issues in the ASEM – Background and Overview*, AEETC, Bangkok, 2002.
61. Chairman's Statement of the ASEM Environment Ministers' Meeting, Beijing, China, 17 January 2002, para. 18, available from http://europa.eu.int/comm/external_relations/asem/min_other_meeting/env_min1.htm.
62. Chair Statement, Fourth ASEM Foreign Ministers Meeting, Madrid, 6–7 June 2002, para. 5, available from http://europa.eu.int/comm/external_relations/asem/min_other-meeting/for_min4.htm.
63. Chairman's Summary, ASEM Environment Ministers' Meeting, Lecce, Italy, 13 October 2003, para. 16, available from http://europa.eu.int/comm/external_relations/asem/min_other_meeting/env_min2.pdf.
64. Ibid.
65. The chairman's statement from the most recent ASEM summit meeting, held in Hanoi, 7–9 October 2004, and the programme of activities submitted to that meeting contain no reference to any further activities on public participation issues. In fact, the work of the AEETC has been discontinued due to lack of sufficient funding after its pilot phase.
66. See Hildén and Furman, note 59 above, p. 140.
67. Barcelona Convention for the Protection of the Marine Environment and the Coastal Region of the Mediterranean, as amended 1995, art. 15, paras 1 and 2 (emphasis added).
68. Although it should be noted that the 1995 amendments, including the new article 15, have not yet entered into force as they have not yet been formally approved by three-quarters of the contracting parties.
69. Another significant subregional development in Africa is the memorandum of understanding concluded in 1999 between the member states of the East African Community (Kenya, Tanzania and Uganda) in which these states express their commitment to

public participation in the management of natural resources and the environment. For a discussion of this instrument see Bruch and Czebiniak, note 51 above.
70. African Convention on the Conservation of Nature and Natural Resources, Maputo, Mozambique, 11 July 2003, art. XVI, para. 1.
71. ACP-EU Partnership Agreement, Cotonou, 23 June 2000, art. 7.
72. Ibid.
73. Ibid., art. 10, para. 1.
74. North American Agreement on Environmental Cooperation Between the Government of Canada, the Government of the United Mexican States and the Government of the United States of America, art. 1(h), available from www.cec.org/pubs_info_resources/law_treat_agree/naaec/index.cfm?varlan=english.
75. CIDI/RES. 98 (V-O/00), OAS Doc. OEA/Ser.W/II.5, 20 April 2000.
76. For a discussion of this strategy and its relevance in the wider context of the ongoing political debate on the proposed establishment of a hemispheric free trade area in the Americas and its impact on sustainable development, see Dannenmeier, Eric (2004) "Trade, Democracy, and the FTAA: Public Access to the Process of Constructing a Free Trade Area of the Americas", *Fordham International Law Journal* 27(3): 1066–1117.
77. UNEP Governing Council Decision 20/4, 4 February 1999.
78. UNEP Governing Council Decision 20/5, 4 February 1999.
79. Malmö Ministerial Declaration, adopted by the Global Ministerial Environment Forum – Sixth Special Session of the Governing Council of the United Nations Environment Programme, Malmö, Sweden, 31 May 2000, para. 16.
80. UNEP Governing Council Decision 21/24, 9 February 2001, paras 6 and 7.
81. Ibid., para. 5.
82. *International legal instruments reflecting provisions contained in principle 10 of the Rio Declaration on environment and development*, Report of the Executive Director, UN Doc. UNEP/GCSS.VII/INF/7.
83. See Report of the Governing Council on the Work of its seventh Special Session/Global Ministerial Environment Forum, UN Doc. UNEP/GCSS.VII/6, 5 March 2002, p. 53, para. 36.
84. Cf. UN Doc. A/CONF.199/L.1, para. 151.
85. WSSD Plan of Implementation (PoI), para. 128. Cf. CSD Decision 9/4, 27 April 2001, para. 4(a), UN Doc. E/2001/29.
86. See also PoI, para. 164.
87. *Report on the Implementation of the Programme for the Development and Periodic Review of Environmental Law for the First Decade of the Twenty-first Century (Montevideo Programme III)*, UN Doc. UNEP/GC.22/3/Add.2, 11 November 2002, p. 3, para. 8 (emphasis added).
88. UNEP Governing Council Decision 22/17, 7 February 2003, section II.B, para. 3 (emphasis added).
89. *Report on the Implementation of the Programme for the Development and Periodic Review of Environmental Law for the First Decade of the Twenty-first Century (Montevideo Programme III)*, UN Doc. UNEP/GC.23/3/Add.3, 4 November 2004, p. 16, para. 79.
90. Panel of Eminent Persons on United Nations–Civil Society Relations (2004) *We the Peoples: Civil Society, the United Nations and Global Governance*, UN Doc. A/58/817, 11 June 2004, p. 42, para. 85.
91. See Accession of non-UNECE Member States to the Convention and advancement of the principles of the Convention in other regions and at the global level, Decision II/9, adopted at the second meeting of the parties held in Almaty, Kazakhstan, 25–27 May 2005, UN Doc. ECE/MP.PP/2005/2/Add.13, 10 June 2005.

9

Promoting enfranchisement: New approaches for the climate talks

Gunnar Sjöstedt

Objectives and analytical approach

This chapter suggests an approach to promote the enfranchisement of developing countries in the UN negotiations on climate change. It builds on chapter 1 of this volume, which outlines many of the challenges that developing countries face in multilateral environmental negotiations. It first describes the general pattern of disenfranchisement in the climate talks. Then it points out the conditions necessary for useful enfranchisement approaches, particularly focusing on the requirements caused by the typical development of a multilateral negotiation process. Finally, it suggests four major empowerment strategies: capacity-building, capability enhancement, process facilitation and coaching.

Enfranchisement of developing countries in the climate talks, as well as in other multilateral negotiation processes, is an important theme for several reasons. One obvious motive for this topic is justice and fairness: developing countries have a right to real participation and influence over international decision-making on global issues that concern all countries. Engagement is also a condition for regime effectiveness; the global reach of climate change calls for the full participation of all countries. In order to achieve this objective, disenfranchised developing countries need to become empowered in such a way that their performance in the climate negotiation is upgraded. The sustainability of international treaties requires that all parties – including those from the developing world – have a reasonable chance of influencing the terms of their own commitments.

Enfranchisement is not easy to accomplish. It entails the support of developed countries, as it inevitably requires the transfer of certain critical resources to disenfranchised nations (e.g. knowledge and experts) and particularly to the large group of least developed countries. However, such aid is not sufficient. Approaches to promoting enfranchisement need to be carefully considered, and this is the main purpose of this chapter. Aid represents *the supply side* in an equation in which *the demand side* has to be carefully analysed as it specifies *how* transferred resources should best be used in order to improve participation and influence. Without a sufficient demand assessment, the supply of support to disenfranchised countries risks becoming ineffective or entirely irrelevant.

Developing countries are disenfranchised in the climate negotiations in that developed countries, especially those of the OECD, have dominated the discussion, as they have in the trade negotiations and most other multilateral encounters. One principal manifestation of their disenfranchisement is that developing countries so far have had little success in promoting an *adaptation* strategy to cope with climate warming and its negative consequences. Adaptation can be described as pre-organised crisis management. The objective of this approach is to counter the effects of climate warming *when they occur*, for example when a river is flooded or when a hurricane begins to pound a coastal area. However, the climate process has given priority to *mitigation*, reflecting the preferences and influence of the developed world. This strategy of prevention and risk management is expressed in the 1997 Kyoto Protocol to the 1992 Framework Convention on Climate Change (FCCC). According to the Kyoto Protocol, the essence of mitigation is the reduction of greenhouse gas emissions into the atmosphere. Shrinking greenhouse gas concentrations will, in turn, halt climate warming and thereby reduce the risk of natural disasters caused by a warmer atmosphere.[1]

Developing countries (DCs) have conveyed a number of reasons why they do not want to take part in the implementation of the mitigation approach of the Kyoto Protocol. DC governments argue that it is unfair that they be assigned the same mitigation costs as developed countries as the latter are primarily responsible for the concentrations of greenhouse gases in the atmosphere because of their much longer history of industrialisation and pollution. Since emissions of greenhouse gases are inevitable consequences of economic expansion and progress, they should be permitted in DCs until they become fully developed.[2]

The need for DC enfranchisement is easy to justify but more difficult to realise. As pointed out in the introduction to this volume, the literature indicates two main approaches to enfranchisement of individual states (or other kinds of actors) in multilateral interaction. One avenue is to increase the capacity of a state to perform effectively. The other approach

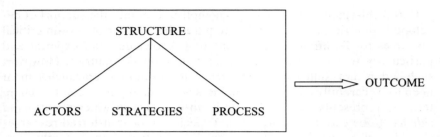

Figure 9.1 Basic elements of a multilateral negotiation

is to make changes in the structural context of the multilateral arena for the purpose of making this external environment more advantageous for the state actor. This chapter will consider both of these approaches in the context of multilateral talks, and will look specifically at the negotiation process to consider ways to increase DC engagement.

In addition to its *outcome*, a multilateral negotiation has four basic elements (fig. 9.1): the *actors* involved in the negotiation; their *strategies* (or more generally their performance); the *process* of negotiation, which is the entire pattern of actor interaction; and its *structure*, which refers to the external factors influencing actors, strategies and process that essentially remain unchanged as long as the negotiation continues.[3]

Changes in the ability of a particular developing country to "influence agenda-setting and decision-making" in multilateral negotiation may in different ways be associated with all its five elements. Thus, all five elements should be considered in the design of enfranchisement strategies. The *outcome* reflects how relatively successful a country has been to shape the agreement forged in the negotiation. Altered *actor properties*, such as greater resourcefulness, may increase the impact of what the country does at the negotiation table, and better-prepared policies and strategies may lead to the same result. One institutional setting (e.g. the UN Conference on Environment and Development, UNCED) may represent a more favourable *structural context* than another (e.g. the World Trade Organization, WTO) for negotiation of a particular package of issues. Finally, the character of the *negotiation process* represents often powerful constraints on what a disenfranchised DC is able to do. The process conditions of negotiations have been somewhat neglected in assessments of what roles DCs are capable of performing in the climate talks, or multilateral negotiations more generally. Therefore, *process conditions* will be highlighted in the analysis that follows. It will be argued that process characteristics represent critical guidelines for the design of enfranchisement strategies.

Coping with disenfranchisement: In search of approaches for enfranchisement

Disenfranchisement in the climate negotiation reflects *powerlessness*, that can conceivably be absolute (or at least almost absolute) or relative and variable. Many of the UN-designated "least developed countries" (LDCs) have been *absolutely powerless* in the climate talks, as well as in other multilateral negotiations, in that they have only been nominal participants and have had no other choice. They have remained virtually passive and have not been able to influence events at the table. Other more resourceful disenfranchised countries have been *relatively powerless*, meaning that their active participation has made an unsatisfactory impact on process and outcome (for a discussion of why this is the case, see Gupta, chap. 1). It is an urgent task to develop enfranchisement approaches to transform absolute to relative powerlessness in the case of the weakest countries and to decrease the relative degree of powerlessness of other disenfranchised states.

In considering the strategies put forth here, enfranchisement means that DCs have lessened or completely removed constraints on participation and influence, and are more capable of defending their own interests. The key question is how such enfranchisement or empowerment can be attained. There are at least two principal perspectives offering answers to this query. The first focuses on the individual (developing) country, and is explained by a traditional political realist analysis. The power of a nation is reflected by its possession of a number of critical resources that may expand or contract over time, including military capabilities, size of population and national economy or technological capabilities.[4] Some authors emphasise issue-specific resources, for example, share of world exports in international trade diplomacy or tonnage in international shipping, as part of the measure of power.[5] The implication of this realist, or neo-realist, outlook is that empowerment is essentially represented by the expansion of critical resources, the growth of *the power base* of a nation. A second perspective on international power relations, highlighting *international structural conditions*, implies that empowerment can be achieved by means of modified structural conditions, for example through the creation of acknowledged norms or institutional reform in an international organisation.

Both the approach of expanding the power base and that of modifying structural conditions are certainly relevant for, and applicable to, the climate negotiations. The two approaches have been discussed in UN circles and some concrete policy measures to implement them have been carried out. Hence, various projects of *capacity-building* have been undertaken to give selected DCs better access to climate knowledge and expertise in the climate talks (*the power base approach*). Institutional reforms in UN institutions for the purpose of increasing the participation of NGOs in processes of cooperation and negotiation are now bringing articulate and competent supporters of DC positions and arguments into the climate negotiations (*structural change*).

Enfranchisement of DCs in the climate talks may occur "automatically" in the sense that no special measures are required. Economic growth and an expanding economy will build up resources with many uses that may, for example, be allocated to support a country's performance in the climate talks. Accordingly, general economic assistance to DCs can be expected to enhance the capacity of their governments to manoeuvre effectively in the negotiations. However, such diffuse spillover effects are not sufficient, even if they do occur. Strategies for enfranchisement require careful design in order to attain specified objectives, and thus be effective.

Cost-effectiveness is also vital for another reason. Meaningful approaches targeting the whole category of disenfranchised countries need support from donor countries, and the only likely candidates are the member states of the OECD. It is realistic to assume that such aid will be forthcoming, particularly from Europe. The European Union and most of its member states are anxious to continue the strenuous work of securing a meaningful international climate regime. The European Union also has a long tradition of economic assistance to many of the most disenfranchised nations, particularly the LDCs least developed countries in Africa. However, such empowerment assistance is not likely to be completely unconditional. Donors can be expected to request cost-effective measures.

Cost-effectiveness begs for clear criteria, thus raising a series of questions. For example, for exactly what operational purpose should aid be used and what concrete operational targets should it have? In order to be effective, aid should help DCs attain the ability to undertake appropriate actions in the climate negotiations in any given situation. Thus, empowerment should basically aim at enhancing the *actor capability* of a targeted DC, not its general strength or its international status.

Actor capability reflects how a given negotiating party – for example a DC – actually performs in the climate talks (or any other negotiation). The requirements for actor capability vary depending on the current circumstances of the negotiation.[6] In the highly variable context of the climate talks, enhanced actor performance may take on a number of different forms and meanings and may also have a variety of effects on other actors, as well as on the negotiation process as a whole. Thus, in the negotiations process, influential parties put forward strategic proposals or counter-proposals in order to give direction to the whole process.

They argue in favour of some proposals and disagree with others. They propose a formula for a compromise between a proposal and a counter-proposal. They go to informal restricted meetings with like-minded countries, or otherwise consult with other actors involved in the negotiation. They take part in decisions on an intermediate or a final agreement, be it by vote or consensus.

As the climate talks unfold over time they change character as different process stages replace each other, moving from pre-negotiation and agenda-setting to final bargaining on detail and formal agreement.[7] Different process stages require somewhat different performance by a negotiating party that strives to be effective. For a given country, the possibility of having influence may be somewhat greater under some process conditions than under others. In sum, a full-fledged actor in an international negotiation needs to do many different things requiring somewhat dissimilar skills and resources depending on the circumstances. This variety of skills should be considered when developing strategies for enfranchisement.

Actor capability is a significant point of departure for empowerment strategies. The critical factor is *impact* on other actors, process and ultimately outcome. The broader and the more solid actor capability a country has, the stronger impact it can be expected to make on the climate talks, "all other things being equal". However, generally things are not equal. We will often find structural circumstances and actor properties (the power base) that amplify or reduce the impact of the actor capability. Together actor capability, an actor's power base and structural conditions represent the drivers on the supply side of an equation causing an impact on actors, process and outcome. The demand side is manifested by *performance requirements*, which, in turn, are conditioned by the patterns in which a multilateral negotiation like the climate talks unfolds. Performance requirements represent irreplaceable guidelines for the development of empowerment approaches.

Performance requirements

Each multilateral negotiation is an individual drama. It is coloured by the issues put on the agenda. For example, economic and environmental negotiations have some important divergent features. Economic negotiations are often guided by a neo-classic economic doctrine and aim to distribute positive values that are easy to quantify and cope with from a technical negotiation point of view.[8] Environmental negotiations are concerned with negative values and risks.[9] They strive to avoid harmful effects caused by pollution and misuse of scarce resources, and their aim is typically to distribute abatement costs, negative values. Negotiation by like-minded countries can be expected to have a different character than bargaining between parties which have a different outlook on a negotiated topic, as developed and developing countries tend to have on the climate issue. For example, like-mindedness facilitates problem-solving in a negotiation. However, multilateral negotiations tend to progress in a recurrent sequence of stages: pre-negotiation, agenda-setting, formula negotiation, negotiation on detail, agreement and post-negotiation.[10]

Process stages in the climate talks: The general pattern

In the climate talks *pre-negotiation* started in the international scientific community, particularly in a broad and growing international epistemic community around the World Meteorological Organization (WMO) and UN Environmental Programme (UNEP).[11] In 1988 these consultations became more structured through the Intergovernmental Panel on Climate Change (IPCC), a new and unique international institution strongly anchored in the world scientific community. Its main function was to identify, frame and assess the issue of climate change for the benefit of the diplomats in the Intergovernmental Negotiation Committee (INC), which marked the beginning of formal climate talks in 1990. Scientific knowledge gathered (framed, summarised and assessed) by the IPCC in the pre-negotiation stage conditioned agenda-setting in the INC considerably.[12]

The 1992 FCCC revealed a shift from agenda-setting to *negotiation of a formula*. The FCCC represented a framework for structuring further negotiation. Ultimately, it included detailed directions for a binding agreement on state commitments to reduce emissions of greenhouse gases (specified volumes and implementation periods). The negotiation formula was further developed at the first Conference of the Parties (COP) and was thereafter gradually transferred into *negotiation on detail* concerning binding commitments by individual negotiating parties.[13] In this process a draft text for a supplementary Protocol to the Framework Convention on Climate Change was hammered out on the negotiation table and eventually accepted and signed at the 1997 COP meeting in Kyoto (the Kyoto Protocol).[14]

The signature of the Kyoto Protocol was followed by a sequence of recurrent COP meetings of *post-negotiation* for treaty completion (on the average occurring every year). One aim of the meetings was to eliminate various impediments to the implementation of the Kyoto Protocol and to establish means of facilitation of emission cuts, for example through the creation of procedures for trade in emission permits and joint implementation. Another goal was to establish other means of controlling concentrations of greenhouse gases in the atmosphere than emission cuts, for example through the employment of carbon sinks, notably forests or the sea. However, it was particularly Washington's refusal to ratify the Kyoto Protocol that necessitated prolonged post-negotiation. Since the United States is the largest emitter of CO_2, a climate regime without full US participation would be seriously crippled.[15]

Like most other multilateral negotiations, the climate talks should be seen in a regime-building perspective. Multilateral negotiations do not typically develop as one single sequence of process stages running from pre-negotiation to agreement or post-negotiation. The signature of the Kyoto Protocol did not terminate the negotiations on climate change, but was followed by post-negotiation that in certain respects has been transformed into pre-negotiation for likely upcoming post-Kyoto talks on new issues and conditioned by new premises.

The formal text of the Kyoto Protocol is *not* a comprehensive representation of all the results that had been achieved in the climate negotiations before 1997. Parties have been affected by the climate talks in other ways than by their formal outcome. The conventional concept of *regime-building* broadens the perspective on the gradually evolving outcome of the climate talks. A regime may be described as an issue-specific governance system around which "actor expectations converge".[16] As seen in this perspective, the emerging climate regime consists of four potentially interacting components, each of which has a special function in the governance system. The treaty provisions of the Kyoto Protocol represent *rules*. The three other categories are *norms, consensual knowledge (regime principles)* and *procedures*, which all give support to the implementation of the regime rules.[17] However, norms and regime principles also have an autonomous role influencing national and international policymakers directly.

The transformation of scientific knowledge into consensual knowledge, primarily in the IPCC, has been of paramount importance in the climate negotiations, and it has sometimes served as a driver in the whole process.[18] When pre-negotiations began in the 1980s in the international scientific community, climate change did not exist as a clearly defined topic on the agenda of world politics. The climate issue was largely constructed in the IPCC in the early stages of the climate talks, essentially on the basis of scientific knowledge and current information provided by hundreds of scientists who had been engaged in the process.[19] The IPCC provided an authoritative description of the climate problem. With the help of sophisticated scientific models, it highlighted and assessed the prospects for climate warming around the globe, as well as the expected negative or disastrous effects of climate warming.[20] Consensual knowledge produced by the IPCC identified the common interest of negotiating parties and identified concrete approaches and methods to cope with the climate problem. By framing the issues the IPCC conditioned diplomatic negotiations in the INC very strongly. Like most other negotiations the climate talks represented a mixture of problem-solving and distribution of values. Problem-solving was closely associated with the development and employment of consensual knowledge. In the distribution game of the climate talks, parties employed a discourse of "knowledge diplomacy" to define positions and develop their arguments.

Norms that have become integrated into the climate regime are not binding in the same legal sense as *regime rules* (e.g. the provisions of the Kyoto Protocol). Nevertheless, when a norm is accepted by a "critical mass" of negotiating parties, it will constrain their choices and in some situations it may have a decisive influence regardless of their legal status. Sometimes international lawyers refer to non-binding commitments in an international treaty as "soft law". Establishment of norms may occur through acknowledgement or formation, or a mixture of the two mechanisms. Norms become *acknowledged* when they already exist in another context and begin to have an impact on the climate regime. Notably, a number of norms concerning "special rights" of developing or least developed countries (e.g. the right of exception to binding, costly commitments) have been transmitted from the general UN context to the climate regime. The 2002 World Summit on Sustainable Development (WSSD) reinforced this process of diffusion and included norms concerning sustainable development. *Formation* creates new norms pertaining to the particular issue and context. It may in reality be the further development of existing general norms, such as those of justice and fairness. An important example is the emerging norms for intergenerational sharing of responsibility for the occurrence of climate change.

Process conditions for enfranchisement

On one occasion, the representative of a small DC, who had won a well-deserved prize for eloquence at the University of Oxford, gave an absolutely brilliant speech at a meeting in a GATT round of multilateral negotiations where a draft text for an agreement concerning non-tariff barriers to trade was discussed. With well-chosen words he pointed at the unfairness of the world trading system with its dominance of industrialised nations and called for radical reforms. This "lecture" caused considerable irritation in the negotiation group and was completely disregarded, by both developed and developing countries. The primary reason for this reaction was not that other country representatives opposed the message of the eloquent speech, but rather that it was completely irrelevant in the context of the negotiation. The talented submission did not contribute anything to the current, difficult negotiation work and was therefore a complete waste of sparse time.

A basic requirement for *actor capability* is a faculty to undertake meaningful actions in a given negotiation situation.[21] In reality, negotiating parties have a limited choice of relevant categories of actions in any given negotiation situation. The result is convergence of performance. Parties tend to behave in a similar way in a given situation, hence generating a distinct pattern of party interaction. Looking at the climate talks five broad patterns of interaction are discirnable, each of which may dominate the process at one time or another.

- *Issue clarification.* This pattern of performance has been both common and important in the climate talks. It has appeared for long periods of time and is also significant in the current early post-Kyoto negotiation. When clarifying the climate issue a principal objective of negotiation parties has been to develop consensual knowledge about its causes, its manifestations and its likely disastrous consequences for many regions and countries around the world, as well as about appropriate abatement methods. From a procedural point of view, interaction representing issue clarification is relatively unfocused. Discussions may take on a character similar to that of an academic seminar. In the climate talks, the negotiation work of individual delegations in the INC was dependent on the input from the IPCC. Written submissions by national delegations were often analytical or conceptual papers or comments on similar submissions by other delegations.
- *Substantive problem-solving* has many specific meanings and applications. For example, it could include discussion of an appropriate negotiation approach that would be helpful to move forward in the process, to build up agreement or consensus, to break deadlocks or to determine the necessary parameters of an agreement. In order to solve substantive problems, parties often need to develop creative strategies by combining issue expertise with other kinds of knowledge regarding, for example, other parties and their interests or the constraints created by process conditions. A solution to a negotiation problem in complex international talks like those in the climate area typically needs to combine two elements that are often contradictory: technical feasibility and political acceptability. Proposals for substantive problem-solving are typically submitted in elaborate papers.
- In this chapter, *bargaining* essentially means "exchange of concessions". In the climate negotiations, bargaining has basically concerned cost-sharing: who shall reduce emissions of greenhouse gases, how much and how quickly? To what extent should industrialised countries give economic assistance to developing or least developed countries, to

help them reduce emissions and take measures to decrease the vulnerability of their ecological systems, society and economy to the negative and disastrous effects of climate warming should they occur? In some way or other, bargaining may be a dimension of almost all interaction within a negotiation. In "pure" bargaining, parties make recurrent requests and offers to specific other actors or groups of actors. Bargaining on the grand issues is typically bilateral or evolving in a small group of especially interested and competent states.

- *Final decision-making* refers to episodes in the negotiation when a formal collective choice is made, as parties did when they established the FCCC in 1992 and the Kyoto Protocol in 1997. Decision by consensus, which is the normal procedure in multinational negotiation, is different from roll calls in the United Nations. All parties are not equally involved when a choice is made.[22] Disenfranchised countries have much greater chances of vetoing a roll-call decision than a decision by consensus. In principle, a consensus decision has been taken when no significant actor is opposing a tabled proposal for an agreement.
- *Debate*. Parties exchange views on the negotiation as a whole or on the various issues it addresses. The general function of debate is to let parties highlight and air their concerns and positions without necessarily committing themselves to a specific policy action. Debates do not need to conclude in a binding agreement but rather produce a general resolution.

Meaningful participation in each of the five types of "negotiation game" requires a particular and varying mix of competence and resources to be effective. Disenfranchisement may result in small and poor countries becoming totally excluded from a specific type of negotiation game, say *bargaining* (e.g. about country-specific reductions of greenhouse gas emissions). However, the same country may not be equally excluded from other patterns of interaction. The significant *performance requirements* may vary considerably across different patterns of interaction. Accordingly, a given country's actor capability is constrained in different ways and to different degrees in the different types of negotiation game. This variation must be carefully considered when enfranchisement strategies are developed.

Of all alternative patterns of recurrent interaction, *debate* is easiest to handle for disenfranchised countries, particularly since it resembles regular UN diplomacy. All countries present at a meeting should be able to debate. Also, LDCs have relatively unproblematic access to a debate in a UN institution. Even vague and general statements are acceptable submissions. Collective action in a coalition of small and weak states is likewise relatively feasible. Coalition members can simply agree on a text to be read by a formal spokesperson, which may contain somewhat diverging views. Regional groups or the Group of 77 can speak for disenfranchised DCs in debates concerning fundamental ethical questions underpinning the grand choices made in the climate talks, for example concerning DC obligations and the question of intergenerational responsibility.

Debates have occurred in the climate negotiations even if they do not represent a dominant form of interaction, as they do in the General Assembly and other central UN institutions. The FCCC was an outcome of UNCED and caused some debate in the preparations for the Rio Meeting of Heads of States and Governments in 1992.[23] This debate increased awareness of the climate issue world wide. Ten years later, the linkages between climate change and sustainable development had become further reinforced. These couplings were debated and assessed at the 2002 WSSD in Johannesburg. Debate therefore has an important function in setting and maintaining the policy agenda, both within and beyond the multilateral arena. However, diplomatic debate has been comparatively rare – and mostly undesired – in the IPCC and other core institutions of the climate negotiations. In this context *issue clarification*, *formula negotiation* and *bargaining* are much more useful and constructive forms of interaction than *debate*, but also more demanding for disenfranchised countries.

A fundamental problem for many DCs, and all LDCs, has been their failing ability to participate effectively, or at all, in interaction that does not have the character of *debate*. *Issue clarification* and *formula negotiation* have represented the most demanding forms of interaction, which have been very burdensome for DCs and therefore kept them on the periphery. In the future, the process of constructing those issues that are of strategic significance will continue to be important. In considering approaches to DC enfranchisement, it is important that they become involved in this issue clarification stage of the negotiations process.

Much of the *bargaining* unfolding in the climate talks, as well as in other similar multilateral negotiations, may be compared to a type of trade between the parties. For example, parties may exchange *threats* or *sanctions* in order to attain concessions of the other side in an ongoing escalation game. In other situations, more typical for the climate talks, parties exchange concessions regarding *requests* and *offers* pertaining to the principal stakes (emission cuts) in a bargaining game. The outcome of such trading games is conditioned by a host of situational factors, events and actions, including threats/sanctions and promises/rewards. However, concessions' trade concerning the stake as such is important, and often probably decisive. For example, the United States' original commitment in the Kyoto Protocol to accept 7 per cent reductions of emissions of greenhouse gases was linked to the 8 per cent reductions pledged by the European Union. The control of the negotiated stakes represents issue-specific power, which is a kind of veto power.[24] The larger the share a country has of current and future emissions, the less value has an international agreement on emission control for other signatory nations if this state does not join it. As compared to OECD countries, DCs emit comparatively small volumes of greenhouse gases into the atmosphere even when their emissions are combined. This situation gives them little issue-specific power that might compensate them for the lack of general "power resources", as has sometimes been the case with certain small "smart" states.[25]

From a legal point of view, participation in *final decision-making* in the climate talks does not represent a great problem for disenfranchised countries. All parties have a prerogative to take part in all formal choices made in the negotiation. DCs also have voting power to carry or block a resolution in most UN institutions. However, in the climate talks, decisions are usually not taken by roll call but by consensus. Consensus decisions may appear to be just as "democratic" as roll calls, because participation is open to all parties. In a general and somewhat misleading sense, consensus may be understood as agreement. In reality, consensus decisions are likely to be steered, or completely controlled, by a "critical mass" of leading nations, which in the climate talks has essentially consisted of the group of OECD countries. The "mass" of countries has become "critical" when the veto power of those that have *not* joined the winning coalition has grown insignificant. In the bargaining about the Kyoto Protocol "the critical mass" may be given a name, the group of Annex I countries.[26] For the OECD countries it was not critical (at least not in the short term) that DCs did not want to reduce CO_2 emissions. Therefore the refusal of DCs to accept binding commitments to reduce emissions of greenhouse gases did not give them any real power, but rather sustained their marginal position in the climate talks.

Issue clarification was of strategic importance in the climate talks and gave far-reaching and quite specific directions for the conduct of the negotiation. To a great extent, this process was a "knowledge game" with deep involvement of scientists in the IPCC as well as in national delegations. Disenfranchised countries with only modest "scientific resources" had great difficulties in making meaningful contributions to the "knowledge game". It was even hard for them to perform effectively in line with their interests as recipients of information communicated by other parties in the context of issue clarification.

Substantive problem-solving represented at least equally demanding performance requirements, which virtually prohibited meaningful participation of many disenfranchised countries. Impact-making interventions required not only a profound understanding of the technicalities of the climate issues but also depended on a deep comprehension of the negotiation process that was virtually impossible for peripheral disenfranchised countries to attain.

Each of the five *patterns of interaction* identified above represents a strong movement towards convergence of individual party performance in any given negotiation situation. A current pattern of interaction need not be completely "pure". Mixed negotiation games may transpire. Brief *debate* incidents have, for instance, occurred in situations even when the climate talks were dominated by *issue clarification* or *bargaining*. However, generally there is a dominant pattern of interaction during the whole negotiation, although this negotiation game changes as the process unfolds.

Hence, there is an association between a dominant pattern of interaction on the one hand and on the other a current process stage of the negotiation, *pre-negotiation, agenda-setting, formula negotiation, negotiation on detail, agreement* and *post-negotiation*. Table 9.1 summarises the likely significant correlations between *process stage* and *pattern of interaction*.[27] The couplings displayed in the table are significant for engagement strategies because they indicate that the degree of enfranchisement of a given country is conditioned by the current process stage.

The circumstances are most favourable for DCs in three process stages, *pre-negotiation, post-negotiation* and *agreement*, when *debate* or *formal decision-making* characterises party interaction. The room for DC influence is restricted also in these phases of the negotiation, but at least *debate* offers an opportunity for "voice". This opening is quite limited, however, as *debate* is only one of several patterns of interaction that may emerge in *pre-negotiation* and *post-negotiation*, and not the most

Table 9.1 Association between *process stage* and *pattern of interaction* in the climate talks

Patterns of interaction	Process stage
Pre-negotiation (debate)	Issue clarification, bargaining and (debate)
Agenda-setting	Issue clarification (debate)
Formula negotiation	Substantive problem-solving
Agreement	Bargaining; formal decision-making
Post-negotiation	Debate; issue clarification; substantive problem-solving

Parentheses represent a clear secondary role for a given pattern of interaction in a given process stage.

important one. DCs are active in the stage of *agreement* but have little weight when decisions are not taken by roll call.

So far DCs have been particularly weak in the strategic process stages of *agenda-setting* and *formula negotiation*, from which they have been virtually excluded due to lacking negotiation strength when the current pattern of interaction is *issue clarification* or *substantive problem-solving*. For example, DCs have argued that more consideration should be given to the issue of adaptation to climate change in rare debate episodes, but they have not been able to bring this topic into *agenda-setting* and *formula negotiation*.

The correlations between type of negotiation game and process stage in table 9.1 paints a bleak picture for DCs struggling to exercise influence. Their actor capability is heavily constrained in all process stages, and particularly in the strategically important phase of *formula negotiation*. The question is whether this negative situation will change if consideration is given to how the outcome is produced in the negotiation. Such an overview can be accomplished with the help of a regime perspective.[28]

The principal objective of the negotiations on the Kyoto Protocol was to establish binding *rules* concerning the reduction of emissions of CO_2 and other greenhouse gases into the atmosphere. Certainly, rule creation influences the entirety of the climate talks. Negotiation on rules can be expected to generate all kinds of patterns of interaction – negotiation games (issue clarification, substantive problem-solving, bargaining, formal decision-making and debate). From this point of view it is not meaningful to separate rule-making from the climate talks generally. However, *procedures, consensual knowledge* and *norms* have to some extent been created separate from the principal negotiation on *rule-making* in the INC. Occasionally the INC agenda has explicitly included *procedural matters*. The IPCC has carried out various tasks in the climate talks, but its main function has been to create and institute regime norms. Examples of such conveyed norms have been polluter pays, the precautionary norm and the norm of sustainable development.

The formation of the four regime elements has had its own specific association with somewhat unlikely combinations of negotiation games – *patterns of interaction*. Although *rule-making* is difficult to distinguish from the climate talks, generally there are two types of negotiation game that have a special significance in this context. *Bargaining* is necessary to reach a formal agreement containing binding commitments. The final conclusion of an agreement requires a formal decision, which is not a prerequisite for the institution of either *regime principles* (consensual knowledge) or *norms*.

Procedures may also be given the form of a legally binding commitment and may be very similar to regime rules. For this reason, proce-

Table 9.2 Association between negotiation on particular *regime element (outcomes)* and *pattern of interaction (games)*

Negotiation outcomes	Negotiation games: Patterns of interaction
Rules	Issue clarification, substantive problem-solving, *bargaining, formal decision-making*, debate
Consensual knowledge	Issue clarification, substantive problem-solving
norms	*Debate*, substantive problem-solving (external opinion-building)
Procedures	Bargaining, formal decision-making (pragmatic precedence)

A pattern of interaction is italicised when it is considered to be particularly significant in relation to a given regime element.

dures may be similarly constructed with a significant role for *bargaining* and *formal decision-making*. Procedures pertaining exclusively to the climate talks are in general of an informal nature and have typically been created by the institutionalisation of useful ways of doing things in negotiation groups or plenary bodies.

In some multilateral negotiations the construction of consensual knowledge – regime principles – has simply been the joint acknowledgement by negotiating parties of well-known facts and established causal relationships. In the climate talks the situation has been quite different. Because advanced knowledge was necessary to begin to understand the climate issue, new special working methods and institutions (the IPCC) had to be established. It may be argued that the broad participation and considerable influence of the world scientific community in the IPCC should to some extent have counterbalanced the strong influence of industrialised countries in the knowledge-building process. However, disenfranchised countries were not in a position to take advantage of this situation. The construction of consensual knowledge was particularly associated with *issue clarification* and *substantive problem-solving*, the patterns of interaction that were most demanding for them (see table 9.2).

To make an impact on negotiation, *norms* need to be well established amongst the parties. The consolidation and reinforcement of international norms may occur in different ways, for example by means of opinion-building by the media, NGOs and other private actors. Such activities have neither been common nor important in the central negotiation bodies of the climate talks. On the other hand, opinion-building associated with the climate talks took place in other forums, for example the 1992 UNCED and the 2002 WSSD.

Norms may also be sustained and bolstered by being recalled in the deliberations in the negotiation process itself. Such references to norms may be part of a *debate*, but may also occur in other patterns of interaction, *issue clarification, substantive problem-solving* or *bargaining*. All things considered, *norms* are the elements of an international regime that are the easiest to address for disenfranchised countries. Firstly, they can count on support from international opinion-building. Secondly, they can contribute to forming or reinforcing norms in the climate regime by acting in other contexts than the climate talks where they have more advantageous positions. Thirdly, *debate* in the process of climate negotiation can be used for norm-building or norm consolidation.

In contrast, the building of regime principles – *consensual knowledge* – has represented the greatest difficulty for DCs, and has seriously crippled their actor capability in the climate talks. In the post-Kyoto situation there may be some new openings for DCs in the strategically important area of knowledge diplomacy, particularly if more consideration is given to adaptation measures than in the past. Such a development would increase the value of knowledge about local conditions around the world, DCs included.

What can be done? Empowerment approaches

Sustainability and effectiveness of the international climate regime need the full participation and commitment of all countries around the world. Accordingly, promoting the enfranchisement of marginalised countries is a necessary but complex approach to this problem. There is a need to take many different factors into consideration pertaining to targeted countries and their interaction with other parties as well as surrounding structural conditions. However, the complexity of promoting enfranchisement is not only a stumbling block, but also points out a potential; a "toolbox" of possible approaches and concrete measures.

The strategies proposed here may target an individual disenfranchised state, particularly its actor capability and its resource-conditioned power base. It may also aim to ease the effect of constraining structural background conditions for constructive performance in the climate negotiation. The most effective strategy cannot be determined a priori. To assess the relevance and expected effectiveness of proposed measures, the performance requirements for winning negotiation tactics and strategies need to be clarified. The accurate appraisal of performance requirements is a key prerequisite for any successful enfranchisement approach.

The above analysis emphasises that performance requirements do not remain constant in an evolving negotiation. The climate talks are no exception. The general strength of performance requirements varies as the climate talks evolve but also, and more significantly, so does their meaning for influenced parties. As seen by an individual party, process-conditioned constraints have altered as the climate negotiations have evolved through process stages, hence requiring changed performance of individual disenfranchised countries. Given these diverse conditions in the climate talks, successful enfranchisement of DCs may be attained with the help of five principal approaches: strategy change, capacity-building, capability training, facilitation and possibly coaching.

Four options for enfranchisement

Ultimately individual DCs need to develop a separate national climate policy and a strategy to pursue in the climate talks. The predicament of, say, Egypt, Fiji and Nepal is quite similar with regard to continued climate warming but also in certain respects quite different. For example, in contrast to their opposite numbers in Fiji and Egypt, decision-makers in Nepal do not have to cope with the threat of a rising sea level. Individual countries need to update strategies constantly, taking developments in the climate talks carefully into consideration, which may require the support of empowerment strategies, *capacity-building, capability development, facilitation* or *coaching.*

Individual climate policies in DCs are closely linked to a common approach that may need to be revised in order to give them a more favourable position in the continued climate negotiation. The essence of this joint approach has so far been to retain the prerogative to refrain from accepting costly commitments to reduce emissions of CO_2 and other greenhouse gases. However, the successful policy of seeking exceptions now begins to take on the character of a Pyrrhic victory. In the longer term tactical gains can be expected to become offset by strategic disadvantages. One shortcoming of an "exceptions" strategy is that DCs should have a long-term interest in developing an effective and robust climate regime. At the same time their predicament is different from that of the OECD countries. Therefore, they need to increase their influence in the climate regime-building process as far as possible, which in the longer term is not possible with an "exceptions-to-rules" strategy.

DC governments should anticipate growing pressure from the OECD countries and other states to begin accepting the costly disciplines of the climate regime. In the longer term "a seeking exception policy" will probably be self-defeating. DCs have little choice but to find better ways of defending their interests in the climate talks than by remaining in the wings and avoiding costly commitments. A shift from an exception-seeking to a commitment-making strategy can be regarded as an element of an empowerment approach.

Capacity-building is usually thought of as the mobilisation (domestic capacity-building) or the cross-country transfer (international capacity-building) of critical resources in order to support analysts, planners, decision-makers or negotiators in an assisted country trying to cope with a certain issue or dealing with a particular policy area. In other words, this assistance may either have the character of self-help within a given country or represent international aid. Several international organisations have established institutions with the task of organising capacity-building in selected developing countries. Similar programmes of capacity-building have been carried out to support negotiation on climate warming, for example by the UN Institute for Training and Research (UNITAR).

Domestic capacity-building has often established competent task forces to assist the government or has undertaken institutional reform for the same purpose. International capacity-building projects have to a large extent involved the transfer of expertise regarding the institutions of the climate negotiation or advanced knowledge drawn from the world scientific community concerning the problem of climate warming as such. Knowledge about the climate issue (causes, effects, countermeasures) can be expected to increase a country's ability to address this issue actively in a negotiation.

Capability development may be closely related to *capacity-building*, but is quite different with regard to both character and purpose. *Capacity* represents favourable conditions for effective performance. *Capability* represents how a given party actually performs in the negotiation. Accordingly, *capability development* has the character of a training programme that may be organised domestically or be part of a programme of international assistance that could be either bilateral or multilateral.

Closely targeted capability development is an important and somewhat neglected approach of strengthening negotiation effectiveness of weak countries. Negotiation games (with or without computer support) represent one approach to attain that objective. This method is certainly not an innovation. However, such negotiation games have usually had a too general conception of the climate talks. One useful approach would be capability training before an actual upcoming negotiation session such as a COP meeting with special consideration given to the issues currently "on the table" and the main issues that are likely to be addressed.

An important part of capability training with weak DCs is to enhance their ability to protect or promote their own interests in a coalition of actors. The principal participants of such coalitions would be states, but other categories of actors might also be included, such as NGOs or other representatives of civic society. One critical condition for this DC capability is an understanding of what different kinds of coalition (ideological coalition; issue-specific coalition etc.) can do in different kinds of negotiation situations. Another crucial condition is a comprehension of what the DC itself can, and cannot, do to make a coalition take care of its own concerns and defend or promote its own interests in the climate talks. Programmes of capability training must, hence, put an emphasis on demonstrating the instrumentality of coalition in negotiation for DCs. Capability training should be supplemented by capacity support to coalition-building directly. Part of the assistance from OECD countries and other sources should be reallocated to prop up DC coalitions in order to make them more effective. Such aid could, for instance, consist of resources to support general administrative tasks, circulation of crucial information amongst coalition members or the holding of workshops in preparation for sessions in the climate talks. Capacity-building efforts could make it possible to recruit climate and negotiation experts to a secretariat serving the coalition.

Facilitation is a third main strategy to enhance the negotiation strength of weak countries. The purpose of other approaches (*capacity-building*, *capability training* and *coaching*) is to increase the ability of a weak country to manoeuvre in the demanding and highly constraining environment represented by an unfolding, complex, multilateral negotiation. The logic of *facilitation* is the opposite; to modify a demanding environment of weak parties.

Understood in this general way, facilitation is by no means an innovation in international negotiation or organisation. For example, a recurrent request for facilitation put forward by DCs at many international conferences is to keep the number of parallel meetings down as far as possible in order to make it easier for countries with very small delegations to participate effectively in the negotiation. However, facilitation measures have been easier to ordain or recommend than to implement successfully. The case of restrictions of parallel meetings is instructive. In a complex negotiation like that on trade or climate change, *process effectiveness* may require not only parallel but also small, restricted negotiation groups working at private meetings. Although it is highly unfair for weak countries that are excluded from restricted meetings, the leading countries do not easily abandon this process organisation. It is impossible to conduct complex multilateral negotiations in only plenary negotiation bodies including all formal participants, like for example the formal COP meetings in the climate talks. Smaller negotiating groups are needed to address important sticking points or to assess particularly complicated stumbling blocks. Smaller negotiation groups typically possess a higher concentration of knowledge than a larger group of countries and also have a larger capacity to act more flexibly than a large coalition of states like the Group of 77. One type of solution might be a flexible representation system letting a limited number of especially interested or competent

Group of 77 countries participate in a particular restricted meeting. However, although facilitation stands out as a promising approach to enhance the actor performance and influence of DCs in the climate talks, this strategy needs to be designed and carried out with the utmost sensitivity to the political realities of the unfolding climate negotiations. Attention should always be given to the constraints and possibilities of the current process stage. Facilitation may possibly include elements of process design, which is different from structural reform. Furthermore, facilitation should not be employed as a separate strategy but should be integrated in a broader, comprehensive programme of assistance to DCs.

Coaching of disenfranchised countries contains certain important possibilities but is probably unrealistic. The whole point of a negotiation is that the parties involved discuss an issue with one another and look for as favourable an agreement as possible, or at least an accord that they can live with. A government negotiating climate change, or any other issue, must have optimum autonomy to make its own assessments and decisions. It is possible for the government to get information and other resources from external sources, but it needs to be in complete control of its own actions in the negotiation process. However, as far as some disenfranchised countries are concerned this autonomy requirement has to be related to another principle: that of active participation and influence in the negotiation. Full control over negotiation performance has little value if it does not lead to meaningful negotiation performance.

The essence of *coaching* is that the international community offers neutral negotiation experts (*guides*) who could participate in the work of the delegation of a disenfranchised country. Naturally, these guides should not be given authority to take formal decisions in the unfolding negotiation process. Nevertheless, they could possibly be given a mandate to act on behalf of a weak country in some negotiation situations when domestic negotiators display very limited capacity and performance capability. This predicament does not necessarily mean that the weak country concerned has poor diplomats in a general sense in its delegation. Imagine, for instance, a negotiation session in the climate talks going on in Geneva. A given DC has a small permanent delegation in Geneva whose job is to cover all international negotiations going on this UN city. The head of delegation is a former surgeon-general who is a specialist in the issue area that is most important to the DC concerned, which is AIDS. The surgeon-general is an effective negotiator in the World Health Organization but not in the WTO or in the climate talks, where he lacks expertise. Under these circumstances it is possible that the negotiation strength of the DC can be enhanced in the climate area with the help of a knowledgeable external coach recruited, say, from a "roster" of experts kept and continuously updated by a UN institution. One role of the coach would be that of an adviser to the head of delegation. However, a coach might also have a more active role at the negotiation table. He or she could take the floor in certain situations when argumentation requires a profound knowledge of issues addressed in the discussions. Such situations may particularly occur when the dominant pattern of interaction can be described as *issue clarification* or *substantive problem-solving*.

Notes

1. Grubb, M., Vrolijk, C. and Brack, D. (1999) *The Kyoto Protocol. A Guide and Assessment*, London: Earthscan.
2. Markandaya, A. and Halsnaes, K. (2002) *Climate Change and Sustainable Development: Prospects for Developing Countries*, London: Earthscan.
3. Kremenyuk, Victor (2002) *International Negotiation: Analysis, Approaches, Issues*, San Francisco: Jossey-Bass Publishers.
4. Knorr, Klaus (1973) *Power and Wealth*, New York: Basic Books.
5. Knudsen, Olav (1973) *Politics of International Shipping*, Boston, MA: Lexington; Keohane, Robert and Nye, Joseph (1977) *Power and Interdependence*, Boston, MA: Little Brown.
6. See Sjöstedt, Gunnar (1977) *The External Role of the European Community*, Farnborough: Saxon House, for a general discussion of the meaning of a state's *actor capability*.
7. Zartman, William (1994) *International Multilateral Negotiation*, San Francisco: Jossey-Bass Publishers.
8. Kremenyuk, Victor and Sjöstedt, Gunnar (1993) *International Economic Negotiation. Theory versus Reality*, London: Edgar Elgar.
9. Sjöstedt, Gunnar (1993) *International Environmental Negotiation*, Newbury Park, CA: Sage Publications.
10. This is the basic pattern. In individual cases of process stages may overlap, be simultaneous or recur. For an overview of the general features of multilateral negotiation see Zartman, note 7 above.
11. See definition and description of *epistemic community* in Haas, Peter (1990) *Saving the Mediterranean: The Politics of International Environmental Cooperation*, New York: Columbia University Press.
12. Skodvin, Tora (1999) *Structure and Agent in the Scientific Diplomacy of Climate Change: An Empirical Case Study of the Intergovernmental Panel on Climate Change*, Oslo: Department of Political Science, University of Oslo.
13. Since 1997 a COP meeting has taken place at least once every year. In December 2004 COP 10 was held in Buenos Aires.
14. Essentially, the 1997 Kyoto Protocol contained specific rules for mitigation: emission reductions and programmes for supportive action, for example joint implementation and trade with emissions rights.
15. The situation is even worse as an American ratification would have put hard pressure on Russia to ratify the Kyoto Protocol.
16. Krasner, Stephen (1983) *International Regimes*, Ithaca: Cornell University Press.
17. *Consensual knowledge* is here given a specific meaning. It is the interpretation of the scientific knowledge about the climate issue that negotiating parties (or a critical mass of them) have accepted.
18. Recall that in Krasner's original analytical language *consensual knowledge* was referred

to as *regime principles*, which specify critical causal relationships in issues addressed by a regime. See Krasner, note 16 above.
19. Parallel issue construction was unfolding simultaneously in individual states, particularly in countries sending influential and many scientists to IPCC meetings.
20. Skodvin, note 12 above.
21. Sjöstedt, note 6 above.
22. In principle, a decision is taken by consensus when the chair of the meeting deems that no (significant) party will oppose a proposed choice.
23. Fermann, G. and Borsting, G. (1997) "Climate Change Turning Political: Conference Diplomacy and Institution Building to Rio and Beyond", in G. Fermann, ed., *International Politics of Climate Change: Key Issues and Critical Actors*, Oslo: Scandinavian University Press.
24. Knudsen, note 5 above.
25. Knudsen, note 5 above, presents the case of international shipping in the 1970s: Due to its large amounts of issue-specific power (control of tonnage), Norway was an equal of the United States and the United Kingdom at the international shipping conferences organised by UNCTAD.
26. Grubb, Vrolijk and Brack, note 1 above.
27. The cross-tabulation between *process stage* and *pattern of interaction* in the climate talks certainly needs to be corroborated by further research but reflects the common knowledge in the literature about the nature and the general development of the climate negotiation.
28. Recall that Stephen Krasner's commonly used definition sees an *international regime* as an issue-specific system of rules, norms, principles (consensual knowledge) and procedures, around which actor expectations converge. See Krasner, note 16 above.

10
Toward inclusion and influence: Strategies for enfranchisement

Jessica F. Green

Introduction

The 1992 Rio Summit was a landmark event for sustainable development governance for a variety of reasons. In addition to the legal agreements – the Convention on Biological Diversity, the Framework Convention on Climate Change and the Convention to Combat Desertification – an important normative shift took hold, emphasising the need for greater inclusion of the developing world and of civil society in addressing the challenges of sustainable development. Despite the commitment to participation elaborated in the Rio Summit and many subsequent agreements, 15 years later there is still much progress to be made in the engagement of the developing world and civil society.

This volume has elaborated some of the persistent obstacles to enfranchisement, identifying two main themes that characterise the difficulties developing countries and non-state actors encounter in their efforts to influence the policy-making process. First, and not surprisingly, capacity remains a serious challenge. For representatives of developing countries, the lack of human and financial resources is a persistent problem. This is often exacerbated by a lack of instructions from developing country capitals, which leaves diplomats on their own to develop a negotiating position, as well as strategies for achieving their goals. In environmental and sustainable development matters, developing country diplomats often find themselves negotiating with technical experts from developed countries. This uneven match of knowledge and tactics generally favours the developed world.

These and other capacity issues are further exacerbated by the workings of the policy-making process. Most policy processes are both complex and continually in flux; following even one of them is a difficult and demanding task. Following many may be impossible for a small or understaffed ministry. Even with adequate training, staff, knowledge and experience, some policy processes related to sustainable development, particularly those outside the ambit of the United Nations, may not facilitate developing country influence.

Civil society actors often face the same capacity problems, though they may be even more pronounced in small, grassroots or informally constituted organisations. Of course, there are many different types of CSOs, and the large Northern-based NGOs tend to have little problem in participating in policy-making. However, the UN system has been slow to distinguish between these very different types of civil society actors, thus creating confusion and further objections to enhancing non-state participation. Why should large NGOs, which are often already serious players in policy discussions, be given more access and potentially more influence? This volume emphasises the different challenges faced by different types of non-state actors, underscoring that one size will not fit all when it comes to proposing measures to promote enfranchisement.

In this light, the second part of the book provides examples of how different actors have attempted to overcome obstacles to engagement, and enhanced their participation and/or influence in different sustainable development regimes. It offers a variety of tactics and strategies to be used in the face of different structural and capacity constraints to enfranchisement.

In chapter 6, Kevin Gray examines the participation of civil society in the proceedings of the World Trade Organization. Noting the traditionally closed nature of the organisation, Gray points out that civil society actors have been both innovative and persistent in creating institutional pathways for engagement. Although the WTO is not subject to any prescribed rules regarding its relationship with civil society, it has, in the recent past, accredited NGOs to attend ministerial meetings and to engage with the secretariat through symposia and briefings. There are still very limited provisions allowing for direct civil society participation in WTO operations, but one area where civil society has made marked progress is in the dispute settlement mechanism. Although, as Gray points out, the use of *amicus* briefs submitted by non-state actors is not explicitly permitted under the rules of the Dispute Settlement Understanding, civil society actors have used the lack of rules as an entry point for their views. The Appellate Body has begun accepting unsolicited briefs and thus transformed this conduit to the WTO, rendering it an acceptable means for receiving civil society input. Gray's chapter is useful in demonstrating that participation must be the first step toward engagement, and illustrating how the creation of new institutional pathways can facilitate this process.

Herman demonstrates in chapter 7 that creating new non-institutional pathways is an effective way of not only gaining access but also exercising influence in international policy-making. The Financing for Development process effectively shifted the institutional venue for discussing international finance issues from the Bretton Woods institutions to the UN system. This was a key component of developing countries' success. Not only were they able to shape the agenda of the discussion, but they were also able to bring a diversity of stakeholders to a new, relatively flexible forum, one where the possibility of political commitment (not just agreement) was considerably higher. Because the negotiation of text was postponed for as long as possible, political differences were debated in informal roundtables. These discussions were documented by designated facilitators, whose job was to produce a compromise text, taking in all points of view. In a sense, Herman's message is a simple one: innovation can be a key factor in engagement. New venues, new formats and new mechanisms for discussion were all ways to help give developing countries more influence over the shape and outcomes of the discussions about financing for development.

In chapter 8, Pallemaerts also examines the role of innovative practices. His analysis of the Åarhus Convention of the Economic Commission for Europe demonstrates that new institutional pathways are being created to promote the enfranchisement of civil society. The Åarhus Convention is the first multilateral treaty on the environment which imposes obligations on states with respect to their citizens. The convention articulates a detailed system of individual environmental rights; although it is a regional agreement, its implementation is already having a considerable impact on national systems of environmental law and administrative practices in many countries. For example, Pallemaerts notes that UNEP is re-examining ways to implement Principle 10 of the Rio Declaration, which affirms the need for public participation in a diverse number of areas. In addition, in its proposed guidelines for public participation in *other* international forums, the Åarhus Convention is poised to have an even larger effect on international governance for sustainable development.

Finally, in chapter 9, Sjöstedt takes up the challenge of promoting greater influence of developing country delegates in the climate change regime. He argues that enhancing actor capability – how an actor actually performs in negotiations, as opposed to its capacity to perform – should be a key strategy in promoting developing countries' enfranchisement in the climate negotiations. He also asserts that understanding the different process conditions that comprise negotiations is a key component of designing effective enfranchisement strategies. Specifically, he outlines five patterns of interactions that are part of the negotiating process: issue clarification, substantive problem-solving, bargaining, final decision-making and debate. Since the ability to undertake meaningful actions in a given negotiation situation is a basic requirement for actor capability, enhancing capability must focus on these five types of interactions and acknowledge that performance requirements may vary considerably across different patterns of interaction. Traditionally, debate is the easiest and most accessible to all; issue clarification and problem-solving are generally the most demanding for developing countries.

To a great extent exercising influence in the climate change process has been a "knowledge game" with deep involvement of scientists in the Intergovernmental Panel on Climate Change, as well as in national delegations. Countries with only modest "scientific resources" have had great difficulty in making meaningful contributions to the "knowledge game". In terms of problem-solving, influencing the discussions requires not only a profound understanding of the technicalities of the climate issues as such, but also depends on a deep comprehension of the negotiation process. Sjöstedt's proposed empowerment approaches, which are detailed in the following section, have to take into account these five stages of the negotiation process, and that each situation will call for enhanced capacity in different stages of the process.

Strategies for enfranchisement

The following section offers a brief overview of some of the lessons to be gleaned from the case studies in the second half of the book. Taken together with the obstacles identified in the first half, it offers the following recommendations for promoting enfranchisement in sustainable development governance.

Developing countries

Voice

As explained earlier, participation is the first step in engaging disenfranchised actors. This means that actors must have access to policy discussions and the information required to understand and to monitor these discussions, and have some degree of voice in them. This basic level of participation can be achieved through both institutional and non-institutional pathways; however since developing country negotiators are agents of the state, proposals to enhance their participation are focused on institutional pathways – ways to improve their voice via modes that are sanctioned by international processes and organisations. To achieve this goal, the following proposals are offered.

Halt negotiation proliferation
The rapid growth in international meetings surrounding issues of sustainable development puts additional strain on what are generally scarce human and financial resources. Treaty negotiations, subsidiary bodies and *ad hoc* working groups are just some of the meetings that require state participation, which in turns means preparation, allocation of human resources and travel to meetings. Back-to-back scheduling of meetings could, at the very least, reduce travel costs, but ultimately reduction of the number of inter-governmental meetings will be required to lessen demands on developing country negotiators. Moreover, as Gupta points out in chapter 1, "the law on the climate change is continuously being revised, and not just at discrete moments such as at the negotiation of the convention and the protocol". Thus continuous attention to the policy-making process is required; again, this fact bolsters the argument that halting negotiation proliferation would go a long way toward easing demands on the diplomats of the developing world.

Another proposal to lessen negotiation fatigue is to halt the renegotiation of text – a frequent occurrence when there is a lack of consensus or willingness to move forward. This could be achieved through a specialised commission to codify principles so that they are not reinterpreted and renegotiated in different processes. It is worth noting that some forums, such as the Commission on Sustainable Development, do indeed defer to agreed language. This, however, can lead to another dead end; simply reciting previously decided text in a new forum does not constitute forward progress.[1]

Change the make-up of executive bodies
Herman's analysis of the Financing for Development (FfD) process underscores the recognition by the International Monetary Fund and the World Bank that developing countries need more voice and representation in decision-making processes that affect them. At the same time, the political reality of this proclamation is that some of the smaller developed countries would have to step aside to allow more developing countries seats on the executive boards of these institutions. Although this proposal has yet to be implemented, the FfD process was able to raise the issue as one that needed to be addressed. As Herman notes, "It is impos-

sible any longer to justify the informal arrangements by which a European is always elected managing director of IMF and a US national always heads the World Bank."[2]

Improve the workings of the G-77
Despite being one of the main engines of a unified developing country perspective, the G-77 is a very small administrative organ. It has a small staff in New York and Geneva, and small chapter offices in Rome, Nairobi, Geneva and Vienna. Greater support for these offices would not only provide more staff but, more importantly, greater coordination between the offices. For example, the New York and Geneva offices have different chairs, and there is minimal coordination between them. Better communication between these offices could promote the circulation of information among them on various inter-governmental processes to craft positions that are coherent across issues. Stronger organisation of the G-77 can only enhance its ability to set forth positions in a myriad of international forums.

Greater use of regional forums
Although the G-77 has proven an important vehicle to ensure that the voices of developing countries are heard, irrespective of their differences in capacity, other institutional pathways can also achieve this effect. Expanding the use of regional forums is one way to increase the opportunities available to developing countries for pursuing their agendas. In this way, the same issue will be taken up in different processes. In addition to improving developing country participation through more institutional pathways to the same discussion, simply expanding the number of forums will also go a long way to improving developing country voices. Although some might criticise this approach for creating redundancy and overlap, it gives greater opportunity for discussion, and may allow circumnavigation of political obstacles that impede dissension in their forums. In addition, coordinating positions among developing countries before they move to the multilateral arena allows issues to be discussed informally and consensus to be reached before the pressures of drafting a text. This is not to say that there will always be uniformity of views among developing countries, but to the extent that there is a consensus among some subset therein, opportunities to coordinate and develop joint positions can help increase voice.

Create "defensive power" through negotiating blocs and "offensive power" through like-minded groups
As indicated by the discussion above, the G-77 is an imperfect instrument, particularly on the micro level, for the empowerment of smaller

states. However, in considering strategies to ensure the participation of developing countries at the international level, negotiating blocs such as the G-77 can be a useful starting point. They can provide resources and information to "lonely" and inexperienced diplomats, who may lack the capacity, training or simply the person-power to participate in all of the discussions at a given meeting.[3] On the opposite side, like-minded states can align themselves around a specific issue, and may be able to leverage greater influence. For example, Benin, Burkina Faso, Chad and Mali joined together and enlisted the aid of a number of NGOs to put the issue of American cotton subsidies on the map in the WTO negotiations. The $3 billion subsidising cotton farmers in the United States renders African cotton producers unable to compete with low US prices, they asserted, and was crushing their already feeble industry. Although they were unsuccessful at getting developed countries to reverse their subsidies, this like-minded group was effective in putting the issue of cotton subsidies on the agenda, and transforming the issue into a symbolic discussion about the extent to which the Doha Round was focused on the poor.

Power

Although the recommendations listed above are an important first step toward enfranchising developing country voices in international policy-making for sustainable development, they must be accompanied by efforts to improve their influence in these discussions; that is, to restructuring the balance of power between developed and developing countries. Of course, the line between enhancing developing country voices and effecting greater influence may be blurry at times. For example, improving support for the G-77 can certainly help them insert their views into more sustainable development-related processes, but in the end a stronger G-77 secretariat may have more staff and resources to consult with members, develop proposals and cultivate alliances. The net result would be greater influence. Thus, the recommendations below are principally aimed at improving developing country *influence*, but at the same time acknowledge that the distinction between voice and influence is not always clearly delineated.

Create new forums for negotiating issues

As suggested in the recommendations above, using regional meetings as a way to enhance interaction, develop positions and cultivate consensus or proposals on particular topics is a first step to improving voice. Creating new forums or moving existing discussions to different ones is another way to achieve this end. As demonstrated in the FfD process, shifting discussions about economic policy from the international financial institutions to the United Nations was an important tactic in recalibrating the power dynamics on development policies. Despite the limited power of the CBD's Working Group on Article 8j, the forum change has had a similar effect – engaging indigenous actors where it was not possible in the trade regime.

Although the tactic of changing forums was recognised as a potentially effective one for enfranchising developing countries, it was also noted that this might be the case because the institutions are themselves disenfranchised from the larger multilateral system. That is, although the FfD process may be counted as a success in terms of the *process* of engaging developing countries – affording them both voice and significant amounts of power (particularly in relation to similar discussions within the international financial institutions) – success in terms of measurable *outcomes* has yet to be demonstrated. In fact, as Herman notes in the conclusion of his chapter, this is now the main test for the FfD. The underlying assumption here is that despite moving this process from one forum to another, the power to impact on outcomes still rests with other multilateral institutions. Although this may seem to be beyond the scope of this project, it is quite germane. Eventually, full enfranchisement must occur across multilateral institutions; otherwise, the potential to relocate decision-making to less hospitable venues will always exist.

Better instruction from capitals
There is consensus that the lack of capacity among many developing country delegates is often exacerbated by a lack of clear instruction or established negotiating position from the capital. Though this link is well understood, it is less clear what measures should be taken to remedy it. One recommendation is to encourage states to promote greater continuity of diplomats on specific portfolios. Frequent changes not only demand that newly assigned diplomats assimilate large amounts of information in short periods of time, but also undermine a sense of history of negotiations within a particular area or regime.

In her discussion of developing country engagement in the climate change regime, Gupta cites the "hollow negotiating mandate" as a key obstacle to developing country power. That is, developing countries may be unsure which ideology should underpin their policies and how to incorporate the many aspects of sustainability into this viewpoint. Moreover, she points out that the agenda is often set in the developed world. This may result in failure to engage fully in discussion on the national level in the developing world, since many issues are not necessarily perceived as a priority. These problems, in addition to a number of others that occur on the national level, give rise to a hollow negotiating mandate: "a bare skeleton of ideas that leans heavily on the national position in other areas".[4] Better instructions from capitals must begin with a clear understanding of the hollow negotiating mandate and be followed by efforts to overcome it, such as those set forth here.

Extensive consultation and exchange of views before drafting
Similar to the idea of facilitation, extensive consultation *before* the drafting of any text has been identified as a successful institutional pathway for developing country influence. In this way, both developed and developing countries can exchange views and move toward consensus (or a mutually agreeable outcome) without the political constraints of a negotiating environment. Certainly, there may be other political constraints, but this type of exchange facilitates not only consensus but also a final agreement to which countries are more fully committed.

Flexibility and ambiguity
In addition to informal consultation and exchange of views, more generally flexibility in the process and its goals can be a key element in keeping communication lines open in the face of potentially controversial topics. For example, the recommendation above underscores the merits of informal discussions to build consensus and commitment before the drafting process begins. In instances where there is a lack of consensus, diplomats often stall for time or recycle previously agreed-upon language. This is a waste of time, energy and funds and may yield little or no forward progress. Instead, flexibility and open-endedness can avoid the traps of "premature specificity" that can put parties and other stakeholders on the defensive.[5] Flexibility has the advantage of building on the momentum of sympathetic parties as consensus is being developed; this tactic is also important for involving multilateral institutions. Flexibility can also be construed as the ability to move policy discussions from one forum to another, or between forums. This fluidity can also help reconfigure constraints in the debate.

More effective use of regional meetings for coordination and advocacy
Just as the use of regional forums can help enhance developing country voices in international policy-making, so too can it improve their level of influence. Regional forums can provide an additional space for discussing specific issues; they can also allow developing countries to coordinate positions before taking them to the international level. Regional meetings can serve as a useful venue for setting the agenda for global meetings, as was the case with the World Summit on Sustainable Development. Finally, inter-regional meetings such as those between the European

Union and the African, Caribbean and Pacific (ACP) countries can facilitate North-South dialogue, again without the constraints of a negotiating atmosphere. In addition, the European Union provides funding for ACP countries to meet among themselves.

Capacity-building and coaching for specific, recurring types of interactions

In his analysis of the empowerment of developing countries in the climate change talks, Sjöstedt points out that negotiations entail five types of negotiation games, and that meaningful participation requires developing capacity and capability in all of them. These five different patterns of interaction – issue clarification, substantive problem-solving, bargaining, final decision-making and debate – mean that capacity-building efforts must acknowledge that performance requirements will vary by pattern, and may change during the course of an evolving negotiation. Thus, capacity-building efforts should be closely targeted to each of these different patterns, and to developing an understanding of what types of negotiation outcomes correspond to which pattern of interaction. For example, the creation of consensual knowledge, which serves as the basis for a future course of action, often takes place through the process of issue clarification. In the climate change talks this was a "'knowledge game', with deep involvement of scientists in the Intergovernmental Panel on Climate Change".[6] Therefore, in this example, capacity-building might be focused on developing country scientists and institutions to enhance their participation, a topic that Chambers raises in chapter 4.

When capacity-building is not possible or practical, "visiting" experts can also help boost developing country influence. Along these lines, experimenting with the use of coaches is recommended. Countries could compile and maintain a roster of experts on specific issues who could advise delegations during negotiations. Coaches or guides could provide neutral negotiation support. They could be especially useful, for example, in instances where diplomats are called upon to participate in negotiations beyond their expertise, or that require in-depth scientific knowledge which they may lack. This has already happened in a number of limited occurrences. The Foundation for International Environmental Law and Development (FIELD) has sat on a number of developing country delegations in the climate change negotiations, notably the Alliance of Small Island States (AOSIS). In this capacity, FIELD lawyers assist by "providing briefing materials on the legal and political issues at stake, informing and training AOSIS members between negotiating sessions, assisting with the drafting of submissions and interventions, supporting delegations during the negotiations, and, when requested, intervening on their behalf".[7]

South-South technical cooperation and consultation

Though it was acknowledged during the course of the project that there is no agreed-upon definition of the global South, at the same time many agreed that it is an empirical reality. The developing world, state and non-state actors alike, experiences marginalisation and a lack of influence in global policy-making. In this sense, close collaboration between civil society actors from the developing world and state actors is a way to promote mutual empowerment. Technical cooperation provided by civil society actors can enhance knowledge and strengthen negotiating positions. At the same time, increased interaction between the two groups promotes greater exchange of views and increases the voice (if not the influence) of civil society actors in the formulation of developing country positions and strategies. Finally, enhanced technical expertise of developing country actors helps to address the imbalance of knowledge when experts negotiate with diplomats.

Not only can civil society and other actors offer technical cooperation, but they can also legitimise developing country negotiating positions. Through consultation with non-state constituencies, developing country governments can demonstrate that they have (at least) considered a variety of viewpoints in formulating their positions. Pressure from non-state actors can force states to invest more time and effort in deliberations over their position, thus lessening the trap of the "hollow mandate" described earlier. That is, civil society and other non-state actors can either facilitate through cooperation, or force through confrontation, governments to expend time and energy in considering the policy problem before them.

More input into the creation of scientific knowledge and consensus

As noted in Sjöstedt's discussion of the climate change regime, much influence lay with those who could shape the scientific knowledge feeding into the decision-making process. As Chambers notes, the underrepresentation of developing country scientists in the IPCC, and in other international networks that promulgate the creation of consensual knowledge, raises legitimate concerns about the extent to which this knowledge is globally consensual. Thus, an important avenue for increasing developing country influence is enhancing their involvement in shaping global scientific knowledge. There are several reasons why this is the case. First, involving developing country scientists in global scientific networks (particularly those based in the developing world) is an important part of their professional development and, in turn, of increasing the research and teaching capacity at the national level. Second, developing country participation may increase legitimacy of the knowledge generated, both on a global and a national level. Nationally, policy-makers may be more likely to take note of scientific knowledge created by one of their own. Finally, some advocates, particularly from the developing world, argue that greater participation of the developing world in the international scientific community would result in different scientific priorities.[8]

To ensure greater participation of scientists from the developing world, there must be greater capacity at the national level to produce and train these actors. Chambers recommends creating graduate programmes in the methodology and processes of conducting interdisciplinary scientific assessments, and greater incorporation of traditional knowledge into scientific assessments and globalised science to help insert a developing country perspective. This will require greater formalisation of traditional knowledge forms. To bridge scientific information and the policy process better, capacity development for policy-makers should focus on how to use science, understand risk and uncertainty and use assessments in their work.

Facilitation in negotiations
Another suggestion to empower developing countries is "facilitated negotiations" to reduce the constraints on them. Instead of enhancing the capacity of developing countries to improve their performance, facilitation aims to loosen the constraints of a demanding negotiating environment. One example is the repeated request from many developing countries to hold the number of parallel sessions to a minimum so that those with small delegations can attend all of the meetings. Another example would be to reduce the number of negotiating parties, so that particularly contentious issues can be discussed in a less politicised way, perhaps through a temporary and flexible representation system. This concept is not a new one. Yet when conceived as a strategy to promote substantive debate in a way that developing countries may perform better in spite of capacity constraints – rather than as a way to expedite a decision – facilitation can be understood as a useful tool for promoting influence.

Leadership
Although leadership cannot substitute for an absence of power, effective leadership can help developing countries "punch above their weight".[9] That is, there are circumstances under which developing country missions may be able to exercise considerable influence, despite past marginalisation. Generally, this level of influence requires that the negotiator have the backing of his or her ambassadors as well as of the capital. Once this support is in place, or perceived to be by other negotiators, developing country leaders may be able to negotiate deals more effectively. Thus it is not simply the effective leadership of developing countries but the perception of leadership that can help empower developing country delegates.

Civil society and other non-state actors

In his response to the report of the Cardoso Panel, UN Secretary-General Kofi Annan illustrates the political difficulty of engaging a variety of non-state constituencies. He stresses that "the United Nations should become a more outward-looking organisation, making more of its role as a global convener of diverse constituencies ... facilitating their input into relevant debates of global significance can only enhance the quality and depth of policy analysis and actionable outcomes".[10] At the same time, the Secretary-General's response highlights that "it is important to stress that the United Nations is and will remain an intergovernmental organisation at which decisions are taken by its Member States".[11]

Thus the recommendations outlined below aim to tread between these two constraints: on the one hand, enhanced participation must be meaningful, improving both the voice and the influence of these constituencies. On the other, in order to be implemented these changes cannot be perceived as supplanting state involvement. Enfranchising civil society and state representatives from the developing world represent two distinct, but equally difficult, challenges. The recommendations below offer some first steps toward a much larger project which has been elaborated by many, including the Secretary-General, to reconceptualise global governance to include non-state constituencies from the transnational to the local levels.

There are a number of institutional pathways for non-state input into policy-making processes. Indeed, many of the Cardoso Panel recommendations focused on this aspect of participation. Thus the recommendations begin with suggestions on how to improve official avenues for engagement through institutional pathways, both to improve their levels of participation (voice) and to enhance their influence in policy discussions (power). Additionally, enhancing the power of non-state actors does not mean that their input should be on a par with nation-states, nor that those non-state actors already deeply engaged in policy debate should be granted further privileges or power. Rather, enhancing power is about levelling the playing field between all non-state actors; none should be significantly more influential, since all are equally unaccountable. This is particularly important given the current imbalance in the participation and influence of civil society and other non-state actors from the developed and developing worlds. Second, as a pre-emptive rejoinder to those who object to the idea of increasing the say of non-state actors, both participation and influence of these actors is absolutely critical, not only to solving the complex problems of sustainable development but also to maintaining the legitimacy and credibility of the multilateral system.

Voice

Expanded, simplified accreditation processes
One of the main focal areas of the Cardoso Panel was on ways to improve the accreditation process for civil society actors. They made several suggestions, including consolidating fragmented processes into one centralised procedure (proposals 19, 20 and 21); focusing on reaching out to different constituencies through a variety of forums (proposals 2, 5, 6 and 9); and making changes in UN staffing and management to support these innovations (proposals 24, 25 and 28). The Secretary-General, in turn, supported a number of these proposals.[12] Changing the accreditation process is thus the first step in easing entry barriers to participation, particularly for non-state constituencies from the developing world for whom extensive accreditation procedures can be particularly onerous.

Another option for amendments to the accreditation processes can be drawn from the Åarhus Convention, which allows all "relevant non-governmental organisations, qualified or having an interest in the fields to which the Convention relates", to participate in the proceedings of any meeting, unless at least one-third of the parties present object.[13] In essence, this loosens the accreditation process even more, allowing all those non-state actors who wish to observe the proceedings to do so, provided that they notify the secretariat. In the case of the Åarhus Convention, this practice also extends to members of the public who wish to observe. While this latter practice may be too problematic in a larger global meeting, the former is a viable proposal. Despite concerns that such a permissive practice would flood the meeting halls this has not proven to be the case.[14]

Amending rules of procedure
As noted earlier, of those NGOs that do participate in inter-governmental proceedings, many complain that the quality of their input is limited by the rules and informal practices of the meeting. As such, a number of proposals were made to amend them to allow more opportunity for input by non-state actors. Some of these suggestions are drawn from the rules of procedure of the Åarhus Convention. First, take speakers in the order they raise their flags, instead of relegating non-state interventions to the last few minutes of discussion. The Åarhus rules of procedure state that this practice should be the norm, though the chair may choose to call upon parties before observers at his or her discretion.[15] Second, allow non-governmental actors to observe the meetings of the bureau and be named as friends of the chair. Third, allow communications from the public and observers to trigger compliance mechanisms. This is another innovative practice of the Åarhus Convention worthy of note.[16] This

practice may not be appropriate for those agreements where non-compliance brings sanctions, but it is a way for non-state actors to get their views on the record.

Institutionalise funding
Funding is another major factor in determining the participation of civil society and other non-state constituencies.[17] The limited budget of CSOs, particularly small groups, is a considerable impediment to their participation; this problem has been widely acknowledged. The Secretary-General has proposed creating a new trust fund to support the participation of non-governmental actors from the developing world.[18] This is an important start. Yet more steps should be taken to institutionalise funding for non-state actors from the developing world. Other proposals that could help address this problem could be to institutionalise funding within the inter-governmental process. For example, the Climate Action Network suggested that a portion of the monies that host countries contribute to support the Conference of the Parties of the FCCC be earmarked for travel costs for civil society from the developing world. The Åarhus Convention has taken a similar approach, where funds to support CSO participation are provided by member governments and apportioned through the secretariat.[19]

Coalition and policy coordination
There are two primary strategies for coordinating activity among civil society actors that have proved effective in exercising voice in various multilateral discussions. First, as demonstrated by NGO networks involved in the FfD process, coordination can be an important tool for targeting one message and elaborating on it through a variety of actors. In this instance, several NGO networks converged in their views and together elaborated a "detailed critique of the dominant Washington/Monterrey Consensus and various aspects of neo-liberal approaches to development".[20] Thus it was a key tactic in promoting coherent input into the negotiations and pre-negotiations consultation processes.

Second, coalition coordination can be an important tool for self-regulation. The European ECO Forum, active in UNECE's Åarhus process, has been an important umbrella group which has engaged very effectively with the secretariat. Moreover, as an informal but widely recognised liaising point between environmental citizen organisations and the Åarhus secretariat and negotiations, it has gained credibility and legitimacy from both sides. Its membership is open to whoever wishes to join, and it has been characterised as "self-policing", again reinforcing its perceived legitimacy from both sides. The ECO Forum was the recipient of funding from member governments, which in turn enabled greater

..rticipation in meetings and negotiations.[21] Both of these aspects of coalition coordination, it should be noted, are important ways to improve exchange and communication with secretariat staff, which can be an important tactic for influencing discussions.

Linking local and transnational civil society actors
The discussion of the impacts of transnational advocacy networks abounds in the academic literature.[22] The case study of the FfD process adds yet more evidence for this strategy of enfranchisement. It can be an important strategy for gaining credibility and legitimacy within policy discussions for those civil society actors participating, and can demonstrate the backing of local and grassroots groups, social movements and other non-state constituencies. Moreover, such linkages can promote influence through non-institutional pathways. As Foster points out in chapter 2, the Mexican host NGOs at the Financing for Development Conference in Monterrey, Mexico, did an effective job of reaching out to domestic media and raising concerns about the social and economic effects of globalisation.

"Technical teams" to interpret proposals and decisions for non-expert civil society actors
In the campaign against the Free Trade Agreement of the Americas, a transnational coalition of civil society actors used their "insider" members, those with expert knowledge, who were often serving on delegations, to relay information about the progress of the discussions and the potential consequences of various proposals.

Increased involvement with parliamentarians
In some senses, engaging with elected officials at the national level is an obvious avenue for civil society to voice its opinions. Civil society pressures elected officials to adopt its position, and then because it has drawn attention to the issue and mobilised constituencies, these officials may be compelled to take these positions as their own. However, parliamentarians should also be viewed as a potential conduit for civil society voices at the international level; this is especially the case in those regimes that still have relatively restrictive rules with respect to the access of non-state actors'. Rather than a combative relationship, where civil society pressure compels parliamentarians to adopt its position, civil society actors should examine the potential for collaborative relationships. This can be viewed as a coalition-building process, where parliamentarians reinforce the strength of their views through broad coalitions between government and civil society.

Power

Extensive consultation and exchange of views before drafting
This strategy was highlighted as an effective one for developing country actors in the FfD process, and has proven similarly useful for civil society actors in the Åarhus Convention. Several participants involved with the Åarhus process described the involvement of the European ECO Forum, an informal umbrella group of environmental organisations. Its participation has been a particularly useful way to channel the views of a number of organisations to the parties and the secretariat. Even in times of disagreement, this has fostered trust and a sense of bottom-up legitimacy to the process. Importantly, these environmental citizens' organisations (ECOs) were involved at very early stages of the negotiations process, which ensured that preliminary draft decisions addressed almost all the issues considered relevant by participating ECOs.[23] It is important to note that although this consultative process has intrinsic value, it does not necessarily lead to identifiable impacts. As Foster notes, "If one of the marks of successful policy consultation is that the parties can identify what impact they have had, the FfD follow-up process still has a good distance to go."[24]

It is also worth noting that in some cases there appears to be a positive feedback system as the quality of participation improves. For instance, in the case of the Åarhus Convention discussions, as ECOs perceived that their input was being taken into account, their input became increasingly more constructive. That is, when civil society actors feel that their voices are being heard, they are more likely to respond positively.

Greater use of regional meetings for coordination, advocacy and exchange
The Johannesburg Plan of Implementation underscored the need for reform of the institutional structures that underpin efforts to implement global policies for sustainable development. As a result of this and other similar policy discussions, there is increased focus on the potential role of regional institutions. In terms of enfranchising civil society, regional meetings can offer the opportunity for building coalitions, networks and consensus in a smaller arena. Tarrow has noted that international meetings can serve as a "coral reef" for civil society actors working on international policy problems, where they can gather and network.[25] The same is true for regional meetings. In addition, smaller inter-regional meetings, such as the EU/ACP sessions mentioned earlier, can foster exchange between civil society actors from the developed and developing worlds.

cooperation to developing country missions to enhance
ge and strengthen negotiating positions

outh cooperation can work both ways, to help enfranchise both nd non-state actors of the developing world. NGOs from the developing world can provide knowledge and expertise, thus aiding states to elop their positions and represent themselves more effectively. Second, greater contact and exchange between the two groups of actors can only improve the personal relationships that, thus far, have proven to be a key element in successful lobbying at negotiations. Finally, such cooperation need not be restricted to the expert communities of the developing world, but can also include grassroots organisations, social movements and other "implementing" actors, including business. These can help provide knowledge of conditions at the subnational and local levels, key knowledge in understanding the effectiveness of current policies and in informing the design of new ones.

Greater interaction and influence with other forums working on the same issues

This is a key issue that was identified by a number of the authors. Empowering indigenous peoples through active engagement in the Working Group on Article 8(j) is an important step in the right direction, but is not sufficient for ensuring their influence on outcomes of laws and policies governing traditional knowledge in the multilateral system writ large.[26] This example raises a number of issues that extend beyond the goals of this volume, but are nonetheless still critical to its success. There must be greater understanding of the power dynamics between multilateral institutions, beyond the simple recognition that they exist. Further investigation into this area of enquiry should also examine the different institutionalised pathways that exist and are available to developing countries and non-state actors of the developing world.

Regional standards and law-making efforts based on Principle 10

The Århus Convention has been highlighted as a potential model for codifying citizen rights of participation and access to information and justice. Similar efforts are under way through inter-regional efforts by the Asia-Europe Meeting (ASEM), which has initiated research on public participation practices in environmental matters and consistently placed the matter on the agenda. There are a number of other examples of guidelines and practices surrounding public participation – in the 1995 amendments to the Barcelona Convention for the Protection of the Marine Environment, and the African Union's recent African Convention on the Conservation of Nature and Natural Resources. The increasing appearance of procedural rights for public participation indicates the possibility of a larger normative shift toward these institutional pathways becoming standard. Such a change, though still a considerable way off, would constitute an important opportunity for enhancing both the voice and potentially the influence of civil society and other non-state actors.

Coalition-building outside the multilateral process
The previous section discusses how civil society actors can enhance their voice in international policy-making through closer coordination of coalitions. This may also be a viable strategy for enhancing their influence. Joining civil society actors together under an "umbrella" that spans across myriad issues can be an effective strategy for mobilising large numbers of people. Although this may often be a temporary confluence of interests, it can be an important tactic for marshalling media attention, getting items on the policy agenda or creating norms through voluntary standards and guidelines.

Notes

1. Marc Pallemaerts makes the argument that the Johannesburg Plan of Implementation did little for moving international law for sustainable development forward, as much of the text simply "recalled" and "reaffirmed" decisions taken elsewhere. Pallemaerts, Marc (2003) "International Law and Sustainable Development: Any Progress in Johannesburg?", *Review of European Community and International Environmental Law* 12(1): 1–11.
2. Herman, this volume.
3. See Gupta, Joyeeta (2000) "Tips and Tricks for the Lonely Diplomat", in *On Behalf of my Delegation ...*, which details how developing country diplomats can cope with the difficulties associated with being the lone representative of a country at a given negotiation. Available from www.cckn.net/www/lonelydiplomat.html.
4. See Gupta, this volume.
5. See Herman, this volume.
6. See Sjöstedt, this volume.
7. FIELD "Support for the Alliance of Small Island States in the Climate Change Negotiations", available from www.field.org.uk/climate_1.php.
8. Agarwal, Anil and Narain, Sunita (1991) *Global Warming in an Unequal World. A Case of Environmental Colonialism*, New Delhi: Centre for Science and Environment.
9. Barry Herman (2004) personal communication, 24 October.
10. "Report of the Secretary-General in Response to the Report of the Panel of Eminent Persons on United Nations-Civil Society Relations", A/59/354, 13 Sept 2004, para. 4.
11. Ibid., para. 2.
12. Ibid.
13. Meeting of the Parties to the Convention on Access to Information, Public Participation in Decision-making and Access to Justice in Environmental Matters. Report of the First Meeting of the Parties: Decision I/1, Rules of Procedure. ECE/MP.PP/2/Add. 2, Rule 5, 2(e) and Rule 6, 2, 17 December 2002. See also Convention on Access to Information, Public Participation in Decision-making and Access to Justice in Environmental Matters, article 10, para. 5.

sare (2004) "NGOs in Non-Compliance Mechanisms under Multilateral Environ-.tal Agreements: From Tolerance to Recognition?", in T. Treves, M. Frigessi de .ma, A. Tanzi, A. Fodella, C. Pitea and C. Ragni, eds, *Civil Society, International /ts and Compliance Bodies*, The Hague: TMC Asser Press, pp. 205–222.

"Report of the First Meeting of the Parties", note 13 above, Rule 27.

"Report of the First Meeting of the Parties, Addendum", ECE/MP.PP/2 Add. 8, Annex, para 18.

This is less of a problem for business actors, since most involved represent large transnational business actors or coalitions thereof, and fewer represent small and medium-sized enterprises.

18. See "Report of the Secretary-General in Response to the Report of the Panel of Eminent Persons on United Nations-Civil Society Relations", A/59/354, 13 September 2004, paras 20–22.
19. See the Lucca Declaration, ECE/MP.PP/2/Add.1, para. 21, and Decision I/13 on Financial Arrangements, para. 7.
20. See Foster, this volume.
21. Of course, one could argue that this funding might compromise their neutrality, but this did not appear to be the case in this instance.
22. See for example, Keck, Margaret E. and Sikkink, Kathryn (1998) *Activists Beyond Borders: Advocacy Networks in International Politics*, Ithaca: Cornell University Press; Fox, Jonathan A. and Brown, David L. (1998) *The Struggle for Accountability: The World Bank, NGOs and Grassroots Movements*, Cambridge, MA: MIT Press; Edwards, Michael and Gaventa, John (2001) *Global Citizen Action*, Boulder: Lynne Rienner Publishers.
23. Discussion at "Engaging the Disenfranchised" meeting, Laxenburg, Austria, 20 June 2004.
24. See Foster, this volume.
25. Tarrow, Sidney (2001) "Transnational Contention: Contention and Institutions in International Politics", *Annual Review of Political Science* 4(1): 1–20.
26. See discussion of Working Group on Article 8(j) in chapter 5, this volume.

Index

Aarhus Convention 179–203
  background and history 180–182
    Convention 181–182
    implementation of procedural rights 181
    Ministerial Conference of Sustainable Development 180
  impact on governance processes 187–190
    application of principles 188–189
    European Community 187–188
    human rights law, similarities 190
    role of NGOs 189
  model for international efforts, as 179
  purpose and scope 182–186
    assistance in exercising rights 185
    citizens' rights 182
    engagement of civil society 182–183
    guarantee of rights 184
    individual environmental rights 183
    institutionalising pathways 185
    NGOs, and 184–185
    requirements 184
  recommendations 198–199
  relevance and influence 190–198
    African perspective 194
    Barcelona Convention 193
    "global multilateral guidelines" 196–197
    Good Practice Document 193
    innovative instrument, as 190–191
    North American Agreement on Environmental Cooperation 195
    promotion of public participation 192
    provisions of African Convention 194–195
    UNEP agenda 195–196
    World Charter for Nature 191
    significance for sustainable development governance 186–187
    "spill over effects" 187
    unique experiment, as 198
Agenda for Development 162

Business
  obstacles to enfranchisement 12–13
Business-society interaction 62–89
  boundary areas of legislation 79–82
    company laws 79–82
    trade laws 79–82
  "business", definition 62
  "civil society", meaning 62
  CSOs' "watchdog" function 84
  CSR and related international codes 65–72
    Caux Roundtable 67
    code of conduct 67
    codes and schemes 66–67

247

.ty interaction (cont.)
    between business and society
        -72
    rate governance 66
      rnational codes, table 68–69
    otivations for 67–70
    new multi-stakeholder approaches 71
    OECD Guidelines 70
    self-regulation 66
    social obligation 65
    socially responsible investment (SRI) 65
enfranchisement of developing country stakeholders 82–84
formal conference diplomacy 64
Global Compact 64
ISO initiative 85
joint problem-solving 65
national action 85
post-WSSD developments 78–79
    environmental NGOs coalition 78
    finer-grained initiatives 78
    ISO-COPOLCO deliberations 79
    UK CSR Minister 79
"public diplomacy", and 63–64
regulatory implications of stakeholder engagement 72–74
    "bolt on" CSR 72
    CSO's "sticks" 72
    NAFTA, and 73
    power of civil society 72
    revision of OECD Guidelines 73–74
    targets of campaigns 72
    Workers Rights Consortium (WRC) 73
stakeholders' preferences 74–77
    approaches 74–75
    consumers 77
    large corporations 75–76
    small businesses 76–77
    sustainability consultants 75–76
    trade unions 76–77

Call of the Earth/Llamado de la Tierra Initiative 124–127
    core activities 125
    formal launch 124
    funding 125
    indigenous participation in IGC 126
    objectives 124–125
    recommendations 127
Canadian Assembly of First Nations (AFN) 120
Cancun Ministerial 144–145
Capability development 222–223
    closely targeted 222
Capacity-building 221–222, 236
Cardoso Panel 56–58
Caux Roundtable 67
Civil society
    civil society international trade community 134–136
    global governance agenda, and 54–56
    meaning 62
    obstacles to enfranchisement 10–12
    WTO, and. see World Trade Organisation
Climate change
    negotiations 25
        membership 29–30
        pathways for influencing 26–30
        proposing policies 26–29
        reporting 30
        responding to policy proposals 29
        voting 29–30
    problem of 24–25
    sustainable development governance, and 23–24
Coaching 224–225, 236
Coalition building 32–33
Company laws
    corporate social responsibility, and 79–82
Consensual knowledge 96–98
    acceptance of knowledge 96
    analysis of assessments 98
    correlation with participation of scientists 96
    developing countries, in 96
    institutional embededness 96
    Northern and Southern participation 97
    participation, defining 96–97
    thematic focus of assessments 98
    transforming scientific knowledge into 211
Corporate social responsibility 62–89, *see also* Business-society interaction
    definition 65

INDEX

Decision-making
  role of scientific knowledge in international 91–93
Decolonisation
  indigenous peoples 111–112
Developing countries
  acceptance on scientific knowledge in 96
  coalition building at WTO 140–141
  delegates of
    obstacles to enfranchisement, as 8–10
  disenfranchisement of negotiators *see* Negotiators, developing countries
  enfranchisement of stakeholders 82–84
  involvement of in scientific assessments 103
  scientists *see* Scientists
Developing world
  need for meaningful engagement 2
Dispute settlement
  WTO, at 142–144

Enfranchisement
  actors enfranchised, whether 6–7
  approaches for *see* Promoting enfranchisement
  definition 3
  developing country stakeholders, of 82–84
  enfranchising initiatives *see* Enfranchising initatives
  indigenous peoples 111–112
    decolonisation 111–112
  obstacles to 7–16
    business 12–13
    civil society 10–12
    developing country delegates 8–10
    indigenous people 14–16
    scientists 13–14
  promoting *see* Promoting enfranchisement
  strategies for 227–246
    capacity, and 227–228
    civil society and non-state actors 239–245
      accreditation processes 240
      coalition building 245
      coalition and policy coordination 241–242
      consultation 243
      exchange of views 243
      funding 241
      interaction and influence with other forums 244
      involvement with parliamentarians 242
      law-making efforts 244–245
      local and transnational actors 242
      power 243–245
      regional meetings 243
      regional standards 244–245
      rules of procedure 240–241
      technical cooperation 244
      technical teams 242
      voice 240–242
    developing countries 230–238
      ambiguity 235
      capacity building 236
      coaching 236
      consultation 235
      creation of scientific knowledge 237–238
      "defensive power" 232–233
      exchange of views 235
      executive bodies 231–232
      facilitation in negotiations 238
      flexibility 235
      instruction from capitals 234–235
      leadership 238
      negotiation proliferation 231
      new forums 233–234
      "offensive power" 232–233
      power 233–238
      regional forums 232
      regional meetings 235–236
      technical cooperation 237
      voice 230–233
      workings of G-77 232
  understanding 2–6
    developing countries 3
    enfranchised, meaning 2–3
    legal rights, and 3–4
    scale 5–6
Enfranchising initiatives 40–60
  Cardoso Panel, and 56–58
    future prospects 56
    global "democratic deficit" 57
    "global policy networks" 58
    implementation of recommendations 56–57
    inclusion 56

initiatives (cont.)
   n shifts 56
   ship 57
   of "partner" 58
   d conference formats 58
   g of sovereignty 42–44
   gents of 44
   commercial law 43
   development of WTO 42
   investment 43
   secrecy of trade negotiations 43
   UN disenfranchised, whether 44
civil society 54–56
   global governance agenda, and 54–56
FTAA 45–49
   institutionalised pathways 46–48
   membership 47
   non-institutional pathways 48–49
   policies 46–47
   procedural rights 47
   proposals 46–47
   reporting 47–48
   voting 47
role of NGOs 40
   coalitions 41
   "consultative status" 41
   "organisational particles" 41
systemic issues for enfranchising NGOs 49–54
   institutionalised pathways 49–52
   memberships 50
   non-institutional pathways 52–53
   proposing policies 50–51
   prospects 53–54
   reporting 52
   responding to proposals 51–52
   voting 50
Environment
  decline in 90
    technological advances, and 90

Facilitation 223–224
Free Trade Area of Americas (FTAA)
   enfranchising initiatives, and. *see* Enfranchising initiatives

G-77
   workings of 232
Global Compact 64
Global policy networks 58
Globalisation

need for global governance, and 1
trade liberalisation, benefits 21
wealth of nations agenda 21
world as third world country 22
WTO, role of 134
Grey literature 101

Human rights law
   Aarhus Convention, similarities with 190

Indigenous people
   global governance and 112–119
   obstacles to enfranchisement 14–16
   participation in sustainable development governance *see* Sustainable development governance
International Monetary Fund (IMF)
   Monterry Process, and 165

Knowledge
   consensual 96–98
   traditional 101–102

Legal rights
   participation, as 3–4
Lobbying 34

Media
   garnering attention of 34
   swaying public opinion 5
Monterry Process 153–178
   aims 154
   attendance at 153–154
   backsliding after 169–173
     business "hearings" 172
     distancing of WTO from UN 170
     ECOSOC/FfD meeting 170
     FfD not on "radar screens" 172
     focus of 2004 ECOSOC discussions 171
     High-Level Dialogue 170–171
     mechanism for follow-up 169
     NGO "hearings" 172
     role for FfD process 169
   different approach to UN diplomacy 161–164
     ad hoc working group 162
     Agenda for Development, and 162
     confrontation 161
     drafting FfD resolution 163

emphasising weakness of South 161
informal dialogues 163
North-South cooperation 161
participation 164
US government 163
engaging stakeholders 164–173
civil society 167–168
civil society input of FfD 168–169
engaging private sector 167
IMF 165
informal meetings strategy 164
inter-governmental processes 165–166
NGOs 168
Philadelphia Group 166
Preparatory Committee 164–165
"systemic" issues 165
World Bank 165
evolution of 159–161
central challenge to UN delegates 160
delegations to UN bodies 159
development assistance activities 159–160
formal texts 160–161
impotence of UN General Assembly 159
FfD preparatory process 154–155
informal international discussions 154
lessons for continued dialogue 173–175
commitment 174
flexibility 173–174
leadership 173
maintenance of leadership and support 174
non-official stakeholders, engagement 174–175
real-world developments 175
policy reform 155–161
central feature of Process 155
donor-advocated domestic policies 157–158
institutional governance, problem in 157
inter-governmental processes 156–157
official development assistance (ODA) 155–156
pledges on development requirements 158–159
political commitments 155–156
post-consultation negotiation texts 158
seats on executive boards 157
"staying engaged" agreement 156

Negotiation
basic elements of multilateral, diagram 206
Negotiators, developing countries 21–39
disenfranchisement of 21–39
climate change negotiations, 26–30, see also Climate change
coalition building 32–33
implications 35
increasing 34–35
international problem-solving processes 35
lobbying 34
media attention 34
mobilising constituencies 34
negotiating power 33–34
organisational forms 32
pathways for influence 32–34
structural imbalance in negotiation 31–32
Non-governmental organisations
enfranchisement initiatives, role see Enfranchisement initiatives
role see Aarhus Convention
systemic issues for enfranchising see Enfranchising initiatives
Non-state actors
recognition in policy making 5

Official development assistance (ODA)
Monterry Process, and 155–156

Participation
consensual knowledge see Consensual knowledge
framework for examining 4–5
landmark documents on 1
link with sustainable development 2
use of term 1
Policy making
institutional pathways for scientists in 91–95
Promoting enfranchisement 204–226
analytical approach 204–206
basic elements of multilateral negotiation, diagram 206
two approaches 205–206
approaches for enfranchisement 207–209
actor capability 208–209
automatic enfranchisement 208

Promoting enfranchisement (cont.)
　capacity-building 207–208
　cost effectiveness 208
　enfranchisement, meaning 207
　impacts 209
　powerlessness 207
empowerment approaches 220–225
　capability development 222–223
　capacity building 221–222
　coaching 224–225
　facilitation 223–224
　performance requirements 220–221
objectives 204–206
　justice 204–205
　mitigation 205
　transfer of resources 205
performance requirements 209–210
process stages in climate talks 210–220
　association between negotiation on regime element and pattern of interaction, table 219
　association between process stage and pattern of interaction, table 217
　bargaining 213–214
　consensual knowledge 211–212, 220
　consensus decisions 216
　debate 214
　faculty to undertake meaningful actions 213
　final decision-making 214
　formula negotiation 218
　issue clarification 213
　"knowledge game" 216
　negotiation of formula 210
　norms 219–220
　patterns of interaction 218
　post-negotiation 210–211
　pre-negotiation 210
　procedures 218–219
　process conditions for enfranchisement 212–220
　regime principles 219
　regime rules 212
　regime-building perspective 211
　requests and offers 215–216
　rule creation 218
　soft law 212
　substantive problem-solving 213
Public symposia
　WTO, at 140

Scientific knowledge
　meaning 91–93
　transformation into consensual knowledge 211
Scientists
　barriers to participation for 98–102
　　addressing gaps in developing countries 99
　　assessments 101–102
　　grey literature 101
　　importance of science 98–99
　　researchers in developing countries, table 100
　　traditional knowledge 101–102
　　use of traditional knowledge 102
　　women's participation in science 100
　benefits of participation for 103
　developing country, of 90–107
　　consensual knowledge see Consensual knowledge
　　decline in environment 90
　　international environmental policy 90–91
　　strengthening role of 103–104
　institutional pathways for 91–95
　　international decision-making, role of science in 91–93
　　pathways bridging scientific knowledge and policy-making 93–95
　　policy-making, in 91–95
　　scientific assessments 95
　　scientific knowledge, meaning 91–93
　　social networks 94–95
　obstacles to enfranchisement 13–14
　significance of scientific knowledge 102–103
Social networks
　scientific knowledge and policy making, and 94–95
Socially responsible investment (SRI) 65
Sovereignty
　ceding of 42–44
Sustainable development
　importance of science and technology for 98–99
　link with participation 2
Sustainable development governance
　climate change, and 23–24
　indigenous participation in 108–130

Ad-Hoc Open-Ended Working Group on Article 8(j) 117–118
barriers to in institutional pathways 119–122
Call of the Earth/Llamado de la Tierra Initiative 124–127
Canadian Assembly of First Nations (AFN) 120
case studies 119
Chief Deskaheh 108–109
current situation 112–119
decolonisation 111–112
denial of access to UN 109
denial of nationhood 110–111
environmental policy making 127–129
full enfranchisement 111–112
Indigenous Caucus 118–119
indigenous declarations 123–124
indigenous knowledge 112–113
indigenous organisations 117
institutional pathways 115–119
non-institutional pathways 122–124
observer status 117
participation in expert groups 117–118
protection of indigenous knowledge 114–115
recommendations for improving 122
refusal to participate 109
role in environmental management 114
side events 119
state delegations 115–117
women 121–122
meaning 3–4
scientists, role *see* Scientists

Trade laws
corporate social responsibility, and 79–82
Traditional knowledge 101–102
link with scientific assessments 103

United Nations
development assistance activities, 159–160, *see also* Monterry Process
distancing of WTO from 170
Environment Programme 195–196
General Assembly, functions 160
Uruguay Negotiating Round 134

Women
indigenous, participation of 121–122
participation in science 100
Workers Rights Consortium (WRC) 73
World Bank
Monterry Process, and 165
World Trade Organisation (WTO) 133–152
Cancun Ministerial 144–145
civil society, and 133–152
civil society international trade community 134–136
amicus briefs 137
arena for NGO consultation 136
"cosmopolitanicism" 135–136
environmental NGOs 135
external versus internal tensions in 136–138
lack of transparency 137
NGO participation 134–135
one-vote system 136
plurality in civil society community 135
development of 42
dispute settlement 142–144
amicus briefs 142–143
judicial interpretation 144
rapid evolution 142
role for civil society 143
role in development of WTO regime 144
distancing from UN 170
institutional mechanisms 138–144
accreditation processes 139–140
coalition-building of developing countries 140–141
domestic mechanisms 138
Marrakech Agreement 139
modalities of participation 138–144
monitoring implementation 141
NGOs at Ministerial Conference 139
non-institutional participation 142
participation in WTO operations 141
prescribed rules 138–139
public symposia 140
standard-setting bodies 141
WTO website 140
international trade system ethos 133–134
membership of 133
role in globalisation 134
Uruguay Negotiating Round 134